ENGLISH LANGUAGE SERIES
TITLE NO 15

Message and emphasis
On focus and scope in English

ENGLISH LANGUAGE SERIES

General Editor: Randolph Quirk

Title no:

Message and emphasis

On focus and scope in English

JOSEF TAGLICHT

Associate Professor of English
The Hebrew University of Jerusalem, Israel

Foreword by Randolph Quirk

LONGMAN
London and New York

LONGMAN GROUP LIMITED
Longman House, Burnt Mill, Harlow,
Essex CM20 2JE, England

*Published in the United States of America
by Longman Inc., New York*

First published 1984

British Library Cataloguing in Publication Data

Taglicht, Josef
  Message and emphasis.—(Longman English language
  series)
  1. English language—Grammar—1950-
  I. Title
  428.2   PE111Z
  ISBN 0-582-29128-3

Library of Congress Cataloging in Publication Data
Taglicht, Josef, 1926-
  Message and emphasis.

  (English language series; title no. 15)
  Bibliography: p.
  Includes index.
  1. English language—Topic and comment. 2. English
language—Discourse analysis. I. Title.
II. Series: English language series; 15.
PE1369.T32 1983   420'.141   82-20858
ISBN 0-582-29128-3 (pbk.)

Set in 10/12 pt Linotron 202 Times
Printed in Singapore by Four Strong Printing Company

Contents

Foreword

The author of this volume is one of a very few scholars in the world conducting specialised and highly original research into the relation between the prosody of English and its grammar, between what we could call – with some obvious simplification – 'sentence sound' and 'sentence meaning'. Dwight Bolinger is another such linguist, M. A. K. Halliday is a third, and Geoffrey Leech a fourth, and these also are authors in the *English Language Series*.

For too long, syntactical and morphological aspects of grammar have been treated as though grammar was fully represented in graphic substance: in phrases and sentences as spelled and punctuated in writing. For too long equally, the swell and sigh of sonority, the rise and fall of musical pitch were closely studied only within the discipline of phonetics, as 'suprasegmental phonology', related more to the motor organs producing acoustic effects than to the subjects and predicates of grammar; the exhortations, statements and questions of rhetoric; the 'exultations, agonies, and love' (as Wordsworth put it) stirring within and articulated by 'man's unconquerable mind'.

Dr Taglicht's book puts the *emphasis* where it is needed in understanding the linguistic structure of every *message*. Though many if not most of his examples are presented in prosodic transcription rather than in the punctuation conventions of written English, it would be a fundamental error to regard *Message and emphasis* as being concerned only with language when spoken. Indeed, the converse could be argued. In speech, and especially in face-to-face speech, the construction and interpretation of a message can reflect almost automatically the main purport (question or instruction or critical comment or friendly praise) and the items that are being highlighted. So automatic is our manipulation of oral/aural devices like intonation, prominence and tempo that we are apt to forget that our message in writing can possibly fail to be read exactly as we would have spoken it. As it must. Even the silent reading of a typically paper-originating text (such as a legal document) demands the assignment of speech prosodies not merely as an aid to comprehension but as a condition of it. Notice how often we have to read a difficult sentence *aloud* before we feel we have understood it. But stumbling as we read is also our common experience. The further context makes us realise that we must have been wrong in our silent re-creation of prosodic features, and we have to go back and read it differently, redistributing our stresses and intonation nuclei.

The careful writer does not forget this, and punctuation choices are made, along with the grammatical and lexical choices, in the hope of cueing the reader to assign the prosody that the writer is silently hearing within as he sets down his sentences. A bold writer, especially in fiction, is sometimes prepared to take liberties with the conventions of punctuation to aid his reader in this process of prosodic reconstruction. For example, in *Ghost Story* (1979), where a woman is telling her lover that she has decided to return to her husband Ricky, Peter Straub is bold enough to write:

> I think it is time I retired into respectability. And. If you cannot see that Ricky has four or five times your significance, then you are deluding yourself.

It is likely that we read that one-word sentence, 'And', with something approaching the prosody and rhetorical weight it would have been given in speech.

But if, as most of us must, we write within the constraints of standard prose, we are obliged to reorganise our sentences both grammatically and lexically to ensure that so far as possible the reader is able to assign an appropriate prosody. This is where devices such as the 'cleft' sentence are essential, where we need to be alert to the careful placing of adverbials, the anticipation of ambiguities over the scope of negation. All these issues are meticulously explored by Dr Taglicht, who brings to bear upon the data in the Survey of English Usage his own insights and those of Firbas, Halliday, Bolinger and others.

There is no language on earth in which it is more important for messages to be correctly and speedily constructed and interpreted. As English has increasingly come into worldwide use, there has arisen a correspondingly increased need for more information on the language and the ways in which it is used. The English Language Series seeks to meet this need and to play a part in further stimulating the study and teaching of English by providing up-to-date and scholarly treatments of topics most relevant to present-day English – including its history and traditions, its sound patterns, its grammar, its lexicology, its rich variety and complexity in speech and writing, and its standards in Britain, the USA., and the other principal areas where the language is used.

University College London   RANDOLPH QUIRK
January 1983

Preface

This book endeavours to treat from a single viewpoint a set of questions that have more often been considered in isolation from one another, but which all bear upon a single central topic: the grammar of *only* and *also*, considered as principal representatives of the class of 'focusing adverbs' ('referential adverbials' in Jacobson 1964, 'focusing adjuncts' in Quirk *et al* 1972). Such a grammar must deal with problems in at least three different areas: in syntax, in semantics, and in what has come to be called 'functional sentence analysis'. The reappraisal of previous work in these areas has led to a number of new ideas, or new configurations of old ones. Hence the book's original title, now regretfully abandoned: 'Not only *only*'.

The chapters on theme and rheme, intonation focus, and the scope of negation make essential contributions to the grammar of the focusing adverbs; but they also have a wider relevance in that they help to show more generally how the English language works – as a device not for the representation of conceptual structures in a vacuum, but for the sending of messages from speakers to hearers.

It is a pleasant duty to acknowledge my indebtedness to those who have helped me in various ways in the writing of this book. The textual data on which this study is based are drawn from the files of the Survey of English Usage, and I am grateful to Randolph Quirk for making this material available to me. In addition, I want to thank Dwight Bolinger, Dick Hudson, Eddie Levenston, Avishai Margalit, Anita Mittwoch, Randolph Quirk, Mark Stein, and Yael Ziv, for criticism and suggestions that have led to many improvements. They are not responsible, of course, for the blemishes that remain. Finally, I am grateful to my wife Margaret for her continued encouragement and support.

The Hebrew University of Jerusalem   JT
December 1982

Acknowledgement

I am indebted to the *Journal of Linguistics* for permission to use my article in Volume 18, No. 2, as the basis for Chapter 3 of this book.

Symbols and notational conventions

*	asterisk: indicates that what follows is ill-formed
?	question-mark: indicates that the well-formedness of what follows is doubtful
[ ]	square brackets: enclose syntactic constituents

PROSODIC SYMBOLS

a. *Crystal and Quirk notation*[1]

#	Marks end of tone-unit
[ ]	square brackets: enclose subordinate tone-unit

The following accents are placed over the (first) vowel letter of the nuclear syllable; they relate to the syllable or syllable sequence that bears the nuclear pitch movement.

′	grave:	falling
\	acute:	rising
ˇ	inverted circumflex:	falling-rising
^	circumflex:	rising-falling

The following letters are placed before the nuclear syllable and indicate width of pitch movement:

W	wider than unmarked nucleus
N	narrower than unmarked nucleus

The following letters are placed after the onset symbol (in non-subordinate tone units) or before a subordinate nucleus; they mark the starting pitch as higher or lower than expected for the unmarked case.

H	high
L	low

The following symbols precede nuclear or stressed non-nuclear syllables (references to pitch mean starting pitch):

/   oblique: onset (first stress) of tone-unit

·   raised period: continuance, *ie* same pitch as previous syllable

:   colon: booster, *ie* higher pitch than preceding syllable, but lower than for 'high booster'

!   exclamation-mark: high booster, *ie* higher pitch than the nearest preceding syllable that is marked by an onset, continuance, booster, or high booster

,   comma: drop, *ie* lower pitch than preceding syllable; pitch difference greater than the unmarked drop

"   double prime: extra strong stress

The following can precede only syllables that have no other mark:

'   single prime: stress

b. O'Connor and Arnold notation (only in Chapter 3)[1]

All the marks precede the syllable to which they relate.

1. nuclear syllables:

\   high descending: fall from high to low

\   low descending: fall from mid to low   } pitch movements

/   high ascending: rise from mid to high   } initiated on the

/   low ascending: rise from low to mid   } marked syllable

ˇ   inverted circumflex: fall-rise

2. stressed, non-nuclear syllables:

ˈ   high vertical stroke: non-low level pitch; in a sequence of two such marks, the second indicates a step down from the preceding pitch-level

ˌ   low vertical stroke: low level pitch

       small circle, low: low level pitch (continuation)

°
°   small circle, high: a. last syllable after (fall-)rise: rising pitch

                                     b. elsewhere: non-low level pitch, continuing contour indicated by preceding mark

c. Halliday notation (only in Chapter 3)[1]

//   double oblique: beginning of 'foot' and of tone-group

/   single oblique: beginning of 'foot'

∧   caret: used after double or single oblique to indicate that the foot has a 'silent ictus' (*ie* that the foot contains no stress)

__   underlining: marks tonic (*ie* nuclear) syllable
4   (after double oblique) indicates a falling-rising tone, starting
          on the tonic syllable (underlined)

Note: Every salient (*ie* stressed) syllable begins a 'foot'; every foot
begins either with a salient syllable or with a 'silent ictus'.

FOCUS AND SCOPE:

_____   underlining: marks focal element
↳ ↲   angle-brackets: enclose the scope of negation
o⁻ ⁻o   small raised o's with hyphens: enclose the scope of *only*
a⁻ ⁻o   small raised a's with hyphens: enclose the scope of *also*

LOGICAL SYMBOLS

Pa   'a has the property P'
P(a,b)   'the relation P holds between a and b'
~   negation symbol
∃   existential quantifier: ∃x Px 'For at least one x, it holds that x
          has the property P'
∀   universal quantifier: ∀x Px 'For any x, it holds that x has the
          property P'
λ   lambda-opeator: λx Px 'the set of all x such that x has the
          property P'
∉   'is not a member of'
≠   'is not identical with'
{ }   curly brackets: enclose sets
x{ }   'x is a member of the set defined in the curly brackets'
∃x   restricted quantification: For at least one x that is not
  x≠a   identical with a, it holds that'

Note

[1]   Items used in this book, not the full repertoire.

To the memory of my parents
Berysz and Sarah Taglicht
and to the memory of
my son Yuval

One

Focus: Between discourse structure and syntax

1.1 DISCOURSE AND THE NOTION OF FOCUS

Human language may be regarded as being simultaneously structured in a number of different ways, one of which is related directly to its use as an instrument of communication, or in other words as a device for the sending of messages from a speaker (or writer) to a listener (or reader). The first impetus to the study of this aspect of language came from the Prague school,[1] who refer to it as 'functional sentence perspective'. The notions of the Prague school have been further developed by other linguists, notably M. A. K. Halliday who lays emphasis on the co-presence of more than one structure even on the textual level (*ie* the level of the message or functional sentence perspective).[2] Halliday distinguishes between 'information structure', which depends mainly on intonation, and 'thematic structure', which is purely syntactic. Quirk *et al* (1972)[3] devote a whole chapter to various aspects of the organization of the sentence as part of a message, including intonational, syntactic and other devices.

The organization of a communication involves not only the semantic and pragmatic linking of successive sentences – what Halliday calls 'cohesion'[4] – but also the assignment of special prominence to parts of sentences. The prominence assigned may be of various sorts, corresponding to the different syntactic and other devices that serve this purpose. I shall use 'focusing' as a general term for the assignment of prominence by phonological or syntactic means. Each focusing device has a 'domain' within which it is effective,[5] and within each domain we may distinguish between (i) the (focus) marker, *ie* the device used to assign prominence, (ii) the focus, or the part to which prominence is assigned, and (iii) the residue, or the part that is not assigned prominence by the marker in question. The focusing options frequently serve to strengthen the linkage between neighbouring sentences, so that cohesion and focusing overlap. Consider for instance the following discourse fragments:

[1] A: /Let's 'bring them a 'pound of :tèa #
     B: They/don't !drìnk much 'tea # /Cŏffee's what they 'usually
        'have #

[2] /John's a :sùrgeon # And his /wife's !àlso a 'doctor I 'think #

In [1] the two sentences spoken by B are linked lexically by the words
tea and *coffee*, and referentially by the anaphoric item *they*. The
double focus on *coffee* (intonation nucleus and focus of identified
relative construction) underlines the contrast with *tea* and so rein-
forces the cohesive bond between the two sentences. In [2] the two
sentences are linked lexically by *surgeon* and *doctor*, and referentially
by *John* and *his*. The intonation focus on the additive focusing adverb
also draws attention to the fact that the two sentences are in some
way parallel in content, and the residual status of *a doctor* in relation
to *also* and in relation to the intonation focus marks it as something
that has been previously mentioned and so as a link with what has
gone before. Usually, as in the present example, the link made by
also is with the immediately preceding sentence, but this is not
necessary.[6] Compare the following sequence:

[3] /John's a :sùrgeon # He /studied in Amèrica # and /that's
     where he 'met his :wìfe # /She's !àlso a 'doctor #

The examples show that a proper treatment of focusing devices must
often take account of the relationship of a sentence to its context.

1.2 FOCUS MARKERS AND FOCAL STRUCTURE IN ENGLISH

The set of focus markers in English includes the following (in the
examples, the focus is indicated by underlining):

1. The cleft-sentence construction (Halliday's 'predicated theme'):

   [1] It was <u>Jack</u> who called yesterday

   [2] It was <u>yesterday</u> that Jack called

2. The equated-relative construction ('pseudo-cleft' in the terminology of transformational grammar and in Quirk *et al*, *GCE* (1972),

'identification' in Halliday):

[3] What they like is <u>beer</u>

[4] <u>Beer</u> is what they like

3. The WH-interrogative:

[5] <u>What</u> would you like?

4. The alternative interrogative:

[6] Would you like <u>tea or coffee</u>? (in the sense of 'Would you like tea, or would you rather have coffee?')

5. The comparative construction:

[7] <u>Mary</u> sings better than <u>Jane</u> does

[8] Mary <u>sings</u> better than she <u>dances</u>

6. The focusing adverbs:
a. exclusive[7], *eg* [9] below
b. additive, *eg* [10] below
c. particularizing, *eg* [11] below

[9] John speaks only <u>English and Spanish</u>

[10] Peter speaks also <u>a number of very obscure Amerindian dialects</u>

[11] He is particularly interested in <u>Potawatomi</u>

7. The intonation nucleus[8]:

[12] He was <u>here</u>

[13] He <u>was</u> here

[14] <u>He</u> was here

8. Marked word order[9]:

[15] <u>His name</u> I never found out

[16] <u>From one of his pockets</u> he produced a small package

The domain of a focus marker usually consists of three elements: the focus marker, the focus, and the residue. In the following examples the focus is underlined and the structure is represented by the letters

M (for marker), F (for focus), and R (for residue):

[17] Only <u>John</u> phoned   M F R

[18] John only <u>phoned</u>   R M F

[19] <u>John</u> also phoned   F M R

[20] John also <u>phoned</u>   R M F

In the next three examples, the residue is divided into two parts (represented in the formula by r . . . r):

[21] Today <u>John</u> also phoned   r F M r

[22] <u>Today</u> John also phoned   F r M r

[23] Today only <u>John</u> phoned   r M F r

It is clear that both word order and intonation are relevant to the identification of the focal element in structures with focusing adverbials like those in [17]–[23] above. The rules are complex and are different for each individual marker. Examples [19] and [20], or [21] and [22], clearly show that word order alone is not a sufficient clue. But neither is the place of the intonation nucleus. Both [21] and [22] could be represented in speech by utterances with the same intonation pattern, as shown in [21'] and [22']:

[21'] Today <u>John</u> àlso phoned #

[22'] <u>Today</u> John àlso phoned #

And [17] could be represented in speech by [17''] as well as by [17']:

[17'] Only <u>Jòhn</u> phoned # (I expected them all to get in touch, but . . .)

[17''] Only <u>John</u> phòned # (They were all worried, but . . .)

Three of the focus markers are combined with the focus: the intonation nucleus, the WH-interrogative, and the alternative interrogative. The combination may be symbolized by '$\frac{M}{F}$', as in [24]:

[24] <u>Who</u> called? $\frac{M}{F}$ R

In the superordinate clause of the comparative construction, the marker is an inflexion (*-er*) or a modifier (*more* or *less*) of the item that denotes the dimension of comparison, *eg young, carefully*. (In phrases like *more people, more room*, the word *more* is a conflation of dimension + marker.) In the subordinate clause (or phrase) of the construction, the comparative marker (*than*) is the initial element and the dimension is omitted:

[25] Harry drives more carefully than
     you do   F r M r – M F R

[26] Jane looks younger than Susan   F R M – M F

Although every focus domain must have a focus marker and a focus, there is sometimes (as in [26] above) no residue. Firstly, it may happen that the whole of a normal complete sentence is intended to be in focus. This is a reasonable interpretation for [27], in the context of, say, 'Just imagine what I found out today!':

[27] Matilda smokes cigars!

But there is also the possibility of ellipsis. Since the residue represents what the speaker is treating as 'background information', it is not unnatural that the residue should sometimes be omitted; and this may in fact happen with all the focusing devices listed above except for the equated relative (pseudo-cleft)[10] and marked word order. In the following examples, the A-sentences provide the context:

1. Cleft focus: M F (R)

   [28] A: Who said that?   B: It was John (who said it)

2. WH-focus: $\frac{M}{F}$ (R)

   [29] A: We are going to Paris.   B: When (are you going)?

3. Alternative focus: (R) $\frac{M}{F}$

   [30] A: I'd like a drink.   B: (Would you like) whiskey or beer?

4. Comparative focus (reduction of subordinate clause): M F (R),
   M (R) F

   [31] I know Susan better than you (do)

   [32] I know Susan better than (I know) you

5. Adverbial focus: M F (R), (r) F (r) M, *etc*

[33] A: Who's coming?   B: Only <u>John</u> (is coming)

[34] A: They've left.   B: (Has) <u>Susan</u> (left), too?

6. Intonation focus: $\frac{M}{F}$ (R)

[35] A: Who made the sandwiches?   B: <u>Màry</u> (made them) #

The omitted residue may have to be recovered from the context at large, rather than the immediately preceding sentence:

[36] A: Why aren't you coming? Don't you like musicals?
B: Oh, I do. It's (just) <u>the date</u> (that's incovenient/ that I can't manage)

In the examples given above, the missing residue can be supplied without altering the sentence in any other way, but sometimes the form of the focal element makes this impossible:

[37] A: Don't you like musicals?   B: Oh, I do. It's just <u>that I'm too busy</u>.[11]

[38] <u>Tommy's</u> bigger than <u>me</u>

[39] A: I'm going out.   B: <u>Me</u>, too

The domain of a syntactic focus marker may be interrupted by parenthetic material, *ie* by something that is not part of the domain and so neither focal nor residual. For example (with the parenthesis marked by '+... +'):

[40] It was <u>John</u>, +of course,+ who arranged the meeting

[41] <u>The boys</u>, +I suppose,+ were also there

[42] Martin, +unfortunately,+ could only stay for <u>an hour</u>

Such parenthetic items, excluded from the domains of other focus markers, may themselves be focus markers in theme-rheme structure (see Ch. 2).

In the chapters that follow, we shall be mainly concerned with the focusing adverbs and with such topics as are most closely bound up with the grammar of the focusing adverbs. This means that of the

focusing devices listed above we shall have to pay particular attention to word order (Ch. 2) and intonation (Ch. 3). In addition, we
shall deal with some aspects of the grammar of the cleft construction (§4.1).

1.3 FOCUS AND MEANING

All the focusing devices give prominence to selected parts of sentences or utterances, and this is itself part of their meaning. But for
each one of the focusing devices the prominence (or 'highlighting', or
'foregrounding') is associated with some other aspect of meaning. It
is convenient here to make use of Halliday's distinction between what
he calls the ideational, the interpersonal, and the textual components
in the linguistic system.[12] The ideational component 'is concerned
with the expression of content'; it 'represents the speaker in his role
as observer'. The interpersonal component 'is concerned with the
social, expressive, and conative function of language, with expressing
the speaker's "angle"', his motive in speaking; it 'represents the
speaker in his role as intruder'. The textual component 'comprises
the resources that language has for creating text', where 'text' (or
rather 'a text') is 'a unit of language in use', its unity being
based on cohesion, or connectedness, between its parts. The textual
component could be said to represent the speaker in his role as
designer.

A focusing device may have ideational, interpersonal, or textual
meaning (and these possibilities are not mutually exclusive). The
comparative construction, and the particularizing and exclusive
adverbs, have ideational meaning. The prominence they give derives
from the content represented.[13] The interrogative focusing constructions have interpersonal meaning. The prominence they give derives
from the speaker's 'intrusion', from the expression of his communicative intent. Focusing by intonation has textual meaning. It serves to
fit the sentence into its context by distinguishing between items
presented as 'new' and items presented as 'given' information (see
Ch. 3). Additive focusing is both ideational and textual. On the one
hand it involves propositional content (see §4.2.8 below), and on the
other it serves to create a link with what has gone before (see [2] and
[3] in §1.1 above). The cleft construction has meaning of all three
kinds. Ideational meaning is involved because the construction

specifies its focus as unique with respect to the content of the residue (*ie* of the relative clause). The interpersonal meaning consists in the selection of the focus as the target, so to speak, of the speaker's communicative intent. And clefting also has textual meaning, because its use, and the selection of its focal item, change the way a sentence coheres with the text of which it forms a part.[14]

Although the meaning of intonation focus is primarily textual, it may serve in addition to mark distinctions between different ideational meanings, by the way it affects the interpretation of particular syntactic structures. For example:

[1] Mary is particularly fond of cherries

may be interpreted as either (i) comparing Mary's fondness for cherries with her fondness for other kinds of fruit, or (ii) comparing Mary's fondness for cherries with other people's fondness for the same fruit. The two intonation patterns [2.a] and [2.b]

[2] a. /Mary's par!ticularly 'fond of :chèrries #
    b. /Mary's par!tìcularly 'fond of 'cherries #

are understood as pointing to (i) and (ii) respectively. This follows naturally from the intonational marking of *cherries* as focal in [2.a] and non-focal in [2.b]. Marked theme is clearly associated with textual cohesion by virtue of its position in the clause. But the cohesive effect goes with the position, regardless of markedness. For example:

[3] a. One was a great success. <u>The other</u> they didn't like very much
    b. One was a great success. The other was not very popular

[3.a] and [3.b] contrast with [3.c]:

[3] c. One was a great success. They didn't like the other very much

The placing of *the other* in initial position strengthens the cohesion in [b], where it is unmarked theme, no less than in [a], where it is marked theme. So where an unmarked cohesive order is available as an alternative, as in this example, we may regard word order focusing as conveying prominence pure and simple.

1.4 FOCUS, SCOPE, AND SYNTACTIC STRUCTURE

In § 1.1 above we introduced the notion of a 'domain' within which a focus marker is effective: its scope or sphere of operation. Within this domain the focus marker picks out a focus, and all the rest is residue. The examples of focus markers in § 1.2 above were all very straightforward, in the sense that the domain of the marker always corresponded to a whole sentence or clause. However, this need not be so. The relationship between domain and syntactic structure is liable to be particularly complex in the case of intonation, but even the domain of a syntactic focus marker may be something less than a clause and need not correspond to any syntactic constituent. Compare the following sequence:

[1] I know that Harry had nothing against it. And it wasn't <u>John</u> that objected

[2] *I know that Harry had nothing against it. And it was <u>John</u> that didn't object

There is no difference between [1] and [2] in the first sentence. The second in both is a cleft sentence corresponding to the uncleft

[3] John didn't object

and *John* is focus of the cleft construction in both cases. Nevertheless, only the first of the two sequences can be part of a coherent discourse. The difference between them is in the domain, or scope, of the cleft construction. In [2] the negation is inside the scope of the cleft construction, whereas in [1] the cleft construction is inside the scope of the negation. Similarly with the following two sequences:

[4] Harry wasn't always on time. But it was <u>John</u> who was always late

[5] *Harry wasn't always on time. But it was always <u>John</u> who was late

In both [4] and [5], the cleft sentence corresponds to the uncleft

[6] John was always late

and both have *John* in cleft focus. Yet the two cleft sentences clearly differ in meaning, and only the sequence in [4] is coherent. Again the difference is in the domain of the cleft construction: *always* is inside in [4] and outside in [5].

In the above examples, the difference in domain corresponds to a difference in syntactic structure. The negative is within the domain of the cleft construction when it is a constituent of the relative clause, but not otherwise; and the same holds good for *always*. But domain (or scope) is not always determined by syntactic structure, as appears from the ambiguity of

[7] Only <u>John</u> has read some of these books

This could mean either the equivalent of

[8] Some of these books, only <u>John</u> has read

or of

[9] Only <u>John</u> has read any of these books

In the reading corresponding to [8], *some* is outside the scope of *only*, whereas in the reading corresponding to [9] it is inside. Again no difference in focus is involved, and this time there is no difference in syntactic structure either: in both readings of [7], *some of these books* is object of the verb and a constituent of the predication. We see, therefore, that the extent of a focus marker's domain (the scope of a focus marker) may or may not be signalled by syntax. The notion of scope in relation to focus markers is analogous to the logical notion of scope that is required for the analysis of negation and quantifiers, as will be seen in Chapters 5 and 6.

To return to our notion of language as a device for the sending of messages (§1.1 above): the concepts of scope and focus enable us to deal with language in action from two complementary points of view – the static, concerned with the message as a body of data, and the dynamic, concerned with the message in transmission from speaker to hearer, the message as it unfolds. The first is based on judgements of 'true' or 'false', the second on discrimination between foreground and background, and on the ordering of the parts in the sequence of discourse. Each point of view brings out one aspect of the organization of the message. The static aspect is the province of logic and without it the message can have no conceptual content; the dynamic aspect is the province of functional sentence analysis and without it the message cannot be sent or received. Both logic and functional sentence analysis, too long neglected by linguists in their preoccupation with syntax, are essential to an understanding of language.

Notes

1. See F. Danes (1964); J. Firbas (1964); and J. Vachek (1966).
2. See M. A. K. Halliday (1967–8:3.199–244). Cf. also W. L. Chafe (1970, Ch. 15), (1974), and (1976); and S. Kuno (1972).
3. R. Quirk, S. Greenbaum, G. Leech and J. Svartvik (1972).
4. See especially M. A. K. Halliday and Ruqaiya Hasan (1976).
5. This use of the term 'domain' is quite distinct from that in Halliday (1967–8:3.207), where it is equivalent to what I have called the 'focal unit' in §3.1.1.
6. This ability to make connexions between non-adjacent sentences is characteristic of cohesion in general. See Halliday and Hasan (1976:14ff).
7. In *GCE* 8.13, the exclusives are associated with the particularizers as subdivisions of a class called 'restrictives'. It is doubtful, however, whether there is good reason for such a grouping. The basis for setting up the exclusives and additives as separate classes is essentially semantic, and from this point of view the class of particularizers is distinct from both the others. The particularizers are probably best regarded as implicit comparatives. Compare the following sentences:

   (i)   a. <u>John</u> likes Mary better (than <u>Tom</u> (does))
         b. John likes <u>Mary</u> better (than (he likes) <u>Jane</u>)
   (ii) a. (Of all the boys) <u>John</u> likes Mary best
         b. (Of all the girls) John likes <u>Mary</u> best
   (iii) a. <u>John</u> particularly likes Mary
         b. John particularly likes <u>Mary</u>

   Like the explicit comparatives (whether this term is taken to include the superlatives or not), the particularizers require a dimension of comparison as an essential part of the structure, and this distinguishes them from exclusives and additives alike.
8. The function of the nucleus as a focus marker is well known. On the focusing function of the non-nuclear accents, see Chapter 2.
9. [15] and [16] illustrate 'marked theme'. For an extension of this notion, and also for the concept of 'marked rheme', see Chapter 2.
10. However, the residue of an equated-relative focus may be emptied of all real content, *eg*

    (i) What happened was <u>that Mary went home</u>

11. Here and in [36] above, a single item is focused on by two markers simultaneously – the cleft construction and the exclusive adverbial *just*. For other examples of such convergence, see Chapter 7.
12. See Halliday and Hasan (1976:26f).
13. I am taking 'content' to mean 'propositional content' in the sense of Lyons (1977:749). For the propositional content of *only*, see §4.2.8.
14. On 'cleft' and 'pseudo-cleft', see Prince (1978:883–906).

Two

Sequential focus: Marked theme and marked rheme

2.1 HALLIDAY'S THEORY OF THEMATIZATION: *PRO* AND *CON*

It has long been recognized that there are two kinds of rules – the grammatical and stylistic – that govern the ordering of words and phrases; or in more technical language, that sequential ordering may be (i) purely syntactic, in the sense that sequence is uniquely determined by syntactic dependency relations, or (ii) syntactic and contextual, which means that considerations of coherence and emphasis, in addition to syntax in a narrower sense, have a part to play. For example, if the three words *do*, *you*, and *hear* are to form an interrogative sentence, they can occur only in the sequence of [1]:

[1] Do you hear?

and this is determined exclusively by the rules of English syntax. None of the other five mathematically possible permutations will yield a well-formed interrogative sentence.[1] If on the other hand we wish to form a declarative sentence using the words *I*, *saw*, and *Mary*, we may opt for either of the two sequences [2.a] and [2.b]:

[2] a. I saw Mary

b. Mary I saw

Both are syntactically well-formed declaratives and the choice between them will be made on contextual grounds.[2]

These observations are neither new nor controversial, but the general awareness of such facts as these did not cause them to figure prominently in linguistic theory until the development of 'functional sentence analysis' by linguists of the Prague school. 'Functional sentence perspective', the component of linguistic organization that was dealt with by 'functional sentence analysis', was incorporated by Halliday in his theory of systemic grammar (see especially Halliday 1967–68), under the general heading of 'theme', in a tripartite division of grammatical organization in which the other major components were 'transitivity' and 'mood'. The three major components are derived in the theory from three major functions of language: 'transitivity' from the 'experiential' (or 'ideational') function, 'mood' from the 'interpersonal' function, and 'theme' from the 'textual' function.[3] Within the network of options that come under the heading of theme, a separate subpart accounted for 'thematization', that is the ordering of clause elements in two major blocks, an initial block containing one or more 'themes',[4] and a final block, the 'rheme'. The Prague discussions of 'functional sentence perspective', though abounding in important insights, had been based on a heterogeneous mixture of analytical criteria, including data not only from syntax but also from intonation and from the contextual interpretation of utterances. It was one of Halliday's important achievements to set up within the textual dimension of language the concept of information structure, phonologically signalled by intonation and proceeding from one network of options, and the concept of thematization, or theme-rheme structure, which depended on the sequential ordering of sentence elements and proceeded from a distinct network of options.[5]

But the theory of thematization that Halliday expounded in his 'Notes on transitivity and theme in English' (1967–68), though it constituted a great advance on the work of his predecessors, suffered from two shortcomings: firstly the failure to sever completely and finally the ties that bound it to its pretheoretical antecedents, and secondly the failure to complement the concept of 'marked theme' with a corresponding concept of 'marked rheme'. The pretheoretical notion to which the concept of theme traces its origin is the old and familiar one of the 'psychological subject' or 'what we are talking about'. This notion, ill-defined though it is, has had an important role to play in the progress of linguistics, since it has led to the formation of three vital theoretical concepts: 'subject' in syntactic structure, 'given' in information structure, and 'theme' in textual structure. Of these three, the oldest and best-established is the subject, of course, and this is also the only one that has been formalized to the general satisfaction of linguists.[6] 'Given' and 'theme' are relative newcomers, and though they now have their acknowledged places in the general scheme of things, their precise outlines remain to be determined and agreed upon. In this chapter, of course, we are concerned only with theme.

Halliday took the crucial step of defining theme in purely sequential terms – the theme or themes always precede the rheme – but the notion that the theme has to represent 'what I am talking about' was not disowned.[7] And indeed, at a certain stage in the exposition, this is not only harmless but very helpful, perhaps indispensable. A good example is the observation (1967–8:3.212) that 'while "given" means "what you were talking about" (or "what I was talking about before"), "theme" means "what I am talking about" (or "what I am talking about now")'. Here the reader is made to sit up and think, to take a second look at something familiar and seemingly simple, and discover that it is not as simple as he thought. But the usefulness of such commonsensical leading-strings always has its limits: eventually the analytical concept must learn to stand on its own feet and go its own way. We may compare the syntactic concept 'noun' and its relationship to the 'name of a person or thing'.

The unwillingness to part company with the idea of theme as 'what is being talked about' has this drawback: it leads easily to the conclusion that if x is the theme of a sentence, all that remains must be 'what is being said about it', the rheme; and though Halliday did not follow this line of thought uncompromisingly – we are allowed sequences of two themes on condition that the first is 'non-cognitive' (see 1967–8:3.221*f*) – he did follow it to the extent of denying thematic status (for example) to *John* in *Did John see the play yesterday?* or in *Yesterday John saw the play* or *The play, John saw yesterday*. Now if the items whose status is in question were merely parts of a string, and otherwise unrelated by any structure, there would be no objection to such an analysis. But the situation is quite different. The statement that the subject is theme and the predicate is rheme in textually unmarked declarative sentences, which is the point of departure for the rules of textual sequence in English, illustrates the organic connexion between sequential order and syntactic dependency. Textual order is not merely linear order, related only to preceding and following sentences (if any) in the text; textual order is linear order in relation to syntactic dependency structure. Now the syntactic dependency relations between *John* and *saw* are exactly the same in [3], [4], and [5]:

[3] John saw the play yesterday

[4] Yesterday John saw the play

[5] The play, John saw yesterday

It is therefore totally unmotivated from a formal point of view to change the textual description of John (from 'theme' to 'part of rheme') as we move form [3] to [4] or [5]. In Section 2 of this chapter I shall attempt to provide a more satisfactory theory of unmarked order.[8]

In the preceding paragraph I criticized the failure to sever the connexion – historically important but analytically harmful – between 'theme' and 'what is being talked about'; we now come to the second of the two shortcomings in the theory of thematization: the conspicuous absence of a concept of 'marked rheme', to complement the concept of 'marked theme'. It is a commonplace of handbooks of composition that 'we may ... emphasize ideas ... by placing important words in the important positions at the beginning and end of the sentence' (Hodges 1951:302). It is also well known that we give emphasis by departing in some way from normal order. Thus the writer of a school textbook remarks, by way of comment on a passage from Macaulay: 'In each of these instances Macaulay has departed from the normal order so as to give emphasis to a particular word or phrase. He could not have secured this effect, however, had there been no normal order from which to depart, so these sentences serve to underline the fact that in English the subject is usually placed first and followed by the predicate' (Pritchard 1934:42). It would seem that one of the obvious tasks of a theory of textual ordering is to incorporate these important insights within a formal framework. Halliday's account of thematization does this for the beginning of the sentence, but fails to provide for the end. I shall try, in the last two sections of this chapter to make good this omission and thus provide a more general (though still incomplete) theory of the textual ordering of elements in the English sentence.

2.2 SEQUENCE IN THE SENTENCE: THE UNMARKED OPTIONS

In what follows I shall take the position that sentences may be divided textually into an initial (or thematic) segment, a final (or rhematic) segment, and a mobile segment, which I shall call 'operator'.[9] In the most straightforward cases, there is one theme and one rheme, and the division corresponds to the traditional syntactic division of the sentence into subject and predicate. In the majority of such simple theme-rheme sentences, the theme corresponds to 'what the speaker is talking about' and the rheme to 'what he is saying about it', and this makes it convenient to go on using the established terms 'theme' and 'rheme'; but these descriptions must not be regarded as definitions. Theme and rheme are textual, not 'psychological' entities, and the division into thematic and rhematic is based on sequential ordering.[10] Of course, the freedom to choose a sequence is limited; it is held in check by the bonds of syntactic dependency, and even when syntactic dependency does not prescribe a particular sequence as the only possible one, it generally (perhaps always) points to one that will be chosen unless there is some pragmatic motivation for preferring another. That sequence of syntactic items which requires no special pragmatic motivation is what we shall call 'unmarked sequence', and a sentence that is represented by an unmarked sequence will be said to contain only unmarked textual elements, where 'textual element' embraces 'theme', 'rheme', and 'operator'.[11] The operator is always an unmarked element in theme-rheme structure (though it may be focal intonationally; see below, Ch. 3).

The following sentences exhibit different types of unmarked sequence, the differences between the types being determined principally, but not exclusively, by the syntactic options relating to speech function: declarative, interrogative, *etc*. The sequence types are arranged in three sets, as follows:

(a) Complete (*ie* containing theme and rheme): Types 1–6
(b) Themeless: Types 7–10
(c) Rhemeless: Types 11–13

In the analysis that accompanies the examples, 'Th', 'Op', and 'Rh' stand for 'theme', 'operator' and 'rheme', '//' marks the end of the initial segment, or the beginning of the final segment, or both, and '/' marks any other division between textual elements.

1. Declarative (with or without operator):

[1] John // is // painting the shed
    Th   Op   Rh

[2] John // painted the shed
    Th   Rh

[3] John // did // paint the shed
    Th   Op   Rh

[4] There // is // a ladder in the shed
    Th   Op Rh

[5] It // will // be necessary to paint the shed
    Th   Op   Rh

2. Polar interrogative:

[6] Is / John // painting the shed?
   Op   Th   Rh

[7] Did / John // paint the shed?
   Op   Th   Rh

[8] Is / there // a ladder in the shed?
   Op   Th   Rh

[9] Will / it // be necessary to paint the shed?
   Op   Th   Rh

3. WH-interrogative, with the subject as WH-element (with or without operator):

[10] Who // is // painting the shed?
    Th   Op   Rh

[11] Who // painted the shed?
    Th   Rh

4. WH-interrogative, with something other than the subject as WH-element:

[12] When / is / he // painting the shed?
    Th   Op   Th   Rh

[13] Why / is / there // a ladder in the shed?
    Th   Op   Th   Rh

5. Positive imperative with subject (without operator)[12]:

[14] You // keep out of my way!
    Th   Rh

6 Negative imperative with subject:

[15] Don't / you // touch that ladder!
    Op   Th   Rh

7. Subjectless positive imperative (themeless, with or without operator):

[16] // Paint the shed
      Rh

[17] Do // paint the shed!
    Op   Rh

8. Subjectless negative imperative (themeless):

[18] Don't // touch the paint
    Op   Rh

9. Elliptical declarative (themeless, no operator):

   [19] // Painting the shed (Context: A: What's he doing?   B: –)
        Rh

10. Elliptical interrogative (themeless, no operator):

   [20] // Painting the shed? (Context: What's he doing? –)
        Rh

11. 'Coded' declarative (no rheme)[13]:

   [21] He // did (Context: A: Did he paint the shed?   B: Yes,
        Th   Op
   he did)

12. 'Coded' polar interrogative (no rheme):

   [22] Did / he? // (Context: A: He painted the shed.   B: Did
        Op   Th
   he? Or as a tag: He didn't paint the shed, did he?)

13. 'Coded' WH-interrogative (no rheme):

   [23] Why / shouldn't / he? // (Context: A: He's going to paint
        Th   Op   Th
   the shed!   B: Why shouldn't he?)

According to the analysis here proposed, the subject is always thematic in unmarked sentences (provided of course that there is a subject). It is clear from [4], [5], [8], [9] and [13] that in the present context 'subject' means 'mood-subject', not 'concord-subject' (see note 6, for the use of these terms). The mood-subject may be said to constitute an 'empty' or 'dummy' theme, since it has no referential function (cf Quirk et al, 1972:958f on 'Existential there as "empty" theme'). It is here that we see the most obvious conflict between the formal notion of theme as a textual element and the pretheoretical notion of theme as 'what we are talking about'.

The finite verb can be part of the rheme, as in [2] and [11], but all the 'special finites' that can function in structures of inversion, negation, emphatic affirmation, and 'code'[13] are taken to be outside the rheme and are labelled 'operator', whether or not they are functioning in one of the structures that make the use of an operator obligatory.

There can be little doubt that where syntax (in the narrower sense) fails to determine some part of the sequential ordering, the choice between the available options is always significant in some way. It is possible, however, that we shall not always be able to point to one of the options as the neutral one. For example, if we compare

[24] a. Take your coat off

with

[24] b. Take off your coat

it may not be immediately obvious whether one of the alternatives should be regarded as textually marked and the other as unmarked. It so happens that this particular problem is complicated by dialect differences (see Hughes and Trudgill 1979:25); but if, for a given variety of English, both choices are neutral, we shall have to regard both the above sentences (or utterance-types) as consisting of one textual element only, *viz* unmarked rheme.

There are also cases of syntactically indeterminate sequence where one choice can be regarded as the neutral one, but the other, though marked, does not involve the use of a marked theme or marked rheme. For example:

[25] I have always liked Mary

[26] I always have liked Mary

There is a difference between the ranges of contexts for which each of these is appropriate, and they have different 'preferences' in intonation structure. Thus we find, typically:

[25'] a. I have /always lìked 'Mary #
b. I have /àlways 'liked 'Mary #

[26'] I /always hàve 'liked 'Mary #

There is also a difference in theme-rheme structure between [25] and [26], as shown in [25"] and [26"]:

[25"] I // have // always liked Mary
   Th   Op   Rh

[26"] I // always / have / liked Mary
   Th   Rh   Op   Rh

[25] has one rheme, and [26] has two, with the operator standing between them. Neither of the rhemes, however, is marked, in the sense in which I shall be using the term (see §2.4 below).

There are many other types of syntactically indeterminate sequences, and all of them would have to be dealt with in an exhaustive treatment of the textual organization of sentences. Here, however, our concern is with marked theme and marked rheme, and it is to these that we shall turn in the sections that follow.

2.3 MARKED THEME

In unmarked sentences, the sequence of syntactic elements is determined solely by the syntactic choices made by the speaker or writer and by the syntactic dependency relations that are set up by these choices. Marked sentences are characterized by the breaking of one or more of the links in the corresponding unmarked sequence and the detachment of a syntactic element from the element or elements with which it is contiguous in the unmarked sequence. The detached item may be initial or final in the marked sentence. If it is initial, it is a marked theme; if it is final, it is a marked rheme.

In the following sentences we have marked themes of the most familiar types ('MTh' stands for 'marked theme'):

[1] a. Yesterday / John // painted the shed
       MTh   Th   Rh

   b. The shed, / John // painted yesterday
      MTh   Th   Rh

In each of these sentence-forms, the marked theme is an element whose unmarked, neutral place is in the rheme, as we see in the corresponding unmarked form of the sentence:

[1] c. John // painted the shed yesterday
       Th   Rh

But the marked theme can also be an item whose unmarked place is within the subject and which can therefore be part of the unmarked theme:

[2] a. Of these sheds, / one // needed painting
       MTh   Th   Rh

Compare the corresponding unmarked form:

[2] b. One of these sheds // needed painting
       Th   Rh

A sequence of two such marked themes makes the sentence ill-formed; *eg*:

[1] d. *Yesterday / the shed / John // painted
      MTh   MTh   Th   Rh

   e. *The shed / yesterday / John // painted
      MTh   MTh   Th   Rh

[2] c. *Yesterday / of these sheds / he // painted one
      MTh   MTh   Th   Rh

   d. *Of these sheds / yesterday / he // painted one
      MTh   MTh   Th   Rh

However, pairs of adverbial phrases seem to make up single constituents and so to function as single marked themes; *eg*:

[3] The other day, at the post office, / I // ran into John
    MTh   Th   Rh

Such phrase sequences may be regarded as quasi-appositional structures; *cf*:

[4] Mr Johnson, the secretary, / you // have // already met[14]
    MTh   Th   Op   Rh

All the instances of marked theme which we have considered so far involve placing an item at the beginning of the sentence, instead of putting it in its neutral position, elsewhere; in terms of transformational-generative grammar they are the result of a fronting transformation. This fronting, however one's theory of grammar may account for it, is subject to syntactic constraints which a comprehensive grammar would have to state. For example, we cannot have a sentence like [5] – and the objections are clearly neither semantic nor pragmatic:

[5] *Seen I haven't Mary, but I spoke to her on the phone last night

On the other hand, a sentence may have as its marked theme an item that from the point of view of syntactic dependency is very remotely connected with the item that follows it in sequential order:

[6] This book / I // remembered your telling me that Mary
    MTh   Th   Rh
    had asked John to buy

I shall make no attempt here to formulate the syntactic rules that govern front-shifting.

Except for the so-called 'non-cognitive' themes (*however, perhaps*, etc), which have no position that could be called neutral other than the initial position itself, all the marked themes recognized by Halliday are of the 'front-shifted' type.[15] However, there is also a way of 'marking' even the subject of a normal uninverted declarative sentence. The subject may be separated from the beginning of the predicate by the intrusion of an element from elsewhere. This element may be one whose neutral position is initial, such as a connective, as in [7] below, for example ('// ____ /' marks the intrusive element):

[7] John, // however, / was // painting the shed
    MTh   ____   Op   Rh

Items such as *however, nevertheless, moreover, therefore*, etc may reasonably be considered to be syntactically outside the clause proper, and thus able to function as 'partitions', so to speak, between the textual elements, without being themselves included in either the initial or the final segment. The 'partition' that sets off the marked theme from what follows it in the clause may also be a vocative or a 'disjunct' (in the sense in which the term is used by Quirk *et al* 1972); eg

[8] That shed, // my dear, / will // have to be painted
    MTh   ____   Op   Rh

[9] John, // of course, / has // been painting the shed
    MTh   ____   Op   Rh

The disjunct may also take the form of a 'comment clause' (Quirk *et al* 1972:778*f*); eg:

[10] John, // you know, / has // painted the shed[16]
     MTh   ____   Op   Rh

The 'intrusive' elements that function as 'partitions' in sentences [8]–[10], like the connective in [7] above, may be regarded as syntactically extraneous, contracting no dependency relations within the clause, and textually parenthetical, neither thematic nor rhematic. We must note at this point, however, that some attitudinal disjuncts (eg *probably, possibly, wisely, foolishly, rightly, wrongly, carefully, carelessly*) have their neutral place in medial position, *ie* after the 'operator' if there is one,[17] and if there is no operator, between the subject and the main verb (Quirk *et al*:517). Such items do not function as partitions setting off a marked theme. Similarly with connectives: some have their normal place in medial position (eg *therefore*) and do not function as partitions when they stand between subject and verb:

[11] a. We // are / therefore // trying a new method
     Th   Op   —   Rh

    b. We // therefore // tried a new method
     Th   —   Rh

2.4 MARKED RHEME

There are three basic types of marked rheme:

(i)   The 'end-shifted' subject;
(ii) An 'end-shifted' constituent of the predicate;
(iii) A final item separated by a 'partition' from the item that would precede it if it were part of the unmarked rheme.

The following are examples of Type 1:

[1] Into the room // came / a strange man
   MTh   Rh   MRh

[2] Even more terrifying // was // his face
   MTh   Op   MRh

In these sentences, in which the subject functions as marked rheme, there is also a marked theme. This is in fact obligatory: unless we introduce a 'dummy' theme (a mood-subject distinct from the concord-subject) we cannot make a subject into marked rheme (or, indeed, into part of the unmarked rheme, either) without simultaneously fronting an element that would be in the rheme in the neutral form of the sentence.[18] Thus we cannot have the following:

[3] a. *Came into the room a strange man
    b. *Came a strange man into the room

[4] a. *Was even more terrifying his face
    b. *Was his face even more terrifying (as a declarative!)

But [3.a], and perhaps also [3.b], become well-formed if *there* is inserted as a dummy theme:

[5] a. There // came into the room / a strange man
     Th   Rh   MRh

   b. ?There // came a strange man into the room
      Th

The structure of [5.a] is normal but stylistically marked, being characteristic of narrative prose. The type of sequence represented by [5.b] is so rare, at any rate in present-day English, that its well-formedness might be disputed.[19] However, the corresponding constructions with BE are quite regularly used as a device for making the concord-subject rhematic. The unmarked sequence (parallel to [5.b]) has already been illustrated in §2.2, sentences [4], [8], and [13]. The contrast between unmarked and marked is illustrated by the following pair of sentences:

[6] a. There // were // a number of interesting points in this
     Th   Op   Rh
    article

   b. There // were // in this article / a number of inter-
     Th   Op   Rh   MRh
    esting points

Sentences [6.a] and [6.b] are textually parallel to [7]:

[7] a. He // had // found a number of interesting points in this
     Th   Op   Rh
    article.

   b. He // had // found in this article / a number of inter-
     Th   Op   Rh   MRh
    esting points

Both [6.b] and [7.b] contain marked rhemes of Type 2.

Sentences with anticipatory *it* (ie *it* as mood-subject pointing to a following subject-clause) resemble existential sentences in allowing the 'real' subject to be part of the unmarked rheme. (The term 'concord-subject' is not appropriate here.) The subject clause, however (unlike the concord-subject in existential sentences), is final in unmarked sequence:

[8] It // was // announced on the radio that the road was
   Th Op   Rh
   blocked

[9] It // was // decided last week to reduce the subsidy
   Th Op   Rh

Object clauses also take the final position in unmarked sequence, *eg*:

[10] They // announced on the radio that the road was
     Th   Rh
    blocked

[11] They // decided last week to reduce the subsidy
     Th   Rh

In [10] and [11] there is an adverbial (*on the radio*, *last week*) between the verb (*announced*, *decided*) and the object (*that the road was blocked*, *to reduce the subsidy*). Nevertheless, the direct object being a clause, the sequence is unmarked. Some clause elements which are final without 'end-shifting' can be made into marked rhemes of Type 3 by the insertion of a 'partition' (see 2.3):[20]

[12] They // prefer, / I think, / a warmer climate
     Th   Th   —   MRh

[13] They are // returning, / however, / to England
     Th Op   Rh   —   MRh

Most marked sequences may be said to involve an element of delay: in sentences with marked theme we are often kept waiting for the subject; in sentences with marked rheme we may be kept waiting for the subject, or for part of it, or for some part of the predicate. But this element of delay does not have the same effect in the two sets of cases. In sentences with marked theme, the delayed item is textually unmarked; in sentences with marked rheme, it is the delayed item itself which is the marked item. So what the marked items have in common is not the delay, but rather a combination of two things: detachment and terminal position, where 'detachment' means non-contiguity with a normally contiguous item or items, and 'terminal' means initial or final.

2.5 MARKED SEQUENCE AND INTONATION FOCUS

Theme-rheme structure depends on the ordering of syntactic elements, whereas intonation structure derives from the division of utterances into major phonological units (intonation units) and the placement of nuclear and non-nuclear prominence within these units. Though the two structures result from distinct systems of choices, their functions overlap: both of them serve to distribute emphasis and to establish cohesion in the text. It is natural, therefore, that the two sets of choices should not be entirely independent of one another.[21]

The relationship between sequential focus and intonation may be stated as follows: every marked theme and every marked rheme must contain an intonation focus, whereas an unmarked theme or an unmarked rheme may be residual in intonation structure. The focus on a marked theme may be either a nuclear or a non-nuclear accent; a marked rheme must receive a nucleus.[22]

For example, with marked theme:

[1] a. /Yĕsterday # /John 'painted the shèd #
    b. /Yesterday 'John 'painted the shèd #

[2] a. The /shĕd # he /painted yèsterday #
    b. The /shed he 'painted yèsterday #

[3] a. /Jŏhn how'ever # was /painting the !shèd #
    b. /John how'ever was 'painting the :shèd #

And with marked rheme:

[4] a. He had /found in this árticle # a /number of 'interesting poìnts #

[5] a. They re/vealed to him !all their sècrets #

[6] a. They'd pre/fĕr I 'think # a /wàrmer 'climate #

In [4a], [5a], and [6a], the final element in the predication is a marked rheme, and it would therefore be anomalous to put it in the 'tail' of the intonation unit, after the nucleus:

[4] b. *He had /found in this àrticle a 'number of 'interesting 'points #

[5] b. *They re/vealed to !hìm all their 'secrets #

[6] b. *They'd pre/fĕr I 'think a 'warmer 'climate #

Contrast [4c], [5c], and [6c], with the final element in the tail of the intonation unit, but as part of an unmarked rheme:

[4] c. He had /found a :number of 'interesting poìnts in this 'article #

[5] c. They re/vealed !all their sècrets 'to him #

[6] c. They'd pre/fĕr a 'warmer 'climate I 'think #

When a clause contains an embedded clause as subject or object, the final position is unmarked (see [8]–[11] in §2.4). It follows that such final clauses may or may not contain an intonation nucleus:

[7] a. It was an/nounced on the :rădio # that the /road was !blòcked #

  b. It was an/nounced on the !ràdio that the 'road was 'blocked #

[8] a. It was de/cided last wéek # to re/duce the sùbsidy #

  b. It was de/cided last !wèek to re'duce the 'subsidy #

[9] a. He ad/mitted quite fránkly # that /hè had done it #

  b. He ad/mitted quite !frănkly that he'd 'done it #

[10] a. I /knew all the 'time who it :wăs # (but I couldn't prove it)

  b. I /knew all the :tìme who it 'was #[23]

It was suggested in §2.2 that there might be some sentences with transitive phrasal verbs (such as *turn off*) that could be ordered in two alternative sequences, both of them unmarked in terms of theme-rheme structure. The relationship that has been shown to exist between sequential order and intonational focusing options corroborates this view:

[11] a. He /dìd turn the 'lights off #

  b. He /dìd turn 'off the 'lights #

[12] a. /Màry 'threw the 'rubbish 'out #

  b. /Màry threw 'out the 'rubbish #

Though the intonation nucleus is on the subject or operator, the a- and b-sequences are both acceptable, which we would not expect if one of them ended in a marked rheme. Contrast the rigidity of the order when the object is a personal pronoun:

[13] a. He /dìd turn them 'off #

  b. *He /dìd turn 'off them #

[14] a. /Màry threw it 'out #

  b. */Màry threw 'out it #.

Yet the b-order (adverbial particle before object) is acceptable when the object pronoun bears the nucleus: *eg*:

[15] a. /He called !mè up #
      b. /He called up !mè #

It is clear that with personal pronouns as objects, the b-order is marked, or (more specifically) that it ends in a marked rheme.

So far we have related sequential marking to marking by nuclear or non-nuclear accents. But accentuation can be interpreted in terms of 'information assessment' (see Ch. 3); and the relation between sequence and information is just as simple but more meaningful: an unmarked theme or rheme may or may not contain information that is assessed by the speaker as 'new', but a marked theme or a marked rheme always contains 'new' information. The choice between marked and unmarked rheme, like that between marked and unmarked theme, is a major factor in textual well-formedness, and textual well-formedness is an essential component in overall acceptability, together with phonological well-formedness, syntactic well-formedness, and semantic well-formedness. But in textual structure the transition from well- to ill-formed is somewhat gradual, and this contributes not a little to the notoriously fuzzy edges of acceptability.

Sequential marking has been included among the focusing devices here examined because like them it gives the marked item a greater prominence than it would have if it were unmarked. It represents a separate set of choices, interacting with (though distinct from) related choices in intonation structure and syntax. The connexion between sequential focus and intonation focus is particularly important, as we have seen in this section. Of the links between sequential and syntactic-semantic choices, those with adverbial focusing are of special interest in the context of this study; see §4.2.7 and §7.2.2.

Notes

1. I am using Bar-Hillel's distinction (1970 : 365) between declarative, interrogative, *etc* on the one hand and statement, question, *etc* on the other. The sentence *You do hear* could be used to ask a question, but it is declarative in syntactic form. See also Lyons (1977:30).

2. Depending on one's use of the term 'sentence', one might call [2.a] and [2.b] either two sentences or two utterance-types corresponding to a single sentence. Lyons (1977:622*ff*) uses the term 'text sentence' for something that normally corresponds to an utterance unit, and 'system-sentence' for the more abstract sense of 'maximal unit of grammatical description' (1977:624); but he regards thematic differences like those between [2.a] and [2.b] above as differences

between system-sentences. Since system-sentences are supposed to be 'maximally decontextualized', this is surprising; but Lyons admits to 'an element of arbitrariness' at this point (page 632).

3. See also Halliday (1970b).

4. The term 'theme' is thus used by Halliday in two distinct senses, either for the whole set of choices serving the textual function, or for one element in the sequential structure of clauses.

5. The elements of structure in information units are Given and New, which Halliday carefully distinguishes from Theme and Rheme (see §3.1–3). The importance of this contribution to linguistic theory was not fully appreciated at the time by linguists at large, and even now it has probably not made the impact that its significance would seem to warrant. The reasons may be divided into two sets. Those in the first set belong to the sociology of linguistics, rather than to the study of language itself, and I shall not be concerned with them here. Those in the second set are more directly relevant to the subject of this book, and to them I shall devote the remainder of this section.

6. The process took longer in English than elsewhere, since it became clear only gradually that 'subject', in English, was not a single individual, but a pair of Siamese twins. They are known by various names, and I shall follow Huddleston (1971) in calling them 'concord-subject' and 'mood-subject'. There is also the 'deep subject' of transformationalist grammar, but with this we are not concerned in the present context.

7. 'The theme is what is being talked about, the point of departure for the clause as a message' (1967–8:3.212).

8. The demand for a treatment of theme rigorously based on syntactic dependency and sequential ordering is not intended to deny the need for a complementary approach from the pragmatic end. For a discussion of topichood (or 'aboutness') as a pragmatic relation, see Reinhart (1980).

9. The use of 'operator' to denote the function of the finite auxiliaries and of the non-auxiliary uses of the finite forms of BE is familiar from Quirk *et al* (1972). The term was introduced by J. R. Firth. 'Operator' as an element in theme-rheme structure is an innovation of the present analysis.

10. 'Left-to-right ordering', though convenient enough for English and other languages written in roman characters, seems rather parochial for a term that should be more generally applicable.

11. The converse does not hold good: a text-sentence that contains only unmarked textual elements may nevertheless exhibit marked sequence; see [25]–[26] at the end of this section.

12. Types 5 and 6 are marked options syntactically (corresponding to the unmarked options represented by Types 7 and 8), but they are unmarked textually, with unmarked elements in unmarked sequence.

13. Types 11–13 examplify 'code' uses of the operator. The term 'code', which is familiar from Strang (1969) and Palmer (1974), was introduced by J. R. Firth.

14. The phenomenon exemplified by [3] was already noted by Halliday (1967–8:3.219). There are clear parallels in cleft focus and adverbial focus (see §4.1.4 and §4.2.3). Alex Grosu has pointed out to me that the special status of sequences of adverbial elements is confirmed by multiple WH-questions. Compare (i) and (ii):

(i) Where and when did you meet?
(ii) *Where and whom did you meet?

15. It is not clear why Halliday considers his 'non-cognitive themes' to be marked rather than unmarked (that he does so is clear from the table on page 222); he

says himself that 'they favour initial position' (page 221), and their marked status is not even mentioned in the text, let alone justified. Presumably there is an unspoken assumption that marked themes cannot follow unmarked ones, and this seems reasonable. Now initial 'non-cognitive' adjuncts may be followed by 'cognitive' adjuncts, whose neutral place is elsewhere and which must therefore be marked themes (eg *However, yesterday John saw the play*). So there would certainly seem to be a problem here. But there is an alternative solution, which I regard as preferable, *viz* that items like *however*, etc are syntactically extraneous to the clause proper (rather like conjunctions) and that therefore they are not part of the theme-rheme structure at all (except insofar as they can function as 'partitions' and so change the status of other sentence elements).

16. We find that here too a sequence of two marked themes makes the sentence ill-formed; *eg*:

   (i)   *Today, John, you know, is painting the shed
   (ii) *The kitchen, he, you know, painted yesterday.

17. Prof. Bolinger has pointed out (private communication) that this formulation is oversimplified, since with some operators it is equally normal, or even more normal, for the disjunct to be placed before the operator (*John probably will leave*). This seems to be partly (but only partly) a matter of Anglo-American differences. According to Quirk *et al* (*loc cit*) the normal position is at 'M2' *ie* '(a) immediately before the [main] verb, or (b) before the complement in intensive BE clauses' (§8.7). This may hold good for some items (*He has been quite rightly dismissed*), but it is surely false for *definitely, indeed, surely, undoubtedly, probably, possibly* (eg *He has surely been dismissed*). Contrast (i) and (ii):

   (i)   He has been definitely informed that . . . (He has received definite information)
   (ii) He has definitely been informed that . . . (It is definitely the case that he has been informed).

   In (i), *definitely* is an adjunct, in (ii) it is a disjunct.

18. This statement holds good for independent sentences. In 'quoting clauses', it is possible to have the structure // Rh / MRh (see note 19). Sentences like *Came the rain* are the kind of exception of which it may justly be said that they prove the rule. Prof. Bolinger (private communication) draws attention to the legalistic archaism of *Comes now John Metcalf and deposes that* . . . as another exception to the rule.

19. Scheurweghs (1961) has a solitary example (page 5), and this, by its awkwardness, tends to reinforce rather than remove one's doubts: 'Nevertheless there would be thrown an additional burden on our balance of payments' (T. [*ie The Times*] 20.11.1954). Jespersen (1909–49) quotes only one example (vii. 112), and this is clearly intended by its author (Stevenson) as an archaism: 'In the ancient days there went three men upon pilgrimages.' Prof. Bolinger, however, (private communication), supplies the following examples, which can hardly be called archaic:

   (i)   There can be found a few villages like that in Austria to this day
   (ii)   There appears to have arisen some small misunderstanding in our dealings
   (iii) There never existed any such creatures on this earth
   (iv)   There comes a time in everyone's life when . . .

20. For the use of focusing adverbs as partitions, see §4.2.7. Not all final elements that follow partitions are marked rhemes; see §2.5. Clauses that function as

partitions are not themselves thematic or rhematic elements in the clauses that contain them. Nevertheless, being clauses, they have their own internal theme-rheme structure. Comment clauses normally have an unmarked theme-rheme structure (eg *you* // *know*; *I* // *think*; *I* // *suppose*), but there is one particular subtype, the 'quoting clause', that may have a marked structure (eg - // *said* / *John*). Vocatives before marked rheme seem to be very rare.

21. This is recognized in Halliday (1967–8, 3 : 199*ff*). But the present analysis differs from Halliday's both in relation to theme-rheme structure (this chapter) and in the interpretation of intonation (Ch. 3). This results, among other things, in a stronger statement of the relationship between sequential order and information assessment.

22. This follows from the final position of the marked rheme. On nuclear and non-nuclear accents, see Chapter 3 below, especially §3.1 3–5.

23. Final embedded clauses are unmarked even after partitions, since they can be treated as 'given'. For example:
    (i) I /knèw of 'course where he 'lived #
    (ii) He /tòld me you 'know that he'd 'done it #.

Additional Note
Green (1980) is a valuable study of sentences with the subject as marked rheme (Type 1 in §2.4), mainly concerned with contextual motivation for the use of the pattern. The author is dissatisfied with the explanatory value of 'some general pragmatic principle, such as the "Old information first, new information last" dictum of some Prague school linguists' (page 583), but unfortunately she seems unfamiliar with Halliday's distinction between 'information structure' and 'thematization'.

Three

Intonation focus and the assessment of information

3.1 INTONATION FOCUS AND NEW INFORMATION

3.1.1 'New information' in a syntactic framework

It is now a commonplace that one of the functions of intonation in English is to divide a discourse into 'units of information' and to structure these units by singling out within each one a focal part which contains what the speaker is presenting to the listener as 'new', in the sense of 'newsworthy' (Halliday, 1967–8, Quirk *et al*, 1972; Bolinger 1958, 1972). The remainder of the information unit (if there is a remainder – some units are all focus) is said to contain 'given' information.[1] According to some versions of the theory, many information units – in fact the majority of those with 'unmarked tonicity' (Halliday), or with the focus in the 'neutral position' (Quirk *et al*) – are ambiguous in structure, and the choice between two or more structural possibilities is made in accordance with the context. The principle is illustrated in the following examples, in which the A-sentences provide the context, the nuclear syllable is marked with an accent, and the focal unit is in capitals (Halliday's term for the focal unit is the 'domain of focus'; Quirk *et al* speak of the 'new element' or the 'unit marked as new'):

[1] A: Who did John phone? B: John phoned MÀRY #

[2] A: What did John do? B: John PHONED MÀRY #

[3] A: What did you want to tell me? B: JOHN PHONED MÀRY #

In all the B-sentences the nucleus is on the first syllable of *Mary*, but the intonation focus extends over *Mary* in [1], *phoned Mary* in [2], and *John phoned Mary* in [3]. This kind of ambiguity occurs in all cases of unmarked tonicity, *ie* whenever the intonation nucleus ('tonic') falls on the last lexical ('open-class') word – provided, of course, that the last lexical word is not also the first word in the intonation unit. If the last word is a grammatical ('closed-class') item, it will not receive the intonation nucleus unless all the preceding lexical words are to be treated as given, *eg*:

[4] John phoned HÈR #

In [4] the focus is only on *her*. The focus is also limited to a single constituent when the nucleus precedes the last lexical item in the unit, but some ambiguity remains if the focal syntactic unit is complex and the nucleus falls on its last lexical item, *eg*:

[5] WILLIAM WÒRDSWORTH is my favourite English póet # (not John Keats)

[6] William WÒRDSWORTH is my favourite English póet # (not William Shakespeare)

Sentences [5] and [6] are from Quirk *et al* (1972: §14.6), as is [8] below. The intonation unit here contains a second nucleus. Such compound units with a 'major' falling nucleus followed by a 'minor' rise are said to have given elements which the speaker nevertheless wishes to make prominent (Halliday, 1970a:44), or 'semi-given' elements (Quirk *et al*, §14.6, note *a*). It is sometimes uncertain whether a particular utterance contains such a sequence of major nucleus plus minor nucleus, or a single nucleus with a distributed fall-rise contour. Apart from this, it is a matter of dispute whether such compound tone-units should not be regarded rather as sequences of two tone units, each with one nucleus, as proposed by Fox (1973), and also by Brazil (1978). But this is not crucial to the discussion that follows. In the following examples, the focal unit is fully determined:

[7] WÒRDSWORTH is my favourite English póet #

[8] ÈMILY Bronte is my favourite English nóvelist # (not Charlotte Bronte)

The differences between the relevant portions of Examples [1]–[3] and [5]–[6] are accounted for in terms of differences of structure, more specifically in terms of differences in the extent of the focal unit. This amounts to saying that the sentences in question are ambiguous, and that we are guided by the context in choosing between the two or more possible meanings.

3.1.2 Objections to the syntactic theory

But the theory as outlined so far will account for only part of the data. This is not surprising, for 'newness' and 'givenness' (like 'information' itself) are primarily contextual, pragmatic notions, based on '(the speaker's assumptions about) the addressee's awareness of things' (Allerton 1978:166),[2] and there is no reason why 'new' and 'given', in the contextual sense, should coincide neatly with syntactic units. Yet though the 'information unit' is clearly not tied to syntactic structure (as everyone has recognized), Halliday and others have tried nevertheless to delimit the 'domain of focus' or 'new element' as a syntactic unit.[3] Examples like [1]–[3] or [5]–[6] above are of course quite easily taken care of, but others turn out to be more refractory. It seems quite impossible, in fact, to reconcile the theory with the data unless we are prepared to recognize as a syntactic unit of some kind any collection of items (within a single intonation unit) which the speaker happens to be presenting to the hearer as 'newsworthy'. Consider for example

[9]   John phoned Máry # and Peter phoned Jàne #

In the second intonation unit of [9], *phoned* is 'given', and *Peter* and *Jane* are 'new', but *Peter* and *Jane* do not constitute any kind of syntactic unit. Similarly with [10], though here we have an example of marked tonicity:

[10]   (How did the message get to Mary?)
        I phoned Jóhn # and John phoned hèr #

In *and John phoned her*, *phoned* is 'given', and *John* and *her* are 'new'. A different combination of elements is 'in focus' in [11]:

[11]   Ǐ wouldn't mind sole # but Mary hàtes fish #

In the second unit of this example, both *Mary* and *hates* must be considered as 'new', while *fish* is 'given'; but we do not want to set up *Mary hates* as a syntactic constituent on that account. In view of problems like these, it seems that we must give up the idea of an information focus defined in terms of tonicity and syntax.

3.1.3 The theory of 'accented words'

What are the alternatives? O'Connor and Arnold (1961) speak of the 'prominence' that is given to words by a phonological feature they call 'accent'. 'Prominence' is given to words that are 'important' in a given context, and 'important' seems to correspond quite closely to what Halliday and others call 'new'. 'Accent' means rhythmical stresss plus pitch-obtrusion, or (in some contexts) rhythmical stress alone. The intonation nucleus always falls on the last accented word.[4] This gives us a theory that differs from those of Halliday and of Quirk *et al* in three ways:

(i)   Syntactic constituency at levels above the word is given no status at all;
(ii) The intonation contour as a whole, not merely the place of the nuclear (tonic) syllable, determines the distribution of prominence – and hence newness.
(iii) There is no provision for ambiguity: accented words are 'important' and unaccented words are 'unimportant'.

The following examples illustrate the approach ('important' words underlined):

[12] 'Come and 'see me to\morrow (*pp*18, 20)

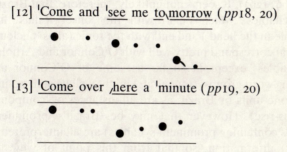

[13] 'Come over /here a 'minute (*pp*19, 20)

Albrow (1968), though he expounds a version of Halliday's analysis of English intonation, does not relate 'newness' to tonicity and syntax or to tonicity alone, but recognizes 'ictus' (stress) as a marker of newness in addition to tonicity. He thus explains not only 'the coincidence of lexical items with the ictus' but also the fact that some grammatical items, *viz* interrogatives and demonstratives, 'very commonly coincide with the ictus' (*pp*20–21).[5] In Albrow's treatment, as in O'Connor and Arnold, there is no mention of ambiguity in information structure.

In O'Connor and Arnold (1973) there is a new definition of 'accent'. All stressed syllables are accented except for those in the 'tail' (after the nucleus) and those in the 'prehead' (*pp*33–5), which 'are usually weakened if not wholly suppressed' (*p*24). In other words, all stresses in the 'head' now qualify as accents, regardless of whether they are pitch-prominent or not. The relationship stated between accent and 'prominence' is unchanged, however: all accented words are 'prominent' and hence 'important', alias 'new'.

Brazil (1978) also relates newness to something like accent rather than to tonicity alone or to tonicity plus syntax. According to Brazil's analysis, the words that are 'prominent', and hence bearers of (new) information, are distinguished not only 'from those which, in the usual distribution, are non-accented' but also from 'those which merely have word accent' (*p*16). It is claimed that 'prominent' syllables show a 'direction-change (rise changing to fall)' in the fundamental frequency contour, while syllables with mere 'word accent' are characterized by a level contour. The sketch copies of f_o traces that are reproduced (*p*11 *etc*) seem to indicate that the direction change referred to as essential to 'prominence' is of a kind that does not necessarily give rise to the auditory perception of pitch change in the syllable (compare Crystal's distinction between stress and accent (1969: 120)). It seems not unlikely, therefore, that Brazil's 'prominent' syllables, which begin with the 'onset' (alias 'first accented syllable in the head') and end with the tonic (alias 'nucleus') would in general correspond pretty well with O'Connor and Arnold's 'accented' syllables, except in so far as some of O'Connor and Arnold's longer 'word groups' (tone units) might well be split up into sequences of tone units by Brazil, as are all instances of 'compound tunes' (fall-plus-rise). However that may be, Brazil's 'prominent' words (*ie* words containing prominent syllables) are all interpreted as items of (new) information, so that from this point of view the treatment of information structure resembles that of O'Connor and Arnold rather than Halliday's.

3.1.4 Shortcomings of the accent theory

The type of analysis favoured by O'Connor and Arnold is clearly able to account for many sentence types which are not adequately represented in the Halliday-type analysis. For example:

[14] 'John phoned 'Mary # and 'Peter phoned ˌJane #

[15] (How did Mary get the message?)

    'I phoned 'John # and 'John phoned ˌher #

[16] ˇI wouldn't mind °sole # but 'Mary ˇhates ₀fish #

But we have difficulties with this system, too. One defect is that it fails to recognize the possible ambiguity (or rather, perhaps, indeterminacy) of the phonological marking of information structure. We can easily find sentences, even in O'Connor and Arnold's own intonation drills, where the automatic equation of 'accented' with 'new' seems hard to accept. For example:

[17] Shall I 'pass them to ⸝Robert?   'Pass them to ⸜me, ⸝rather (1961 : 97)

[17'] Shall I 'pass them to ⸝Robert?   'Pass them to ⸜me, ₒrather (1973 : 117)

[18] I've 'lived here a ⸜long ⸝time.   Yes, but 'have you 'lived here 'all your ⸜life? (1961 : 103)

[18'] I've 'lived here a ⸜long time.   Yes, but 'have you °lived here °all your ⸜life? (1973 : 122)

The words that are accented (and hence 'important') are the same ones in both versions: in [17] and [17'] *pass*, *Robert*, *pass*, and *me*; and in [18] and [18'] *lived*, *long*, *have*, *lived*, *all*, and *life*. Now the context of the response in [17] makes it hard to accept the second *pass* as 'new', yet the accent on *pass* sounds right. And similarly with [18]: *lived* in the response is hard to accept as new, yet the version with the accent on *lived* seems eminently natural. The motivation for the accent on *pass* seems to be bound up with the effect of the accent on the intonation contour and its attitudinal effect, while the motivation for the accent on *lived* seems purely rhythmical. In [17], without the accent on *pass*, we would have, according to O'Connor and Arnold's account (*p*48), a pattern 'typically convey[ing] *detachment, a lack of involvement*, which may be variously interpreted as *coolness, dispassionateness, reserve, dullness*, and possibly *grimness* or *surliness*', whereas in the pattern as given we have (*ibid*) and 'effect . . . of very considerable *power* and *strength*, in addition to . . . definiteness and completeness . . . This power may lend itself to utterances of a *categoric, weighty, judicial, considered* kind'. While others might use different terms to characterize the attitudes conveyed by the two intonation patterns that are here contrasted, it will be generally agreed that the attitudes are markedly different, and that the speaker could not afford to disregard this difference in choosing the intonation of the response. The speaker, therefore, is not free (in this case) to mark the word *pass* as 'given', even though he is not interested in marking it as 'new', either.

The stress on *lived* in [18] has no better contextual motivation than that on *pass* in [17], and its removal would not necessarily affect the intonation contour at all. It would, however, produce an awkward unstressed sequence *you lived here*[6] which would give, by contrast, an exaggerated emphasis to the preceding *have*. If the reply had been:

[19] Yes, but 'I've lived 'all my 'life in this ₀place

the word *lived*, coming now between two stressed syllables, and still lacking contextual motivation for stress, would naturally be pronounced weak.

An examination of transcriptions of recorded speech, from the files of the Survey of English Usage,[7] provides further examples of the ambivalence of non-nuclear accents[8] ('accents' in the sense of O'Connor and Arnold (1973)). For example:

[20] it was /only in 'tended as a dràft # (S.11.1.56)

Here *intended*, in spite of the stress, is contextually given, since the interpretation is equivalent to that of *It was intended only as a draft*. In the following example:

[21] in which /we can 'only 'help . a 'small amòunt # (S.11.2.37)

the word *small* must be intended as 'new', whereas *help* is clearly 'given'; yet both words have the same kind of stress. Similarly with:

[22] /Manchester Unìted # /only de'feated 'once this sèason # by Èverton # (S.10.2.67)

In [20]–[22] the motivation for the stresses on the given items is presumably rhythmical (in [21] the brief pause after *help* points to a slight hesitation, which could be a contributory factor); but other motives seem to be involved in the following:

[23] it's /not only a'bout wórds # /it's a'bout !Nfèelings # and /it's a'bout !Nhìstory # /it's a'bout an in:terpre'tation of a !whole ... (S.5.7.24)

In the second, third, and fourth units, *it's*, an item normally quite unstressed, is placed in the onset position of the contour, though neither information distribution nor rhythmical considerations of the sort previously noted could be thought to motivate this. We are concerned here with the building up of a rhetorical pattern extending over a sequence of intonation units, a pattern in which both the distribution of stresses and the pitch contours play their parts.

3.1.5 A synthesis

Examples [17]–[23] show that we can neither discount non-nuclear accent nor treat it as a reliable indicator of contextual newness. The natural way out of our difficulty is to recognize 'accent' as relating to the contextual concept of 'newness' but not fully determining the distribution of 'new' information in an utterance. The situation may be summed up as follows:

(i)   Items bearing nuclear accents are always 'new';[9]
(ii) Items bearing no accent at all are always 'given';
(iii) Items bearing non-nuclear accents are, from the listener's point of view, 'potentially new', and their interpretation depends on his assessment of the total context.[10]

From a theoretical point of view, this means a clear separation between 'intonation structure' (where 'intonation' is given a wide sense, to include features of rhythm) and 'assessment of information'. The 'intonation structure' includes the division into 'intonation units' (or tone units, or tone groups) and the separation of 'focal' items, marked by 'accent', from 'residual' items, unmarked by accent. The 'assessment of information' (from the listener's point of view) is part of the total pragmatic import of the message, arrived at by extracting the 'new' information from the set of 'focal' items. Intonation structure, in this sense, is a purely linguistic level of description, as opposed to assessment of information, which is now clearly set apart as a pragmatic concept.[11]

The linguistic level of intonation structure is concerned with both phonological and non-phonological entities. The phonological entities (tones, accents) are the markers and the non-phonological entities are the items marked. It now remains to be a little more specific on the subject of these non-phonological entities. According to Halliday they are syntactic units, but this view we found unsatisfactory. According to O'Connor and Arnold they are words, but this is not quite satisfactory, either. Consider, for instance, the following:

[24] What are you doing? I'm reading

Here *reading* is the word that bears the accent in the response, but the focus is on the lexical item *read*. The progressive aspect component of the verbal group, represented by *'m -ing*, is residual. Here, then, the focal item is only part of a word. But it can also be more than a word, as in:

[25] I /won't put :ùp with it #

Here the accent on *up* serves as a marker, not for the word *up* alone, but for the complex lexical item *put up with*. It follows that the focal item can consist of part of a word together with one or more other words, *eg*:

[26] I'm /not putting :ùp with 'this #

Here the focal item marked by the accent on *up* is again *put up with*, though *put* does not stand as a separate word in this sentence.

We must therefore allow the focal entities to be lexical items of different degrees of syntactic complexity, correlating in various ways with syntactic constituency structure, including word division.

But it is not only lexical items that can be focal. Of the grammatical items, interrogatives and demonstratives (as noted by Albrow) are frequently marked as 'new' by non-nuclear as well as by nuclear accents. Other grammatical items, *eg* personal pronouns, are rarely focal unless they are used contrastively. The verbs require special notice. The finite auxiliaries, or rather the 'operators' (see Quirk *et al* §3.6), are typically quite unstressed; but they may also bear accents, even nuclear accents. When they do so, it is usually not the grammatical function of the individual operator that is marked as focal, but rather the 'invisible' component that is common to the whole class, *viz* the 'assertive' component of the operator. For example:

[27] Why haven't you phoned John? – But I hàve (phoned him)!

The word accented in the response is *have*, but the focus rests neither on *have* as marker of perfect aspect nor on *have* as marker of present tense (if present tense can be considered to have a marker in English); the focus rests only on *have* as marker of assertion. The position is even more complicated in cases like the following:

[28] This book ought to be reprinted. – But it's bèen reprinted!

The nucleus in the response is on *been*, but the item that is marked as focal is the perfect aspect component of the verbal group, represented by the 'stem' of *'s* and the 'past participle' suffix of *been*. The stem of *been*, which is part of the representation of passive voice in the verbal group, is not part of the focal item.

We see, therefore, that the grammatical focus-bearers, like the lexical ones, may be syntactically complex and may enter into complicated relationships with the syntactic constituency structure. Such are the non-phonological entities involved in 'intonation structure' in the present account. It will be apparent that in relating the status of 'focus' to lexical and grammatical items in the sense indicated above, we have related 'focus' directly to the linguistic entities on which the semantic interpretation must be based. The plane on which these entities 'exist' is surely the right 'habitat' for what has been called information structure – which I prefer to call 'intonation structure', in order to distinguish it more clearly from the pragmatic concept of 'information assessment'.

To sum up: we have considered two conflicting schemes of analysis, represented chiefly by (i) Halliday, and (ii) O'Connor and Arnold, which may be outlined as follows:

(i)   Focus is marked by the tonic (nucleus) and delimited by syntactic constituency. The size of the constituent is frequently undetermined by phonological marking of any kind, giving rise to ambiguity in information structure, which must be resolved with the help of the context.

(ii) Focus is marked not only by the tonic (nucleus), but also by other 'accents' (which are phonological features or combinations of phonological features). Focus extends over the accented words and there is no ambiguity in information structure.

Neither of these of these analyses is adequate: what is required is something that may be called a version of (ii) modified so as to account for the factor of ambiguity (present in (i)), and also to account for focal items larger than words or smaller than words. We thus obtain (iii):

(iii) Focus is marked by the tonic (nucleus) and by other accents. It extends, not over words as such, but over the lexical or grammatical items that include or are included in the accented syllables. 'Information' is a pragmatic concept. All 'new information' is represented by focal items, but not all focal items represent 'new information'.

3.2 INTONATION AND CONTRAST

3.2.1 Bolinger's theory of contrast

In 'Intonation Focus and New Information' (§3.1) I have adopted the common practice of using the label 'new' to denote whatever is presented by the speaker to the hearer as particularly deserving of attention, and I have not distinguished between the different contextual reasons that a speaker may have for conferring 'new' status on part of an utterance – except for incidental mention of the contrastive use of focus on certain grammatical items (p40).

'New' does not mean that the part so designated 'cannot have been previously mentioned, although it is often the case that it has not been'; it is simply that 'part ... of a message block' which 'the speaker ... wishes to be interpreted as informative' (Halliday 1967–8:3.204). Correspondingly, 'given' means 'predictable' rather than 'already mentioned'. Both 'informative' and 'predictable' relate to the manner in which the speaker presents the items, and this is based on his assessment of them in the immediate context of utterance.[12]

Within 'new' Halliday and others distinguish a subcategory 'contrastive'. The use of intonational highlighting for contrastive emphasis is well known, having been first pointed out, it seems, by Coleman (1912), and it is generally agreed (*pace* Chafe 1976) that there are no phonological or phonetic features that by themselves force a contrastive interpretation. A question that does arise, however, is 'What mappings of accents onto grammatical or lexical items make a contrastive interpretation (a) possible and (b) necessary?'

To answer this question, we must first decide in which of several possible senses we intend to use the term 'contrastive'. Bolinger (1961a:83) speaks of 'the familiar phenomenon of contrast, by which two or more items are counterbalanced and a preference indicated for some members of the group'. His examples include the following (pp83,88; the notation, both here and in [31]–[32] below, is the present writer's):

[29] This whiskey was not ĕxported from Ireland; it was DÈ-
ported

[30] I said to repòRT the trouble, not BRŎADcast it

Both of these exemplify what Bolinger calls 'contrastive accent'; the
first, but not the second, also shows what he calls 'contrastive stress'
(what might be called 'marked salience' in Hallidayan terms, on the
analogy of 'marked tonicity'). The two sentences contain uncon-
troversial examples of pairs of words used contrastively, but the
definition quoted above is open to criticism. Firstly, one might want
to regard contrast as an essentially binary relationship (Bolinger's
examples are in fact all binary). Secondly, the indication of a
preference, though typical of contrast, is not essential to it. Bolinger
himself, in the same article, gives examples that lack this feature,
eg(*p* 89):

[31] The phenomenon we are noting may be called the relationship between length and ŭNfamiliarity, or between
condensation and FÀMiliarity (or . . . famìLiarity)

[32] On the one hand you have the densest ŭNintelligibility, and
on the other the clearest ìNtelligibility (or intèLLigibility)

Two further points call for comment. The first is that in his examples
of contrastive accent Bolinger ignores those instances of contrast that
do not bear 'the main accentual prominence'. Thus pairs like *one* . . .
other and *densest* . . . *clearest* in [32] are not dealt with, presumably
because 'the main accentual prominence' is on *unintelligibility* and
intelligibility. In our terms, this may be equivalent to saying that for
Bolinger contrastive accent implies 'nuclear accent'; but even this
may not be strong enough, since *on the one hand* . . . *on the other
hand* are in fact more likely than not to be pronounced with nuclei *on
one* and *other*. The second point is that the use of 'contrastive' in
'contrastive stress' to mean simply 'a shift in stress' from its normal
position in the word (*pp*88,96) is inconsistent and confusing: if we
distinguish, as Bolinger does, between marked tonicity and contrastiveness, we should distinguish similarly between marked salience
and contrastiveness (Bolinger does not use the terms 'tonicity' and
'salience', but this does not affect the issue). Contrastive use is no
doubt the most important occasion for marked salience, but it is not

the only possible one. Here are two non-contrastive examples:

[33] I've/CHĒCKED it # and/DŌUBLE-checked it # and/RÈ-
checked it #

[34] There's/STRÉPtomycin # and/NÉomycin # and
/AÙreomycin #

Unless we equate 'contrastive' with 'marked', these are no more
contrastive than:

[35] There's/TÓM # and/DÍCK # and/HÀRry #

3.2.2 Contrast in Halliday's theory of grammar

Halliday also uses the term 'contrastive' in more than one way. In
'Notes on Transitivity and Theme in English' it is simply the
contextual interpretation of 'marked focus' (1967–8:3.206–8):
'Marked focus may be focus on a reference or other closed system
item, whether final or not, or on a lexical item that is not final; here
what is structurally new is informationally contrastive.' In *Intonation
and Grammar in British English*, on the other hand, a distinction is
made: 'The marked information point is either contrastive, or new by
reference to another item as given: //∧ I/saw/<u>him</u>// either = "not her"
or is in answer to *who did you see*?' (1967:38).

In addition to these contextual uses of the term, 'contrastive'
figures as a element in the labels attached to terms in grammatical
systems (the 'contrastive' term being expounded by tonicity in System
12, by tone sequences in 3, 3.1, and 5); but the labels, of course, are
chosen for convenience and are not a reliable basis for conclusions
about the theory; witness System 2 (NEGATION TYPE), where the label
'transferred negation' is given to an option which certainly deserves
to be called 'contrastive' from a contextual point of view (*eg*
'//4 ∧ I/didn't/come because he/<u>told</u> me// (= "it wasn't because he
told me that I came")' (1967:34).

In one case, Halliday's terminology is not merely inadequate but
seriously misleading from a contextual point of view. In 1967:39
he says: 'Note that non-tonic *does*/*do*, *did* are non-contrastive:
// ∧ he/did/<u>ask</u>//, with tonicity neutral, is non-contrastive marked
positive'. The choice of term here seems singularly unfortunate;
for contextually, we must distinguish between//∧ He/did/<u>ask</u>//∧ but

he/didn't/wait for an/answer//, with *did* contrastive, and // ∧ I/did
en/joy that//, with *did* intensifying. So if the pattern is to have a single
systemic label in the grammar (which is questionable) the element
'contrastive' ought to be kept out of it altogether.

Of the two contextual uses distinguished in the last paragraph but
two, the first is also the one adopted by Quirk *et al* (1972: §14.3,
*pp*938–9, §14.5, *pp*940–41), while the second is compatible with a
more generally accepted sense (*cf* Bolinger 1961). The first sense (*ie*
as in 1967–8:3.208) seems inappropriate in contextual-pragmatic
analysis, for it would lead us to include [36] below (which we surely
want to exclude):

[36] (A: Are you expecting anyone?) B: /Yès # /Jòhn said
     he'd come #

and it makes no provision for [37]–[40]:

[37] The/South is fértile # and the/North is bàrren #

[38] /You go fírst # and/I'll fòllow #

[39] Well it/looks 'fine on the :ŏutside #

[40] He/didn't :leave because he was afrăid #

These types must surely be included if 'contrastive' is to make sense
in cognitive terms. In [37]–[40], all the tonics are contextually
contrastive, though none are 'marked', and in [37]–[38] we have in
addition the obvious contrast between *South* and *North*, and between
you and *I*, which do not bear tonics at all, let alone marked tonics. It
follows that 'contrastive', if defined as corresponding to marked
focus, is really a pseudo-contextual category. One might compare it
to a would-be semantic division of relative clauses into restrictive and
non-restrictive, made on the basis of intonation structure (see
Taglicht 1977).

To sum up this part of the discussion, a satisfactory account of
contrast must satisfy two conditions: (i) its basis must be intonational
and contextual, not intonational and syntactic; and (ii) it must not
trivialize the notion of contrastiveness by admitting the possibility of
non-binary contrast – this may be convenient elsewhere (*cf* Lyons
1977:279), but in the present context it would render virtually useless
a familiar and very convenient term.[13]

3.2.3 A contextual and intonational theory of contrast

In what follows I outline a provisional sketch for an account of contrast in the framework of information assessment.

1. 'New' items may be contrastive or non-contrastive. 'Contrastive' means 'presented as one of a pair of opposites'. The hyponymous relation of 'contrastive' to 'new' is the link between contrastiveness and intonation structure, since 'new' entails 'focal in intonation' (though the converse does not hold good, see §3.1.3).

2. 'Oppositeness' is a contextual-pragmatic concept. It may be represented by opposite terms in semantic structure, *eg* 'pos':'neg', 'alive':'dead', 'hot':'cold', 'up':'down'; but this is not necessary: thus 'green (light)' and 'red (light)' are opposites in the context of traffic regulation, regardless of whether we perceive them as (diametrically) opposite hues or not (on opposites in semantics, see Lyons 1977: 270*ff*). Oppositeness is characteristically expressed by the use of syntactically parallel items, *eg popular* and *unpopular* in *Peter was popular and Paul was unpopular*; but this, too, is not necessary: *cf Everyone disliked Paul, but Peter was a universal favourite.* Note also the following series, with *new* and *old* as opposites in all three sentences: (i) *He gave him the old one and got a new one*; (ii) *If you give me the old one, you can have a new one*; (iii) *New lamps for old*!

3. Oppositeness may be primary or secondary. Primary opposites are opposed to one another by virtue of their own meaning in the context of use, *eg* 'pos':'neg'; 'hot':'cold'; 'green (light)':'red (light)'. Secondary opposites are opposed to one another only by virtue of their relationship with primary opposites, *eg He* and *they* in *He votes Conservative and they vote Labour*.

4. An opposite is contrastive if and only if it is 'new'. Thus in /Í didn't do it # /hè did it # the opposite semantic elements 'neg' and 'pos' are not contrastive, because they are non-focal in intonation structure and hence 'given' in information assessment.[14] It follows that in this case both the secondary opposites ('I', 'he') but neither of the primary opposites ('neg', 'pos') are informationally contrastive. The same happens in (*I was right and you were wrong. – No, not at all.*) /Í was right # and /yòu were wrong #. Here the 'given' primary opposites (the second occurrences of 'right' and 'wrong') are represented by lexical items. The converse situation – two 'given' secondary opposites and two contrastive primary opposites – is vanishingly rare. The reason is not far to seek: primary oppositeness, which is

inherent, is more easily 'taken for granted' (and hence presented as 'given' information) than secondary oppositeness, which depends on its relationship to an instance of primary oppositeness. The following is imaginable: (*I suppose he ate the carrots and left the peas*) – /*Nò* # *he* /*léft the carrots* # *and*/*àte the peas* # But this is much less likely than . . . /*Nò* # *he* /*ate the* !*pèas* # *and* /*left the* !*càrrots* #. (*Ate* and *left* of course, represent (pragmatic) primary opposites, since *left* – in the context – means 'didn't eat').

5. Contrastiveness may be explicit or implicit. If it is explicit, both members of the pair of opposites are present in the utterance; *eg* /*Í didn't do it* # /*hè did it* #. If it is implicit, only one of the pair of opposites is present, but the form of the utterance conveys the implication of something unsaid which would have contained the other member of the pair: *eg* /*Í didn't do it* #. It is often hard to determine whether implicit contrast is present or not in a particular utterance.

6. Explicit contrastiveness may be bilateral or unilateral. If it is bilateral, A is contrastive to B and B to A (where A and B are a pair of opposites and A precedes B), eg /*One was únderexposed* # *and* /*one was* !*òverexposed* #. Here both the primary opposites ('over-' and 'under-') and the secondary opposites ('one' and 'one') are mutually contrastive. The relationship may be represented thus: A ↔ B. If the contrastiveness is unilateral, either A or B is 'given'; eg /*Yǒu 'know him* # /*I* !*don't* #. Here the primary opposites are the semantic elements 'pos' and 'neg', and only 'neg' is used contrastively. The secondary opposites, however (*you* and *I*), are mutually contrastive. The instance of unilateral contrastiveness is in this case of the type A ← B; by A → B is also possible; eg (*I keep telling you:*) /*John* !*dìdn't go* # / *Ì went* #. Here the 'neg' in *didn't* has a double function: on the one hand it contradicts something said or implied in the preceding context, and on the other it contrasts with 'pos' in the following clause (but 'pos' is 'given' and hence non-contrastive).

The principal options mentioned in 1–5 above may be diagrammatically represented as follows (braces and brackets as in standard systemic notation):

Note: 'Contrastive' is not a term in a system but indicates the co-selection of [opposed] and [new] in Systems 1 and 2 respectively, or in other words it represents the intersection of the classes defined by the features [opposed] and [new]. This is shown here by the

Fig 1

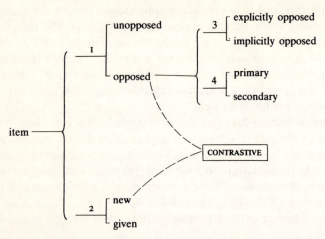

broken lines leading to the box labelled CONTRASTIVE.

It follows from what has been said above that in the present scheme there are four types of contrastive items that are distinguished from one another contextually:

(i)   primary, explicitly opposed, eg *unfamiliarity, familiarity* in [31] above;
(ii) secondary, explicitly opposed, eg *exported, deported* in [29];
(iii) primary, implicitly opposed, eg *outside* in [39];
(iv) secondary, implicitly opposed, eg *afraid* in [40].

The terms 'bilateral' and 'unilateral' do not appear in the network above, since they describe not 'items' but configurations containing two mutually opposed items. The study of configurations of opposites – the antitheses of the rhetorician – is beyond the scope of the present inquiry. A study of antithesis would necessitate a theoretical distinction that has only been hinted at so far (note 13): between 'contrastive' as a feature, or rather feature-complex, of single items, and CONTRAST as a function performed by one or more items that are used contrastively. Thus in *You know, and I know; but does the dog know?* both *you* and *I* are contrastive; but they represent jointly one side of the opposition {*you, I*} : *dog*. (One might compare the coordination of two subjective nominals in SUBJECT function; eg *He and I know*.) Such a study would deal also, of course, with various kinds of multiply contrastive configurations, of which the simplest are the double contrasts (*eg* [38] and [39] above).

We can now return to the question that was asked earlier, *viz* What kinds of items (a) can, or (b) must be contrastively interpreted if suitably accented? The answer to the first part is now straightforward: any item that can be 'new' can also be contrastive, though the contrastiveness may depend on a 'secondary' opposition (see *pp*46–47 above). The accentuation may be nuclear, *eg* on *fertile* and *barren*, (*go*) *first* and *follow* in [37] and [38] above, or non-nuclear, *eg* on *South* and *North*, *You* and *I* in the same sentences. The second part of the question is harder to answer, since it is often difficult to draw the line between 'implicitly opposed' and 'unopposed'. The best candidates for obligatory contrastiveness are morphemes that indicate binary choices and bear 'marked salience' in the utterance – provided that marked salience is defined in such a way as to exclude rhythmical stress-shift in premodifiers–the most obvious examples being those where marked salience coincides with marked tonicity, *eg* *un-* in [41]:

[41] He was /selfish and ùnkind #

But non-nuclear marked salience suffices to force a contrastive interpretation for *un-* in [42]:

[42] He was /unkind and sèlfish #

Where the stress-shift is rhythmically conditioned, the interpretation is normally non-contrastive, *eg*:

[43] a. /undue ìnfluence #
      b. an /unfair quèstion #
      c. of /unsound mìnd #

We see that just as there are types of contrastive items that differ from one another contextually (see Fig. 1 above), so there are types that are distinguishable intonationally. The options are shown in Fig. 2:

This means that there are six phonological possibilities:

(i)   marked tonicity, marked salience, eg *exported* in [29];
(ii) marked tonicity, unmarked salience, eg *report* in [30];

Fig 2

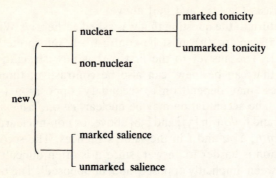

(iii) unmarked tonicity, marked salience, eg *familiarity* in [31];
(iv) unmarked tonicity, unmarked salience, eg *broadcast* in [30];
(v)   non-nuclear, marked salience, eg *unkind* in [42];
(vi) non-nuclear, unmarked salience, eg *selfish* in [41].

The examples in [41]–[43] show how easy it is to overgeneralize when attempting to formulate rules for the contextual interpretation of intonational phenomena. The writing of precise rules for the contrastive interpretation of utterances, insofar as it is possible at all, will require a great deal of further research. What I have tried to do here is to prepare the ground for such research and to provide a theoretical framework within which it might be carried out.

Notes

1. Allerton (1978) distinguishes three kinds of givenness: (i) of a linguistic item, (ii) of the particular referent, and (iii) lack of news value. It is news-value givenness that is meant here. In Chomsky (1969:199*ff*) 'presupposition' is used in this sense. The idea of a distinction between 'new' and 'given', marked by differences in stress, goes back at least as far as Sweet (1898: §1884); but the function of pitch as a marker of prominence seems to have been first noted in Coleman (1912).
2. In Halliday's formulation, the function 'new' means ' "treated by the speaker as non-recoverable information": information that the listener is not expected to derive for himself from the text or the situation' (1970b:163).
3. See Halliday (1967–8:3.207): 'The domain of focus is [...], in general, the highest rank constituent within which the syllable that is tonic is the last accented syllable.' Also Quirk *et al* (1972:940, §14.5); Chomsky (1969:201); and

Akmajian (1979:197*ff*). The account in terms of surface syntactic constituents is criticized in Lakoff (1971:260–62), where it is suggested that 'derived structure at some earlier point in derivations is relevant'.

4. This formulation applies, properly speaking, only to 'simple tunes'. But O'Connor and Arnold, like Halliday and others, allow also for compound intonation units with two nuclei. On pitch change as a factor in stress and accent, see Crystal (1969:113*ff*) and the references there.

5. It must be acknowledged that at one point in Halliday (1967–8:3.208) recognition is given to the connection between stress and information. '["Given-new" and "new"] tend[...] to be distinguished in informal speech; either by tone [...] or by rhythm, the given-new having no salient syllable before the tonic [...] compare (*what do they do*?) // ∧ they / teach / classics// with (*what do they teach*?) // ∧ they teach / classics//' (*p*208). But the point is developed no further. If the principle had been applied consistently, it would have necessitated abandoning the notion that syntactic constituents as such are units that function as 'new' or 'given'.

6. There is of course nothing inherently awkward in a sequence of three unstressed syllables as such, but not all sequences of vowels and consonants are destressed with equal ease: thus '*Did he come a'long*? is more likely than '*Have you lived here 'long*? (other things being equal). This 'phonological resistance to destressing', as it might be called, leads of course to the development of the 'weak forms' of grammatical words like personal pronouns, auxiliary verbs, *etc*. But the process is not limited to grammatical words. Lexical words that are frequently low in informational content may be subjected to reduction in the same way; *cf* OE *macode* > ME *made* 'made' with OE *slacode*, *wacode* > ME *slakede*, *wakede* 'slaked', 'waked'. *Make* was relatively 'empty' in many collocations, *eg make mirth, joy, sorrow, dole*.

7. The following symbols are used in the quotations:-'′' and '`' for falling and rising nuclei; '*N*' for narrow pitch-movement; '#' for end of tone-unit; '/' for onset (first prominent syllable) of tone-unit: '″' for stress with 'unmarked' downstep; ':' for stress with a step up in pitch; '!' for stress with a step up above level of preceding onset or step up; '.' for brief pause (shorter than one stress-group).

8. Prof. Bolinger (private communication) suggests that the interpretation of what I have called non-nuclear accents (such as that on *lived* in [18] above) might depend on the degree of accentuation (by pitch prominence). This raises an important question of principle: Are we justified in regarding all non-nuclear accents as equal (as in the interpretation suggested here), or must we add a further distinction or distinctions, and if so how many? The same question is raised by the 'booster' system as set up by Crystal and Quirk (1964). I must admit that so far it is not clear to me what further refinements are desirable (or, indeed, possible, as long as we wish to stop short of representing gradience).

9. Even this is too strong if 'new' is understood in a narrow sense as 'informative in content'. Some nuclear accents fall on items, *eg actually*, *surely*, which may convey only what Brazil (1978:44*ff*) calls 'social' information, *ie* information on the state of the relationship between speaker and hearer. Compare also Halliday (1970a:41–2): '... "new information" is not confined to the communication of facts; the "message" may be of any kind, such as *how do you do*? where the "new information" is simply that the speaker is well disposed and is acting within accepted social conventions.'

10. We can make a stronger statement for items which are without stress in the unmarked case (*eg* personal pronouns). When a non-nuclear accent falls on an item in this class, the interpretation is normally 'new'. Consider, for example, the

two following discourse fragments:

(i) A: /How did you 'get the 'message to :Màry #
     B: I/phòned her #
(ii) A: /How did the 'message 'get to :Màry #
     B: /I !phòned her #

In (i) the second speaker is 'given' in the context of A's question, and so 'I' is unaccented. In (ii), it is more natural for the second speaker to be 'new' – there seems to be no assumption on A's part that the message was delivered by B – and so 'I' is accented. The reply in (ii), with 'I' obligatorily interpreted as 'new', would be pragmatically ill-formed in (i), unless the wider context is calculated to lead A to presume that the message was delivered by someone other than B.

11. This is not intended to suggest that pragmatics is outside linguistics, but rather that it is a marginal area, like phonetics.

12. See also Allerton and Cruttenden (1979). A satisfactory comprehensive analysis of 'newness' does not yet seem to be within reach. Chafe (1974 and 1976) proposes redefining 'new' as 'what the speaker assumes he is introducing into the addressee's consciousness by what he says' (1976:30). It is not clear how this proposal would work out in detail. Prince (1981) develops a taxonomy based on the notion of 'assumed familiarity', with a primary distinction between three values ('new', 'inferrable', and 'evoked') and further subdivisions. These categories are likely to prove valuable for the comparison of different varieties of written discourse, or of written discourse with spoken, since they are not based on intonation structure. Prince's analysis has little in common, of course, with the assessment of information in the sense in which I have used this term.

13. A single binary contrast may contain more than two contrastive items, eg:

     (A: Don't worry; barking dogs don't bite.)
     B: Well/yŏu know that # and/so do !Ì # but/does the !dòg know #

Here you and I contrast jointly with dog.

14. Since didn't is in the 'tail' of the intonation unit, the accentual pattern marks the negation as 'given', which seems counterintuitive. The reason is that here the choice of tone comes into play. A rising or falling-rising tone on a declarative clause, if it ends on a high pitch, produces a challenging or contradictory effect, and this gives extra prominence to the negation even though the operator (with its negative suffix) is unaccented.

Four

Syntactic focus: the focal segment

4.1 CLEFT FOCUS

4.1.1 Ordinary and narrow cleft focus

Intonation structure, as we saw in Chapter 3, is to some considerable extent independent of syntax, both in the delimitation of its units and in the selection of what is highlighted in each unit. The syntactic focusing devices have much less freedom of choice in both these respects. In the cleft-sentence construction, the focus is usually something that corresponds to the relative constituent in the embedded clause,[1] or to the theme (alias 'topic') in the structurally analogous independent clause.[2] For example (with focal segments underlined):

[1] a. It was <u>John</u> who called Peter
    b. It was <u>Peter</u> that John called

[2] a. It was <u>yesterday</u> that we met in the park
    b. It was <u>in the park</u> that we met yesterday

[3] a. It was <u>Mary</u> that we spoke about
    b. It was <u>about Mary</u> that we spoke

Such sentences, and also [4.a] below, exemplify what we shall call 'ordinary' focus, as opposed to the 'narrow' focus in [4.b]:

[4] a. It was <u>John's car</u> that was stolen yesterday
    b. It was <u>John</u> whose car was stolen yesterday (relative constituent: *whose car*)

In [4.b] the focus (*John*) corresponds to only a part of the relative constituent (*whose car*), rather than to the whole of it as it does in [1]–[3] and in [4.a]. Though [4.a] and [4.b] differ, accordingly, in the width of the focal segment, both correspond to the simple sentence:

[4] c. John's car was stolen yesterday

The question naturally arises how [4.a] and [4.b] differ from one another semantically, and the same question may of course be asked about the sentence pairs in [1]–[3], where the corresponding simple sentences are not, indeed, identical, but differ only in theme-rheme structure; *eg*:

[1] c. John called Peter (corresponding to [1.a])
    d. Peter, John called (corresponding to [1.b]).

To answer such questions, we must try to state what meaning is conveyed by cleft-focusing.

4.1.2. The meaning of cleft focus

Semantically, the typical cleft sentence may be thought of as an equation, with a value (represented by the focus) assigned to a variable (represented by the residue – *ie*, in this case, by the relative clause). But such a description is inadequate in two ways: first, it applies only to sentences that have a nominal phrase as cleft focus, *eg* [1.a,b,] or [3.a] above, but not to sentences like [2.a,b] or [3.b], where the focus is an adverb or a prepositional phrase; and secondly, it fails to bring out the communicative raison d'être of cleft sentences. To understand the latter, we must first distinguish two components in the semantic structure of all sentences (cleft or non-cleft), *viz* the propositional content and the communicative attitude.[3]

The communicative attitude may be regarded as a semantic operator that includes the whole propositional content within its scope but normally focuses on only part of it. It is this part – what we may call the communicative focus – that is asserted in a declarative sentence, questioned in an interrogative sentence, and wished for in an optative sentence. The residue of the propositional content is not asserted, questioned, or wished for, but taken for granted, presupposed. In the following sentences, for example,

[5] a. He locks his room when he goes out
    b. He doesn't lock his room when he goes out
    c. Does he lock his room when he goes out?
    d. I wish he'd lock his room when he goes out
    e. I wish he wouldn't lock his room when he goes out

the proposition in the embedded clause *when he goes out*
('he goes out sometimes') is equally taken for granted everywhere,
though the sentences are, respectively, a positive and a negative
declarative, an interrogative, and a positive and a negative optative.

Of course it is not only embedded clauses that may contain
presuppositions. Nominal phrases that constitute definite descriptions always presuppose something.[4] Thus *his room* in [5.a–e]
contains a presupposition that may be formulated as follows:

> 'There is an entity x, such that (i) x is a room, and (ii) x is "his",
> and (iii) x can be identified by the recipient of the message on
> the basis of (i) and (ii) (*or*, and (iii) in the immediate context of
> the communication, there is no entity y, such that (i′) y is a
> room, and (ii′) y is "his", and (iii′) y ≠ x).'

Such presuppositions are excluded from the communicative focus.

Using the term 'communication' for the category that subsumes
statement, question, wish, *etc*, we can say that the communicative
focus equals the propositional content of a communication minus its
presuppositions.

A cleft construction is a syntactic device that singles out part of the
propositional content as containing the communicative focus of a
sentence and designates the residue as presupposed.[5] Thus if we
compare the sentences in [6]

[6] a. It was <u>John</u> who called Peter
    b. It wasn't <u>John</u> who called Peter
    c. Was it <u>John</u> who called Peter?
    d. I wish it had been <u>John</u> who called Peter
    e. I wish it hadn't been <u>John</u> who called Peter

we see that the differences between [a]–[e] leave quite unaffected the
status of the proposition 'someone called Peter' which is implicit in
the relative clause *who called Peter*. What varies as we move from [a]
to [e] is the attitude to the assignment of the value 'John' to the
variable 'who called Peter' (*ie* 'x, such that x called Peter'). Similarly
with sentences like [2.a,b] or [3.b] above, where the semantic relation
of the cleft focus to the residue seems best regarded not as equative
(*ie* identifying) but as attributive ('Our meeting was yesterday/was in
the park', 'Our conversation was about Mary').

We can now specify without further difficulty the difference between the sentences in [4] above. [4.a] presupposes[6] 'Something was

stolen yesterday' and identifies 'John's car' as the value of the
variable 'which was stolen yesterday'; [4.b] presupposes 'Someone's
car was stolen yesterday' and identifies 'John' as the value of the
variable 'whose car was stolen yesterday'. The differences between
the sentence pairs in [1]–[3] above can be specified in the same way,
mutatis mutandis.

4.1.3 Cleft focus and context

We can now return to the syntactic restrictions on the choice of cleft
focus. We used the term 'narrow' to describe the focus *John* in [4.b]
above, because the relative item corresponding to *John* in this
sentence is not an immediate constituent of the relative clause, but
only a constituent of the first immediate constituent (*whose car*). If
we try to produce other types of 'narrow' cleft focus, we find that
there is one that seems to be syntactically well-formed, though it is
extremely rare,[7] with the relative pronoun embedded in a prepositional phrase:

[7] It was <u>Mary</u> about whom we spoke

Apart from the two types represented by [4.b] and [7], 'narrow' cleft
focus seems to be impossible. Consider, for example:

[8] *It was <u>red</u> which wine I asked for[8]
[9] *It's <u>the name</u> that/which of the shop I've forgotten.[9]

However, though the communicative effect that [8] and [9] seem to
be aiming at simply cannot be attained in English by purely syntactic
means, we do have another way of saying what amounts to the same
thing, pragmatically:

[10] It was /RÈD wine that I asked for # (not white)

[11] (I remember where it was all right) It's the/NÀME of the shop
that I've forgotten #

The capitals used for RED in [10] and NAME in [11] mark the intonation
focus, as distinct from the focus selected by the cleft construction.
Here the intonation structure is used in order to relegate to the
background part of the focus of the cleft sentence, and by so doing it
serves to mark the (pragmatic) narrowing of the focus as delimited
by the syntax to the part that is required by the context. Where
intonation is absent (in ordinary writing), the interpretation of the

context alone will in effect narrow the focus by backgrounding the 'superfluous' part. Similarly we can have:

[4] a′. It was /JÒHN's car that was stolen yesterday #

with a cleft focus of ordinary width, part of which is backgrounded by the intonation, as against:

[4] b′. It was /JÒHN whose car was stolen yesterday #

where the intonation focus and the cleft focus correspond fully. In unaffected speech, [4.a′] is more likely to occur than [4.b′]. It is mainly in formal writing that [4.b] is likely to be found, and here it has of course the advantage of greater precision. Since formal writing tends to avoid the use of underlining for emphasis that is so common in private correspondence, the pragmatic import of the normal printed form of [4.a] can be clarified only by the context. Even so, [4.a] would be preferred to [4.b] in many styles of writing. When we compare our other example of narrow focus, *It was Mary about whom we spoke* (=[7] above), with the corresponding ordinary-focus sentence *It was Mary that we spoke about* (=[3.a] above), we see that the narrow-focus version is not superior to the other in clarity. However, [3.a] has a 'stranded' preposition (*about*). It is significant that the speaker (or rather, typically, the writer) who is trying to avoid 'the preposition at the end' will normally prefer the ordinary focus of *It was about Mary that we spoke* to the narrow focus of *It was Mary about whom we spoke* even if the contextual focus is *Mary* rather than *about Mary*.

The two patterns represented by [4.a′] and [4.b′] are close enough in meaning for the choice between them to be, to all intents and purposes, a stylistic one – as is implied in the preceding paragraph; but they cannot be regarded as fully equivalent. Though in [4.a′] the maximum global prominence is given to JOHN's, where nuclear focus and cleft focus coincide, the focal segment of the cleft construction is still *John's car*. *John's car* represents the 'identifier', whereas, *John's* represents 'new', *ie* foregrounded, information.[10] Identifier and New, being conceptually distinct, can correspond to entirely separate parts of an utterance, as in [12]:

[12] a. It/WAS John's car that was stolen # (whatever they say)
     b. It was /NÒT John's car that was stolen # (whatever they say)

In both [12.a] and [12.b], as in [4.a'] above, the segment foregrounded by the cleft construction is *John's car*, whereas the intonational foregrounding picks out *was* in [12.a] and *not* in [12.b].[11]

4.1.4 Multiple focus

There are examples of cleft sentences that suggest that we should
admit the possibility of a focal segment encompassing more than one
clause element. For instance, we can certainly have sentences like
[13]:

> [13] It was three years ago, in London, that I first met him

Here the focus would appear to extend over two adjuncts: an adjunct
of time (*three years ago*) and an adjunct of place (*in London*).
Similarly in [14] and [15]:

> [14] It was rather infrequently, in Paris, that we met after that

> [15] It was over a period of several months, in Jerusalem, that
> we worked together on this project

We see that the time adjunct involved may denote 'time when', or
frequency, or duration. In [16] below, no adjunct of time is involved
at all:

> [16] It was by pure accident, at a football match, that I saw him
> again

It seems, then, that various sequences of adjuncts may constitute focal segments in cleft constructions. However, other combinations of clause elements seem to be barred. Object + object,
object + prepositional object, object + complement, and object +
adjunct (or adjunct + object) appear to be equally inadmissible:

> [17] *It is Maud the garden that he is showing

> [18] *It is the garden to Maud that he is showing

> [19] *It is Tweedledum for Tweedledee that she may mistake

> [20] *It is Arnold director that they have appointed

> [21] *It is Paul here that we are meeting[12]

> [22] *It is here Paul that we are meeting

In view of the ill-formedness of [17]–[22], it may be worth taking another look at [13]–[16]. As to the focal status of *three years ago* and *in London*, in [13], and of the corresponding elements in [14]–[16], this can hardly be doubted. [13]–[16] are of course quite different from [23], for instance, where a sequence of time adjunct + place adjunct occurs in the same position but not in the same structure:

[23] It was usually <u>in London</u> that we met

Here the time adjunct (*usually*) is not in focus any more than it is in [23']:

[23'] Usually, it was <u>in London</u> that we met

How is it, then, that [13]–[16] admit a sequence of two clause elements in focus, something that is impossible in the patterns represented by [17]–[22]? An answer is suggested by the punctuation of [13]–[16] and the probable intonation patterns of the corresponding spoken sentences:

[13'] It was /three yèars ago # in /Lòndon # that I /first mèt him #

[14'] It was /rather infrèquently # in /Pàris # that we /met after thàt #

[15'] It was over a /period of several mònths # in Je/rùsalem # that we /worked together on this pròject #

[16'] It was by /pure àccident # at a /fòotball match # that I /saw him agàin #

It seems reasonable to suggest that what we have been considering as a sequence of constituents (*eg* time adjunct + place adjunct) should rather be regarded as a single constituent, to be labelled, perhaps, 'circumstantial adjunct', and consisting of two or more phrases in apposition. This would be a somewhat loose manner of using the term 'apposition', since we do not have identity of reference here between the members of the appositive set; so 'asyndetic co-ordination' would be better than 'apposition'. At any rate, there is a good deal to be said for the idea that such sequences of phrases with adverbial function can make up single constituents. It has been noted before (Halliday 1967–8 : 3.219) that in general there can be only a

single 'marked theme'[13] in a clause, and that nevertheless sequences
of time adjuncts and place adjuncts may stand in thematic position:

[24] a. John I met last year (Marked theme: *John*)
      b. Last year I met John (Marked theme: *Last year*)
      c. *John last year I met
      d. *Last year John I met

[25] a. John I met in Birmingham (Marked theme: *John*)
      b. In Birmingham I met John (Marked theme: *In Bir-
          mingham*)
      c. *John in Birmingham I met
      d. *In Birmingham John I met

[26] a. Last year in Birmingham I met John
      b. In Birmingham last year I met John

If *last year in Birmingham* and *in Birmingham last year* can be taken
as single constituents, the rule for marked theme will clearly be
simpler. And we shall see in §4.2.3 that a similar 'structure of
apposition (or co-ordination)' functioning as a single constituent
seems to be required by the rules for the focus of *only*. So the
evidence for the constituency analysis suggested above for the
sequences of adjuncts in [13]–[16] seems to be adequate; but whether
this analysis is accepted or not, we clearly need a term to refer to the
special type of focal segment that occurs in these sentences. We shall
use 'multiple focus' for this prupose, both here and in relation to the
focusing adverbs (§4.2.3).[14]

4.2 ADVERBIAL FOCUS

4.2.1 Ordinary focus

We shall distinguish here, as we did in §4.1.1, between 'ordinary
focus' and 'narrow focus', but the definition of 'ordinary focus' in
relation to focusing adverbs is not identical with that which is
required for the cleft construction.[15] 'Ordinary' focus will be used to
mean focus that extends over an immediate constituent of the clause,
eg subject, initial adjunct, or over the predication (in the sense of
Quirk *et al* 1972, 'verb phrase' in transformational-generative terminology), or over an immediate constituent of the predication, *eg*
object, adjunct. The following are typical examples (focal segments

underlined):

[1] a. Only <u>John</u> phoned Mary
  b. Only <u>on that occasion</u> did John phone
  c. John only <u>phoned</u>
  d. John only <u>phoned Mary</u>
  e. John only <u>spoke to Mary</u>
  f. John only <u>told Mary the news</u>
  g. John only <u>asked Mary for advice</u>
  h. John only <u>phoned in the evenings</u>
  i. John phoned only <u>Mary</u>
  j. John spoke only <u>to Mary</u>
  k. John phoned only <u>in the evenings</u>

[2] a. <u>John</u> also phoned Mary
  b. <u>Yesterday</u> he also phoned Mary
  c. John also <u>phoned</u>
  d. John also <u>phoned Mary</u>
  e. John also <u>spoke to Mary</u>
  f. John also <u>told Mary the news</u>
  g. John also <u>asked Mary for advice</u>
  h. John also <u>phoned in the evenings</u>
  i. He phoned also <u>his cousin Mary</u>
  j. He spoke also <u>to Mary</u>
  k. He phoned also <u>in the evenings</u>

[3] a. <u>John</u> particularly liked Mary
  b. <u>Yesterday</u> he was particularly happy
  c. John particularly liked <u>Mary</u>
  d. He was particularly happy <u>yesterday</u>

Where *only* or *also* stand before a predication that contains another element or elements in addition to the verb (*eg* [1.d–h], [2.d–h]), the whole predication has been marked as focal (except where it is all non-focal, *eg* [2.a–b]). The problems involved here will be discussed in §4.2.2.

The constituency analysis of phrases like *spoke to Mary* is complicated by the phenomena of passivization, relativization, *etc.* We shall see that the syntax of focusing provides support for the view that the NP, even though it is an immediate constituent of the clause when it stands clause-initially, is a constituent of a prepositional phrase (rather than object of a 'prepositional verb') when it follows the preposition. In other words, it seems that rather than 'different, but equally valid and complementary ways of looking at the same structure' (Quirk *et al* 1972 : 819) we have here two different types of structure with complementary functions. Evidence in favour of this view is provided by the constraints on what we shall be calling 'narrow' focus (see §4.2.4) as opposed to the 'ordinary' focus defined and exemplified above.

It is already evident from the examples in [1]–[3] above that the adverbs differ from one another in their 'focusing syntax'. Thus *only* and *also*, but not *particularly*, can focus on whole predications; *only*, but not *also* or *particularly*, induces inverted order when it focuses on an initial item other than the subject (as in [1.b]); and *also* and *particularly*, but not *only*, can focus on a clause-initial item from which they are separated by the subject.[16] Further differences will be dealt with below.

4.2.2 Adverbial focus: Syntax, semantics, and context

Sentences like [1.d–h] or [2.d–h] are of course notoriously ambiguous, or rather (if the word 'ambiguous' is to be used in a stricter sense) are open to more than one interpretation. This is particularly noticeable in writing, but there may by some indeterminacy even in speech. Apart from the version with *John* as focus, there would seem to be three possible representations for a sentence like [1.d], repeated here as [4]:

[4] John only phoned Mary.

(a) with *phoned Mary* as focus, as shown above, (b) with *Mary* as focus, and (c) with *phoned* as focus. In speech, (c) would usually be distinguished from (a) and (b) by the nucleus on *phoned*, but (a) and (b) could sound the same; see [5.a–c]:

[5] a. /John 'only 'phoned Màry # (He took no other action)
    b. /John 'only 'phoned Màry # (He phoned no one else)
    c. /John 'only phòned 'Mary # (He did not write to her, for example)

The three representations in [5] seem perfectly satisfactory from a common-sense point of view, and they are undoubtedly simple and convenient. But we shall see that (as in the cleft construction) there are grounds for distinguishing between a syntactic concept of focus, which forms part of the basis for the semantic interpretation of sentences, and a contextual concept of focus, which belongs to the pragmatic interpretation of utterances. To take [5.a] and [5.b] first, it is evident that in a context in which *phoned* represents 'given information', the sentence *John only phoned Mary* will be pragmatically equivalent to the sentence *John phoned only Mary*.[17] There is accordingly no need to distinguish between [5.a] and [5.b] in terms of syntactic focus or semantic representation. The same argument applies to the comparison of [5.a] with [5.c]. The latter is pragmatically equivalent (as far as the interpretation of the focus is concerned) to [6]:

[6] /Mǎry # he only /phòned #

Of course, the intonation pattern of [5.a] does not allow us to interpret it as [5.c]. But since intonation functions primarily as an indicator of information assessment, and this is a pragmatic concept, the relationship between [5.a] and [5.c] is no different, in principle, from the relationship between [5.a] and [5.b]. We see, therefore, that the marking of the focus in [1.d] and [4] is adequate, as far as syntax and semantics are concerned, for all the versions of [5], which may be regarded as different utterance types representing a single sentence. For each utterance there is a global interpretation which integrates the contributions of the syntactic form with those of the context and the phonological form. This global interpretation is of course 'the meaning of the sentence' in the ordinary non-technical use of this expression, but it must be distinguished from 'the meaning of the sentence' in the technical sense of a semantic representation. To avoid confusion, it will be useful to distinguish between the syntactic-semantic focus on the one hand, and the contextual-pragmatic focus on the other. This distinction applies to *also* and other focusing adverbs, as well as to *only*. Just as [4] can be interpreted in the three ways distinguished in [5.a–c], with the placement of the intonation nucleus distinguishing between [a] and [b] on the one hand and [c] on the other, so [2.d] is similarly open to the three interpretations in [7.a–c]:

[7] a.   /John 'also 'phoned Màry # (apart from the other things he did)

   b.   /John 'also 'phoned Màry # (apart from the other people he phoned)

    b'. /John 'also phoned Màry # (=[b])
    c. /John 'also phòned 'Mary # (apart from writing to her)

Here, as in [5.a–c] above, we can distinguish between the syntactic focus of the adverb, which is *phoned Mary* throughout, and the contextual focus of the adverb, which is *phoned Mary* in [a], *Mary* in [b], and *phoned* in [c]. The same will hold good for similar sentences with *just* or *even* instead of *only* or *also*.

When the syntactic focus extends over a predication with three immediate constituents, as in [1.f–g] and [2.f–g] above, one or two of the constituents will usually be 'backgrounded' by the context (it is less usual for the contextual focus to be co-extensive with the syntactic focus):

[8] a. He /only told !Màry the 'news # (He didn't tell Joan) –
       CONTEXTUAL FOCUS: 'Mary'
    b. He /only 'told her the :nèws # (He didn't ask her for advice as well) – CONTEXTUAL FOCUS: 'told the news'

[9] a. He /also asked !Màry for ad'vice # (apart from asking Joan) – CONTEXTUAL FOCUS: 'Mary'
    b. He /also 'asked her for ad:vìce # (apart from telling her the news) – CONTEXTUAL FOCUS: 'asked for advice'

In [8.b] the contextual focus extends over the verb and the direct object, and in [9.b] over the verb and the prepositional object, and in both cases it is discontinuous. Other patterns are exemplified in [10.a–b] and [11.a–b]:

[10] a. He /only 'sent flòwers to 'Mary # (He didn't visit her as well) – CONTEXTUAL FOCUS: 'sent flowers'
     b. He /only sent :flowers to Màry # (He sent nothing to anyone else) – CONTEXTUAL FOCUS: 'flowers to Mary'

[11] a. He /also 'sent flòwers to 'Mary # (He didn't only visit her) – CONTEXTUAL FOCUS: 'sent flowers'
     b. He /also sent :flowers to Màry # (apart from sending chocolates to Joan) – CONTEXTUAL FOCUS: 'flowers to Mary'.

We have seen that sentences like [1.d–h] and [2.d–h] above may be regarded as (pragmatically) indeterminate, rather than (semantically) ambiguous. The focal segment can in each case be regarded as extending syntactically and semantically over a whole predication ('verb phrase'), in which one or more constituents may be relegated to the background by the interpretation of the context (with or without help from the intonation). If such backgrounding takes place, we may say that the focus of *only* or *also* is reduced, or narrowed, by the context. Similarly, the interpretations of [8]–[11] will depend on whether any part or parts of the focal segment are contextually backgrounded. This analysis is preferable for a number of reasons to the superficially simpler view which is taken for granted by most grammarians, *viz* that [1.d], [2.d], *etc* are ambiguous, and that [5.a–c], [7.a–c], *etc* are sets of different semantic readings rather than of different contextual interpretations of a single reading. We may note firstly that we needed a similar distinction – between syntactic-semantic focusing on the one hand and contextual focusing (with intonational correlates) on the other – in our analysis of cleft focus. If the same general principles can be shown to apply also to focusing by adverbs, this clearly means an overall simplification for our theory.

In our analysis of adverbial focus, we have so far given only examples of sentences in which a relatively wide syntactic focus can be pragmatically narrowed by the context. But we can also show that (as with cleft focus, see §3.1.3) it is possible for the whole of the syntactic-semantic focus of an adverbial focus marker to be backgrounded by the context, *eg*:

[12] He's /àlso coming #

Here *he* is the syntactic-semantic focus of *also*, but it is treated by the intonation as background information – the only 'new' element being the word *also* itself. Such a sentence cannot be accounted for unless we have a concept of syntactic focus which is distinct from intonational and contextual foregrounding. The necessity for this distinction is brought out even more clearly by the instances (admittedly not so common, but perfectly well-formed for all that) in which the focus of *also* is subjected to the most extreme form of backgrounding, *viz* total omission. For example:

[13] They now entered a second tunnel, also dimly lit with candles (= <u>which</u> was also dimly lit with candles).[18]

Finally, we have the restrictions on adverbial focus that are dealt with in §4.2.3 and §4.2.4. These are clearly restrictions on syntactic, not on contextual focus, and they are most naturally accounted for by the analysis here put forward.

4.2.3 Multiple focus

We saw in §4.2.2 that by superimposing contextual interpretation on predication focus (*ie* focus encompassing a whole predication, or 'verb phrase'), we obtain a large variety of pragmatic focusing possibilities. We shall now see that the purely syntactic options are much more limited. Corresponding to the restrictions we noted in §4.1.4 on sequences of clause constituents in cleft focus, we find there are parallel restrictions on sequences of predication constituents in adverbial focus. Consider the following examples, all syntactically ill-formed[19]:

[14] *He showed only <u>Maud the garden</u> (not Anne the conservatory as well)

[15] *He showed only <u>the garden to Maud</u> (not the conservatory to Anne as well)

[16] *She mistook only <u>Tweedledum for Tweedledee</u> (not the Red Queen for the White Queen as well)

[17] *They have elected only <u>Peter Secretary</u> (they are still discussing the other appointments)

[18] *He showed also <u>Anne the conservatory</u> (not only Maud the garden)

[19] *He showed also <u>the conservatory to Anne</u> (not only the garden to Maud)

[20] *She mistook also <u>the Red Queen for the White Queen</u> (not only Tweedledum for Tweedledee)

[21] *They have elected also <u>Peter treasurer</u> (apart from electing Paul secretary)

The ill-formedness of [14]–[21] is clearly a matter of syntax, not of the meanings conveyed. Compare [14'] below with [14], and [18'] below with [18]:

[14'] He only <u>showed Maud the garden</u> (he didn't also show Anne the conservatory)

[18'] He also <u>showed Anne the conservatory</u> (apart from showing Maud the garden)

[14'] and [18'] are normal examples of predication focus. But though the verb is syntactically part of the focal segment, it is here backgrounded by the context; and so, pragmatically, the sentences [14'] and [18'] come to the same thing as the ill-formed sentences [14] and [18].

Again, as with cleft focus [see §3.1.4], there is a set of apparent exceptions. Consider the following pairs of sentences:

[22] a. They /played only <u>at wèekends</u> # at /hóme #
     b. They /played only <u>at wèekends</u> # <u>at</u> /<u>hòme</u> #

[23] a. They /played only <u>for fùn</u> # with /frìends #
     b. They /played only <u>for fùn</u> # <u>with</u> /<u>frìends</u> #[20]

In each of these pairs there is a clear difference of meaning between the a-sentence and the b-sentence: whereas in the a-sentences the prepositional phrase immediately following the *only* is in focus and the second prepositional phrase is residual, in the b-sentences both the prepositional phrases are in focus. [22.a] and [23.a] are equivalent to [24] and [25] respectively:

[24] At /hóme # they played /only at wèekends #

[25] With /frìends # they played /only for fùn #

[22.b] and [23.b], on the other hand, are equivalent to [26] and [27] respectively:

[26] They /played only at wèekends # /only at hòme #

[27] They /played only for fùn # /only with frìends #

In view of the paraphrase relationships with [26] and [27], we seem to be justified in treating the sequences of prepositional phrases in [22.b] and [23.b] as structures of apposition or co-ordination that make up single constituents in their respective predications (as we did in the corresponding section on cleft sentences, §4.1.4). In further support of this analysis we may cite also the fact that in such sentences the order of the two focal phrases is immaterial: *cf* [22.b] and [23.b] with [28] and [29]:

[28] They /played only at hòme # at /wèekends #

[29] They /played only with frìends # for /fùn #

Again we shall use the term 'multiple focus' to denote constructions like these. Actually, only double focus seems to be at all common, but triple and even quadruple focus can be perfectly acceptable; *eg*:

[30] She actually saw him only <u>once</u>, <u>in 1939</u>, <u>outside the Albert Hall</u>, <u>after a concert</u>

In multiple-focus constructions, as in the corresponding expanded versions, *eg* [26] and [27], each of the focal phrases must be an optional element in the structure of the predication; hence the unacceptability of [14]–[21] above and the unacceptability of the expanded versions, *eg* [14″] and [15″]:

[14″] *He showed only Maud, only the garden

[15″] *He showed only the garden, only to Maud

We can accordingly formulate a syntactic constraint on adverbial focusing, as follows:

[31] The focal segment cannot extend over more than one immediate constituent of the predication ('verb phrase') unless it is co-extensive with the whole predication; but sequences of optional phrases with adverbial functions (time, place, purpose, *etc*) may have the status of single constituents.[21]

It is natural to ask whether this rule can be made to apply not only to the predication and its constituents, but also to clause constituents apart from the predication, and the following sentences suggest that it can:

[32] a. It was discussed also <u>by Matthews</u>, <u>in 1968</u>
    b. It was discussed also <u>in 1968</u>, <u>by Matthews</u>
    c. <u>In 1968</u> Matthews also discussed it
    d. <u>In 1968</u> Matthews also discussed it
    e. *<u>In 1968</u> Matthews also discussed it

Each of these sentences contains a phrase denoting the actor and a phrase denoting the time of the action. In [a] and [b] these two phrases can form a single constituent, in accordance with the second part of the rule formulated in [31], and can therefore jointly constitute the focal segment of *also*. But in [c], [d], and [e], the actor is subject and unmarked theme (see Ch. 2) and the time phrase functions as marked theme. This means that though the two phrases are adjacent, they form separate constituents of the clause, and so cannot jointly constitute a focal segment. The ill-formedness of [32.e] contrasts with the well-formedness of [33.a–b]:

[33] a. <u>In 1968</u>, <u>in Birmingham</u>, it was also discussed
    b. Only <u>in 1966</u>, <u>in Leeds</u>, was it ever discussed

This suggests that the syntactic constraint first formulated in [31] above can be extended as follows:

[34] i. The 'ordinary' focal segment is always co-extensive with a complete syntactic constituent of the clause or of the predication.[22]
    ii. A phrase sequence that can function as a single constituent in the predication can function also as a single clause constituent.[23]

But we can go still further. In §2.3 and 4.1.4 it was suggested that initial sequences of adverbial phrases (eg *last year in Birmingham*) should be regarded as single constituents, *inter alia* because this meant that we need make no exception to the rule that allows only one marked theme per clause. We can now test this hypothesis with the help of our rule for focal segments as reformulated in [34]. If an initial string of phrases can be a sequence of marked themes, then it should be possible to focus on one of them, since each one would be a complete clause constituent. But in fact this is impossible: the focus can only be on the whole string, not on one phrase without the other.[24] So we have, for example, in contrast to the well-formed sentence [33.a], the ill-formed sentences [35.a–d]:

[35] a. *<u>In 1968</u> in Birmingham it was also discussed
    b. *In 1968 <u>in Birmingham</u> it was also discussed
    c. *<u>In Birmingham</u> in 1968 it was also discussed
    d. *In Birmingham <u>in 1968</u> it was also discussed

If we want to focus on one of the adverbial phrases in thematic position, we have to place the other elsewhere, as in [36.a–b]:[25]

[36] a. <u>In</u> /Birmingham it was àlso discussed in 1968 #
    b. <u>In</u> /<u>1968</u> it was àlso discussed in Birmingham #

We can accordingly strengthen [34.ii] as follows:

[34] ii′. A phrase sequence that can function as a single constituent in the predication is always a single constituent
of the clause when it is placed in thematic position.[26]

Rule [34] seems to be valid for all the focusing adverbs. But of course
there are also differences in focusing options. Some have already
been noted in §4.2.1, and others will be dealt with below.

4.2.4 Narrow focus

The three sentences [37]–[39]:

[37] I only met him at one of the lectures

[38] I met him only at one of the lectures

[39] I met him at only one of the lectures

could all have the same contextual focus, viz *one*, but they differ in
syntactic structure and range of possible interpretations. In [37] the
focus of *only* could extend over the whole of the predicate (*met him
at one of the lectures*) and in [38] it could be the whole of the
following prepositional phrase (*at one of the lectures*). Both [37] and
[38] can therefore be taken as instances of ordinary focus (in the
sense of §4.2.1). [39], on the other hand, represents a variety of
narrow focus. *Only*-constructions with narrow focus are subject to a
special constraint: the focal segment must represent a point on a
scale. Typically, it is the scale of number, with the point on it
represented by a cardinal numeral or by *a few*, or a scale of
measurement, such as length, weight, price, or time, with the point
on it represented by a numeral, or *a few*, or the indefinite article,
followed by the noun denoting the unit of measurement.[27] [39]
exemplifies the first alternative, while the second is exemplified by
[40]–[42] below:

[40] He stayed for only <u>two days</u>

[41] He stayed for only <u>a few days</u>

[42] He stayed for only <u>a day</u>

Though the focal segment in [40]–[42] is a whole nominal phrase, the
focus is 'narrow' because the phrase in question is not an immediate

constituent of the predication or of the clause. Sentences [43] and [44] below show the syntactic ill-formedness that results from narrow focus of this kind without the requisite type of focal item:

[43]   *We saw him on only <u>Sunday</u> (Narrow focus)

[43']   We saw him only <u>on Sunday</u> (Ordinary focus)

[43"]   We only <u>saw him on Sunday</u> (Ordinary focus)

[44]   *He stayed for only <u>the party</u> (Narrow focus)

[44']   He stayed only <u>for the party</u> (Ordinary focus)

[44"]   He only <u>stayed for the party</u> (Ordinary focus)

In [43] and [44] the prepositional phrases are of the type that may be said to have clearly adverbial functions, more specifically of the type classified as adjuncts by Quirk *et al* (1972:Ch. 8). In phrases of this sort the preposition is not generally separated from the nominal phrase. But even those prepositional phrases which are not usually regarded as adverbial and are sometimes called 'prepositional objects' must be regarded as constituents of the predication by the criterion of the narrow-focus constraint when the preposition is followed by its nominal phrase – even though they are often 'split' by relativization, interrogation, topicalization, and even passivization.[28] Compare the following sentences:

[45]   He paid for only <u>one day</u> (narrow focus; scalar)

[46]   *He paid for only <u>Sunday</u> (narrow focus; non-scalar)

[46']   He paid only <u>for Sunday</u> (ordinary focus; non-scalar)

[47]   He spoke to only <u>a few</u> of his friends (narrow focus; scalar)

[48]   *He spoke to only <u>his friends</u> (narrow focus; non-scalar)

[48']   He spoke only <u>to his friends</u> (ordinary focus; non-scalar).[29]

So far, the examples of narrow focus have all been constituents of prepositional phrases; but a narrow focal segment can also be a constituent of a nominal phrase that is an immediate constituent of the predication or of the clause. For example:

[49]   They have an only <u>slightly</u> larger model

Contrast this with [50], which has ordinary focus:

[50] They have only a slightly larger model

The scale involved in [49] may be labelled 'amount of difference'. The sentence corresponding to [49] without *slightly*, *ie* with *only* focusing on *larger*, does not seem to be well-formed, though it would make perfectly good sense:

[51] *They have an only larger model ('They have one that's just like it, only larger')

Contrast the well-formed sentence [52], which corresponds to [50] without *slightly*, and has ordinary focus:

[52] They have only a larger model ('They haven't got this size')

There is ambiguity of focus in utterance types corresponding to [49] above, if *only* is not preceded by a constituent of the nominal phrase. For example:

[53] a. They have only slightly larger models
     b. They have only slightly larger models

[53.a] corresponds to [49], whereas [53.b] corresponds to [50].

   This ambiguity disappears (as one would expect from [51] above) when *slightly* is omitted:

[54] a. *They have only larger models ('Just like this, only larger')
     b. They have only larger models ('They haven't got this size')

It is interesting to note that [53.a] and [53.b] cannot be equivalent in meaning, even pragmatically, unlike a set of sentences such as [37]–[39] above. Even if we make *slightly* the contextual focus in both [53.a] and [53.b], they still belong to different contexts. For example:

[55] A: I suppose they have some models that are not twice as large as this one.
     B: Oh, yes. They've /got only slìghtly larger models #

[56] A: I suppose they don't have any models that are twice as
           large as this one.
      B: Oh, no. They've /got only s̲l̲i̲g̲h̲t̲l̲y̲ ̲l̲a̲r̲g̲e̲r̲ ̲m̲o̲d̲e̲l̲s̲ #

The reason for this contrast in pragmatic import is that [53.a] and
[53.b] differ not only in the focus of *only* but also in its domain
(scope).[30]

The additive focusing adverb *even* resembles *only* in its capacity for
being associated with scalar properties and also with narrow focus,
but the details differ. Compare the following sentences:

[57] This was mentioned in only t̲w̲o̲ reports

[58] *This was mentioned in even t̲w̲o̲ reports

[59] John wrote an even l̲o̲n̲g̲e̲r̲ essay

[60] *John wrote an only l̲o̲n̲g̲e̲r̲ essay

With *also*, narrow focus in barred altogether.[31] Compare the following sets of sentences:

[61] *We saw him on also t̲h̲e̲ ̲f̲o̲l̲l̲o̲w̲i̲n̲g̲ ̲d̲a̲y̲ (narrow focus)

[62] We saẁ him also o̲n̲ ̲t̲h̲e̲ ̲f̲o̲l̲l̲o̲w̲i̲n̲g̲ ̲d̲a̲y̲ (ordinary focus)

[63] We saw him also t̲h̲e̲ ̲f̲o̲l̲l̲o̲w̲i̲n̲g̲ ̲d̲a̲y̲ (ordinary focus)

[64] *He paid for also t̲h̲e̲ ̲l̲u̲n̲c̲h̲ ̲o̲n̲ ̲S̲u̲n̲d̲a̲y̲ (narrow focus)[32]

[65] He paid also f̲o̲r̲ ̲t̲h̲e̲ ̲l̲u̲n̲c̲h̲ ̲o̲n̲ ̲S̲u̲n̲d̲a̲y̲ (ordinary focus)

[66] He paid also t̲h̲e̲ ̲b̲i̲l̲l̲ ̲f̲o̲r̲ ̲S̲u̲n̲d̲a̲y̲ (ordinary focus)

Sentence [64], like [46] above, points clearly to the analysis [paid
[for Sunday]], not [[paid for] Sunday]. But the narrow-focus constraint is inoperative in [67] and [68] below, which seems to show
that the nominal phrase governed by a preposition is not a part of
the prepositional phrase when the nominal phrase stands initially
in the clause.

[67] T̲h̲a̲t̲ ̲d̲a̲y̲ he also paid for

[68] Then they had some drinks, w̲h̲i̲c̲h̲ he also paid for

That day in [67] is marked theme, and *which* in [68] is the relative
element, which makes both of them immediate constituents of the
clause, and hence not 'narrow' but ordinary focal segments.

The narrow-focus constraint does not apply to coordination by *and also*; cf the following pair of sentences:

[69] *After also a period of rest, he returned to work

[70] After a full recovery and also a period of rest, he returned to work

Nor does the constraint apply to the use of the correlative pair of coordinating expressions *not only . . . but also*; cf [71] and [72]:

[71] *He received an also inaccurate report

[72] He received a not only incomplete but also inaccurate report

With prepositional phrases, as with predications, we distinguish between syntactic focus and contextual focus. When the syntactic focus is a prepositional phrase, the contextual focus may be (a) the phrase as a whole, (b) the nominal phrase, or (c) the preposition. For example:

[73] a. We looked also behind the cupboard (not only under the sofa) – CONTEXTUAL FOCUS: *behind the cupboard*
      b. We looked also behind the cupboard (not only behind the sofa) – CONTEXTUAL FOCUS: *the cupboard*
      c. We looked also behind the cupboard (not only underneath) – CONTEXTUAL FOCUS: *behind.*

In [73.b] and [73.c] the focus is contextually narrow but syntactically ordinary. The contrast in well-formedness between [73.b] and [73.d] below confirms once more the correctness of the decision to distinguish between the two concepts of focus:

[73] d. *We looked behind also the cupboard

4.2.5 Ambiguity of focus

In § 4.2.2 and § 4.2.4 we drew attention to the existence of different relationships between the syntactic and the contextual analysis of sentences, or, more explicitly, between the syntactic analysis of sentences as a basis for the semantic representation, and the contextual analysis of utterances of these sentences as a basis for the pragmatic interpretation. In one set of cases, for instance, the syntactic focus of an adverb is reduced, or narrowed, by the backgrounding of a part or parts of the focal segment (*eg* [5], [7]–[11], and [73] above); in another set the whole of the syntactic focus is contextually relegated to the background (*eg* [12] above). Neither of these relationships between syntax and context involved the notion of syntactic or semantic ambiguity.

Various contextual interpretations were deemed to be superimposable on a given semantic representation, but the semantic representation remained the same in the different contexts. (Such relationships between syntax and semantics on the one hand and context on the other were noted also in the analysis of the cleft construction, §3.1.)

But there is also ambiguity of focus, either (a) semantic, or (b) syntactic. In (a) a single syntactic structure corresponds to different semantic representations, and in (b) a single string of morphemes corresponds to different syntactic structures (and also, of course, to different semantic representations). In both (a) and (b) we have (strictly speaking) as many different sentences as there are semantic representations, though the word 'sentence' is often used loosely to denote the utterance-type, regardless of any syntactic or semantic ambiguity. The context, with or without the assistance of the intonation, will usually tell the hearer which of the possible sentences is intended by the speaker. In writing, it is usually the context alone that points to the meaning intended. The following examples of ambiguity of focus have already been given:

[74] a. <u>John</u> also phoned Mary (=[2.a] above)
     b. John also <u>phoned Mary</u> (=[2.d] above)

[75] a. <u>John</u> particularly liked Mary (=[3.a])
     b. John particularly liked <u>Mary</u> (=[3.c])

[76] a. They have only <u>slightly</u> larger models (=[53.a])
     b. They have only <u>slightly larger models</u> (=[53.b])

In all these cases, we posit two distinct semantic representations, not a single representation on which different pragmatic interpretations can be superimposed. No common semantic representation underlies utterances of [74.a] and [74.b].[33] Such a common meaning would not be logically odd in any way; it can even be expressed by a simple English sentence, *viz*:

[77] Also, <u>John phoned Mary</u>

which we would gloss as:

[78] 'Apart from everything else, there was a phone-call from
John to Mary'

But the meaning indicated in [78] cannot be expressed by [74]. The
reason is plain – if we were right in claiming (§4.2.3) that the focal segment must always be a complete syntactic constituent: *John
phoned Mary* is a complete syntactic constituent in [77], but not in
[74]. The same kind of argument applies to [75], but even more
forcibly. Here we would need *John Mary* as our putative focal
segment, and the gloss would have to be something like:

[79] 'A particularly strong liking was John's for Mary'

Not even a permutation of the words in [75] could give us the
required sense.

The question now arises of distinguishing between the two types of
ambiguity, (a) (purely) semantic and (b) (semantic and) syntactic.
Though we are concerned here with what would be called 'surface
structure' in a transformational grammar, it is not always obvious
which of two or more structural descriptions is the best. [74.a] and
[74.b], for instance, might be analysed syntactically as [80.a] and
[80.b] respectively:

[80] a. [John] [also] [phoned Mary]
     b. [John] [also [phoned Mary]]

with *also* as a clause constituent in [80.a], corresponding to focus on
John, but not in [80.b], which corresponds to the reading with predication focus. Alternatively, we could say that either [80.a] or
[80.b] corresponds, on the syntactic plane, to both [74.a] and [74.b],
but that it has two distinct semantic readings. To justify the former
alternative, we clearly need some support extraneous to the focusing
phenomenon itself. This support could be general, such as a claim to
the effect that distinct semantic readings always depend on distinct
lexico-syntactic structures, or particular, relying on distinct syntactic
properties attributable to [74.a] and [74.b]. The general claim is
clearly false, and we need not even go beyond the grammar of
focusing to prove its falsity. Thus we see, for instance, that:

[81] That we could also do

is ambiguous between (a) focus on *that* and (b) focus on *we*.[34]

Another example is:

[82] John was particularly cheerful yesterday

This is ambiguous between (a) focus on *John* and (b) focus on *yesterday*, with *particularly* functioning in both cases as a modifier in the adjectival phrase *particularly cheerful*. It would be absurd to posit two different syntactic structures, corresponding to the two different readings, either in [81] or in [82]. And we have more direct evidence against a syntactic differentiation like that in [80]: the fact that the ambiguity of [74] is preserved in [74']:

[74'] a. <u>John</u> has also phoned Mary
       b. John has also <u>phoned Mary</u>

A syntactic differentiation between [74'.a] and [74'.b] would be even more forced than that suggested in [80]. We can therefore take [80.b], with *also* syntactically part of the predicate phrase, as representing both readings of [74].

We have seen that any attempt to represent ambiguity in adverbial focusing as always syntactic is bound to fail. But it is also impossible to represent the ambiguity as always purely semantic. [76] above is an instance where the two semantic representations must derive from different syntactic structures. This comes out more clearly in [83.a–b]:

[83] a. They have an only <u>slightly</u> larger model
       b. They have only a <u>slightly larger model</u>

In [76] the ambiguity of focus is linked to ambiguity of scope (see Ch. 6); but this need not be so. *Only* (unlike *also*) cannot skip over a preceding auxiliary to focus on the subject,[35] and corresponding to the ambiguous form:

[84] They only complained

we have the two forms:

[85] a. <u>They</u> only have complained
       b. They have only <u>complained</u>

It follows that the two readings of [84] probably do correspond to two syntactic structures, as shown in [86.a–b]:

[86] a. [They only] [complained]
       b. [They] [only complained]

Utterances with syntactic or semantic ambiguity of focus are of particular interest because in them the function of intonation, which we have taken to be primarily and essentially pragmatic, seems to be capable of taking on the more centrally linguistic function of distinguishing otherwise homophonous sentences. Thus:

[87] a. <u>John</u> also phoned
b. John also <u>phoned</u>

will be represented, typically, by [88.a] and [88.b] respectively:

[88] a. /John àlso 'phoned #
b. /John 'also phòned #

Two points are worth making here. Firstly, although the peak of phonological prominence falls within the focal segment in [88.b], it does not do so in [88.a], so that there is no straightforward correspondence even here between syntactic focus and phonological focus. Secondly, by placing the nucleus on *John*, as in [88.c] below, we do not disambiguate the utterance:

[88] c. /Jòhn 'also 'phoned #

The utterance [88.c] would be interpreted as [87.a] in the context of:

[89] A: Did anyone else phone?
B: Yes. John also phoned

But it would be interpreted as [87.b] in the context of:

[90] A: I know they all sent messages, but did anyone phone as well?
B: Yes. John also phoned

In fact, it is extremely doubtful whether disambiguation by intonation pattern can ever be more than probabilistic. Some combinations of phonological and semantic patterning may have a very low probability of occurrence, but it is by no means clear that any can be altogether excluded.[36]

4.2.6 Contextual narrowing: *Only*

In §4.2.2 we saw that a distinction must be made between the syntactic-semantic focus of an adverb on the one hand and its pragmatic focus on the other. It was pointed out that the focal·

segment as delimited in the semantics could often be narrowed down by the interpretation of the context, and that the intonation structure sometimes indicated such narrowing, by backgrounding part of the semantic focus (as in [5.c] and [7.c]), and sometimes remained neutral between different contextual interpretations (as in [5.a–b] and [7.a–b]. In all the cases of contextual narrowing discussed in §4.2.2, the intonation structure could be said to harmonize with the contextual interpretation, in the sense that in all these cases the point of greatest intonational prominence (within the domain of the focusing adverb) was located within the adverb's contextual focus. For example, in:

[5.a–b] /John 'only 'phoned Màry #

neither the syntax nor the intonation make it clear whether *phoned* is part of the contextual focus of *only* or not, but there is no doubt about *Mary*, which bears the sole intonation nucleus. *Mary* in [5.a–b] is unambiguously 'new' in terms of information assessment and also clearly a part of the contextual focus of *only* in both utterance tokens. One might be inclined to generalize, on the basis of such examples, that any item that was (a) within the syntactic-semantic focal segment of an adverb AND (b) unambiguously marked as 'new' information by an intonation nucleus must be part of the contextual-pragmatic focus of the adverb.

But this is not the case. When the focusing adverb is *only*, there is sometimes a conflict between the contextual narrowing of the adverbial focus and the general information assessment as marked by the intonation. Consider for example the following text fragment:

[9] They had /quite a !nĭce little 'place in the 'country # But there was /only an 'outside :làvatory #

The word *lavatory* receives the intonation nucleus in the second sentence because in the information assessment it is the sanitary arrangements that are the speaker's principal concern at this point. Nevertheless, in the contextual interpretation of the *only*-focus, the word *lavatory* represents a background item, something taken for granted, and the contextual focus of *only* is accordingly represented by *outside*. The second sentence in [91] can be roughly paraphrased, therefore, as [92]:

[92] The sani/tătion was 'primitive 'though #

We may describe the situation in the *only*-construction in [91] by saying that the contextual focus of *only* has been 'upstaged' by another contextual focus, though both are located textually within the syntactic focus of *only*.[37]

The following text fragment represents another pattern of this kind:

[93] A: /Maybe !Màry 'found it # . /when she was 'sweeping
     the :flòor #
     B: I /dŏubt it # She /only !swèpt the kítchen #

Here the second sentence in B's reply means that the kitchen was the only place that Mary swept. The contextual focus of *only* is therefore 'the kitchen'. But in the information assessment, *swept* is nevertheless 'new', and the intonation marks it as more prominent than *kitchen*. In this way the speaker indicates that in his opinion Mary is unlikely to have found the object in question on the floor of any room unless she swept it. The pragmatic importance of 'sweeping' in this situation accounts for *swept* getting a greater share of the limelight than *kitchen*, although it is 'the kitchen' that constitutes the contextual focus of *only*.

Utterances like that of the *only*-sentence in [93] are open to different interpretations according to the context as assessed by speaker and hearer. Consider the following example:

[94] A: Was everything spotless?
     B: I /dŏubt it # – She /only !swèpt the kítchen #

If it is assumed that what was needed was a thorough sweeping out of the whole cottage, then the contextual focus of *only* is again 'the kitchen', as in [93]; but if it is assumed that the kitchen floor needed scrubbing, then the contextual focus of *only* is 'swept'. And of course, if the hearer's assumptions do not tally with the speaker's, the communication will be misinterpreted. In [93] the context was sufficiently explicit to preclude such misinterpretation: *only* had to be taken as focusing pragmatically on 'the kitchen'; in [95] below it is the other way round: the context forces us to take *only* as focusing pragmatically on 'swept':

[95] She scrubbed the front steps, but she /only !swèpt the kítchen #

The patterns of interplay between syntactic, intonational, and con-textual focusing that are exhibited by [91] and [93] above are not in any way abnormal, though they are relatively uncommon. Also uncommon, though less so, is the type represented by [96]–[98] below, with focus on numbers:

> [96] He /only had 'one :jàcket # (He had several pairs of trousers, but ...)

> [97] He /only 'had one :jàcket # (He was worried because ...)

> [98] He /only !hàd one jácket # (He would have taken it to the cleaners, but ...)

As can be seen from [97] and [98], the item that the context requires as focus of *only* (here *one*) may be quite clearly marked as 'given' by the intonation structure. The interpretation of focus, in these cases, works in two opposite directions: what is unambiguously marked by the intonation focus as 'new' (*jacket* in [97], *had* in [98]) is required to be residual in relation to *only*; and what is focal in relation to *only* (viz *one*) is marked by de-stressing as 'given' information.[38] (Sen-tences in which *only* focuses on numbers, or on scalar values in general, seem to require a different semantic analysis from other *only*-sentences. See §4.2.8–9.)

Only-sentences like the one in [93] are often criticized as having the *only* 'misplaced'. It is true that the purely theoretical indeterminacy of [93] and the (possibly) real indeterminacy of [94] can be obviated by changing the order of the words to *swept only* and so narrowing the syntactic focus. But this order is not always stylistically appropri-ate, and no change of order can cure the indeterminacy of *only had one jacket*, in so far as it derives from the uncertain status of *jacket*. The pedantic 'correction' to *had only one jacket* officiously proffers help where none, as a rule, is needed (by excluding *had*), and fails where the uncertainty may be real. Here, as so often elsewhere, we depend on the context.

4.2.7 Adverbial focus and theme-rheme structure

The focusing adverbs differ from one another not only in where they may stand in relation to their focal segments but also in the effect they have on the textual structure of the sentence when they are placed in particular positions. Compare the following sentences:

[99]   They visited only <u>Rome</u>

[100]   *They visited, too, <u>Rome</u>

At first sight it may seem that *too*, unlike *only*, cannot focus on a following sentence element but only on one that precedes, as for instance in:

[101]   <u>They</u>, too, have visited Rome

But this is not so. *Too* does on occasion focus on a sentence element that follows it, as we can see from such an example as:

[102]   They admired, too, <u>Michelangelo's 'Last Judgement' in the Sistine Chapel</u>

The explanation for the acceptability of [102], as against the un-acceptability of [100], is a simple one. The word *too* is a connective,[39] but one that has its normal, unmarked place – unlike most connectives – at the end of the sentence. When it stands anywhere else it functions as a 'partition', either between the marked theme and the textual element that follows it, or between the unmarked rheme and the marked rheme. (See §2.3–4 on 'partitions' in theme-rheme structure.) This means that *too* can stand, for example, between the verb and its direct object, but only on condition that the direct object is functioning as marked rheme. The ill-formedness of [100], therefore, is textual: the monosyllable *Rome*, even though it is a proper name, and an impressive item from a pragmatic point of view, is not substantial enough textually to function as a marked rheme after a parenthesis. There is no such difficulty with the object in [102], and this example is therefore textually well-formed.[40]

Also, like *too*, can function as a connective; but unlike *too*, it is normally medial: in declaratives its unmarked position is after the operator if there is one, and between the subject and the main verb if there is no operator. It would seem that in this position it can be regarded as a constituent of the predicate, unlike *too*, which normally follows the predicate and is treated as a parenthesis when it stands medially. Apart from the connective function that is common to both words, there is a second point of resemblance between them. *Also*, like *too*, can be displaced from its usual position so as to stand before some constituent of the predication and focus on it; and when it does so, the weight of the focal segment is clearly a factor in the textual well-formedness of the sentence. Compare:

[103] ?He invited also <u>Jane</u>[41]

with:

[104] He invited also <u>his wife's cousin Jane</u>

To make a textually well-formed sentence, it seems that the final element that follows *also* must be heavy enough for a marked rheme, as is shown by the oddity of [103], as against the relative normality of [104]. This is explained automatically if *also* in [103] and [104] does not form a single constituent together with the following nominal phrase, and so serves to separate the verb from its direct object.

The need for a heavy focal element is not felt when the focus marker that follows the main verb is *only* or *even*. See [99] above, and also [105] and [106] below:

[105] He invited only <u>Jane</u>

[106] He invited even <u>Jane</u>

Furthermore, we find that *only* and *even*, unlike *too* and *also*, may focus on a non-final object, as in:

[107] They sent only <u>John</u> to a boarding-school

[108] They sent even <u>John</u> to a boarding-school

The undisputed acceptability of these sentences contrasts strikingly with the unacceptability or oddity of the corresponding sentences with *too* or *also*:

[109] *They sent, too, <u>John</u> to a boarding-school

[110] *They sent also <u>John</u> to a boarding-school

It seems natural to explain these facts by saying that *only* and *even* in [99] and [105]–[108] – unlike *too* and *also* in [100], [102]–[104], and [109]–[110] – form syntactic constituents together with the nominal phrases on which they focus; that the objects in these sentences are *only Rome* in [99], *only Jane* in [105], *even Jane* in [106] etc; and that consequently these sentences, unlike the ones with *too* and *also*, contain no marked rhemes (see § 2.4 for the definition of 'marked rheme').

We must now consider a problem that has been glossed over so far, *viz* the difference in acceptability between [103] and [110] above, with *also*, and [100] and [109], with *too*. It is probably felt by most people that the sentences with *also* are definitely more acceptable than those with *too*. The sentence types represented by [103] and [110] are a puzzle: though it seems that they never (or hardly ever) occur naturally, they meet with varying degrees of toleration if artificially constructed and presented to informants. The reason is probably the syntactic similarity between *also* on the one hand and *only* and *even* on the other. *Also*, like *only* and *even*, has its unmarked position between the subject and the main verb (after the operator if there is one). And again like *only* and *even*, if focuses syntactically (from its unmarked position) on the whole of the predication, relying on the interpretation of the context to select the pragmatic focus from the syntactic focus. And finally, again like *only* and *even*, it may sometimes follow the main verb, thus narrowing the syntactic focus, leaving less work for the contextual interpretation, and producing an utterance that will be judged as both better and worse: 'better' because more 'precise', 'worse' because more 'pedantic'. Sentences like [103] and [110] assign to *also* yet another property that belongs to *only* and *even*, but one that is not established (so far, at any rate) for *also*.[42]

The use of focus markers to produce sequences ending in marked rheme is not uncommon, but it is found predominantly in the more formal varieties of written English. The same seems to be true of the use of focus markers in such a way as to produce sequences beginning with a marked theme; *eg*:

[111] <u>They</u>, too, were opposed to this scheme

In familiar speech and informal writing the general tendency is to sacrifice the semantic precision of the pattern in [111] to the greater naturalness of *too* in final position, and to rely on context and intonation to convey the pragmatic focus intended, as in:

[112] /Thèy were a'gainst the i'dea # /tòo #

Also characteristic of certain styles of writing is the use of focus structures like these:

[113] Remarkable, too, was <u>his gift for mimicry</u>

[114] The text has also been published <u>of the new Education Act</u>

[115] Also present at the meeting was <u>the leader of the Macedonian trade delegation, Mr Vladimir Slivovic</u>[43]

It seems to be a rule that when the whole concord-subject, as in [113] and [115], or part of the concord-subject, as in [114], functions as marked rheme, the focus markers *also* and *too* must focus on the marked rheme, even though they are separated from it in sequence.

The above rule does not apply, it should be noted, to sentences with anticipatory *it* and a clausal subject in final position. In this construction the subject-clause is in its unmarked position, and so is not a marked rheme at all. Here the main verb is included in the syntactic-semantic focus of *also* (though not necessarily in its pragmatic focus). For example:

[116] It is common knowledge, of course, that he is lazy and incompetent, but it is also <u>suspected that he is dishonest</u>

It is clear that the focus in [116] must include both *suspected* and *that he is dishonest*, just as it does in the corresponding active construction:

[117] They knew all along, of course, that he was lazy and incompetent, but now they also <u>suspected that he was dishonest</u>

If we are right in supposing that focal segments must be syntactic constituents,[44] it seems to follow from sentences like [116] above that the subject-clause in sentences with anticipatory *it* is (paradoxically) a part of the predication in constituency structure. There is of course another common sentence-type in which the concord-subject is part of the predication, *viz* the unmarked existential sentence; here, too, the syntactic focal segment encompasses the whole predication (how much is included in the pragmatic focus depends on the context, of course, as it does in the patterns represented by [116] and [117] above). For example:

[118] There's also <u>some beer in the fridge</u>

[119] There's also <u>a party in the evening</u>

However, when the concord-subject is marked rheme, it monopolizes the focus:

[120] There is also, in such cases, <u>the problem of corroborative evidence</u>

We have seen that there are two sides to the interaction between adverbial focus and textual focus. On the one hand, the choice of adverbial focus may entail a concomitant choice of textual focus (marked rheme or marked theme), and on the other hand, a choice of textual focus may help to determine the adverbial focus.

4.2.8 The logical form of sentences with only and also

So far we have been content to work with informal and intuitive notions of what is meant by the focus of *only* or *also*. We shall now consider the problem of representing the logical form of sentences in which *only* and *also* function as focus markers. A sentence with *only* as focus marker may be regarded as containing, on the semantic plane, a pair of propositions with the following properties: one proposition is positive and contains the focus of *only* plus the residue, and the other is negative and contains what we may call the 'anti-focus' – again plus the residue.[45] For example:

[121] John watched only tennis

can be crudely represented as containing a conjunction of two propositions (A) and (B) as follows (with the focus underlined in (A) and the anti-focus underlined in (B)):

[121'] '(A) John watched tennis & (B)
John didn't watch anything but tennis'

The relationship between (A) and (B) has been represented in various ways. According to Kuroda (1969) and G. Lakoff (1970a), they are jointly asserted. According to Horn (1969), the positive proposition is presupposed and only the negative is asserted. According to Karttunen and Peters (1978), the positive proposition is one of 'a large set of cases that have been called presupposition [and] are really instances of conventional implicature'. The term 'implicature' derives from Grice (1975), as does the distinction between conversational implicature on the one hand, based on norms of co-operative behaviour and cancellable, and conventional implicature on the other hand, based on the form of the sentence and not cancellable. For example:

[122] John has stopped beating his wife

conventionally implicates:

[123] 'John beat his wife'

but

[124] John has not stopped beating his wife

though it also implicates [123], does so only conversationally. This conversational implicature is cancelled in:

[125] John hasn't stopped beating his wife – he never beat her at all

No such cancellation is possible for [122]. The two kinds of implicature have an important property in common: neither is part of what a speaker is understood to be asserting when he makes a statement. But what distinguishes them is no less significant: the conversational implicature is merely something that the hearer will naturally infer from the assertion in the absence of any indication to the contrary, whereas the conventional implicature is something for which the speaker is bound to accept responsibility as long as he upholds the assertion. It is natural, therefore, to include conventional implicatures, together with assertions, in the semantic representation of sentences, and leave conversational implicatures to the pragmatic interpretation of utterances.

In the semantic representations that follow, I shall aim at showing propositional content without trying to account for the differences in communicative focus that are reflected in the distinction between assertion and conventional implicature. One result of this is to enable us to represent the two propositions in [121'] above as conjoined, even if only one of them has the communicative status of an assertion, and similarly with other sentences (eg with *also*, *either*, *too*, *even*) that are analyzable in terms of assertions and conventional implicatures. In the case of *only* we can go even further, perhaps, and claim the status of assertion for both propositions, in view of such possibilities as:

[126] Each of them stuck to one drink; Bill drank only whiskey and Harry drank only beer

[127] Human beings can subsist on all kinds of diets: the inhabitants of Ultima Thule eat only seaweed.

Such examples are hard to reconcile with the claim that the positive proposition in *only*-sentences is not part of the assertion.

Having given reasons for continuing to posit two conjoined propositions for *only*-sentences, we can now attempt a more formal representation of [121] above. We shall use the symbols 'f' and 'R' as specified in [128]:

[128] a. Let 'f' be the argument focused on by *only*.
b. Let 'R' be the residual predicate, *ie* the sentence excluding *only* and 'f'.

This yields for:

[129] He watched only tennis (=[121] above)

the representation:

[130] R *only* f

and for the propositional content of [130], the formula:

[131] Rf & $\sim\exists x \atop x \neq f$ Rx

In order to represent *only*-sentences with focus on the predicate, *eg*:

[132] He only watched tennis

we shall use the following special symbols (in addition to 'Φ' for a predicate variable):

[133] a. F = focal predicate
b. r = residual argument

We can now represent [132] as:

[134] r *only* F

and the propositional content of [134] as:

[135] Fr & $\sim\exists\Phi \atop \Phi \neq F$ Φr

When there are two residual arguments, *eg* in:

[136] Tennis he only watched

we can represent them as r_1 and r_2. Thus [136] will be:

[137] $r_2 r_1$ *only* F

and its propositional content will be:

[138] $F(r_1,r_2)$ & $\sim\exists\Phi \quad \Phi\,(r_1,r_2)$
$$\Phi \neq F$$

When *only* focuses on a scalar item, such as a number or a point in time, the propositional content of the sentence is slightly different. Consider, for example:

[139] John paid for only three tickets

with *only* focusing on *three*. The positive proposition will be:

[140] 'John paid for three tickets' or 'There are three tickets that John paid for'.

But the negative proposition we shall take to be not:

[141] 'There is no number of tickets other than three such that John paid for that number of tickets'

(which would be analogous to the negative propositions in [121'] *etc*) but rather:

[142] 'John did not pay for any number of tickets greater than three' or 'There is no number of tickets greater than three that John paid for'.

When *only* focuses on an expression denoting a point in time, the sentence is ambiguous, because points in time can be treated as scalar or as non-scalar items. For example:

[143] Only on Monday did John get in touch with us

can be interpreted in two different ways. If the focus is taken merely as one of a set of points whose order is irrelevant to the statement being made, the content is something like:

[143'] a. 'John got in touch with us on Monday & John did not get in touch with us on any other day.'

But if the focus is taken as a scalar item, as essentially a place in a linear sequence, the propositional content is something like:

[143'] b. 'John got in touch with us on Monday & John did not get in touch with us earlier than Monday.'

It seems, therefore, that the adverb *only* can be regarded as corresponding to two distinct entities on the semantic plane. We have:

(i) 'Exceptive *only*' – with non-scalar focus
(ii) 'Limiting *only*' – with scalar focus.

When the focus is a disjunction of two points in time, *eg*:

[144] Only on Monday or Tuesday will he be able to phone

we have the same ambiguity as in [143], but when it is a conjunction, as in:

[145] Only on Monday and Tuesday will he be able to phone

the focus must be non-scalar, or in other words [145] must contain 'exceptive *only*'.

The ambiguity of *only* may be observed also in such sentences as [146] (from Horn 1969:102):

[146] Brigitte Bardot is only pretty

The two different readings are brought out by the a- and b-continuations in [147]:

[147] a. ... – she isn't beautiful
      b. ... – she isn't intelligent

Sentences in which *also* functions as a focus marker resemble *only*-sentences in that they can be similarly regarded as containing two conjoined propositions on the semantic plane, one containing the focus plus the residue and the other containing the 'anti-focus' plus the residue. But whereas in *only*-sentences one proposition is negative and one positive, the two propositions in *also*-sentences are both positive. For example:

[148] Mary also watched tennis

can be represented as follows (with underlining for the focus in (A) and for the anti-focus in (B)):

[148'] '(A) <u>Mary</u> watched tennis &
        (B) <u>At least one person other than Mary</u> watched tennis.'

Here it is evident that only (A) is asserted and that (B) is an implicature. Thus we could not say, for instance:

[149] *It wasn't only Mary that watched – Mary also watched.

If we use 'f' and 'R' as defined in [128] above – substituting *also* for *only* – we can represent [148] as:

[150] f *also* R

and the propositional content will be:

[151] Rf & $\exists x$ Rx
$\qquad\qquad x{\neq}f$

In [152] the focus of *also* is on the predicate:

[152] Mary also <u>watched tennis</u>

Using 'F' and 'r' as defined in [133] above, we can represent [152] as:

[153] r *also* F

and its propositional content as:

[154] Fr & $\exists\Phi$ Φr
$\qquad\qquad \Phi{\neq}F$

In [155], as in [136] above, the focal predicate is represented by the verb alone, and we have two residual arguments:

[155] Tennis she also <u>played</u>

This can be represented (with 'r_1' and 'r_2' again standing for the residual arguments) as:

[156] $r_2 r_1$ *also* F

and its propositional content as:

[157] $F(r_1,r_2)$ & $\exists\Phi$ $\Phi(r_1 r_2)$
$\qquad\qquad\qquad \Phi{\neq}F$

There is a further difference between *also* and *only*, apart from those noted above: the focus of *also* is always a non-scalar item. We may contrast *also* with *even*, which always has an additional scalar implicature (see Karttunen and Peters 1978:29*ff*).

4.2.9 *Only* once more: Semantic and contextual focus

In our analysis of adverbial focus in §4.2.2 we assumed that sentences like:

[158] John will only phone Mary

[159] Peter will only show Sue his collection of Ancient Greek coins

are semantically vague, or underspecified, but not ambiguous, each having only a single syntactic-semantic focus (*phone Mary* and *show Sue his collection of Ancient Greek coins*). The semantic focus was taken to be the widest possible, within the limits imposed by syntactic constituency, and the different interpretations of such sentences that are prompted by different contexts were assigned to the pragmatics rather than the semantics.

Such an analysis has the advantage of assuming a minimum of ambiguity for the syntax and a minimum of complexity for the semantics – a small number of relatively simple semantic structures for each syntactic pattern, as against the much larger number of structures, some of them much more complex, that would be required if we assumed that for every possible choice of contextual focus there was a structure with the corresponding semantic focus.

But we found in §4.2.4 that the rules of syntax are not identical for all kinds of *only*-focus, and in §4.2.8 we saw that the adverb *only* corresponds to two distinct semantic entities – 'exceptive *only*', which focuses on non-scalar items, and 'limiting *only*', which focuses on scalar items. The distinction between the two *only*'s enables us to propose a more comprehensive rule for the delimitation of the semantic focus of *only*:

[160] (i) For 'exceptive *only*': widest possible focus, within the limits imposed by syntactic constituency.[46]

(ii) For 'limiting *only*': widest possible focus, within the limits imposed by the scalarity requirement.

Thus [161] below has two different semantic readings, [161.a], with exceptive *only* and non-scalar focus, and [161.b], with limiting *only* and scalar focus (semantic focus underlined):

[161] a. He only <u>asked me for one of those magazines</u> (That was the only <u>reason he came in</u>)

      b. He only asked me for <u>one</u> of those magazines (He
         didn't ask for more than one)

The focal segment in [161.a] can of course be contextually narrowed,
as in [162] for example (with contextual focus in capitals):

[162] He didn't want anything to eat. He only <u>asked me for ONE</u>
     <u>OF THOSE MAGAZINES.</u>

Contextual narrowing of scalar focus is illustrated by [163]–[164]:

[163] a. It took only <u>THIRTY seconds</u>⎫
      b. It only took <u>THIRTY seconds</u>⎬ (Not forty-five)

[164] a. It took only <u>thirty SECONDS</u>⎫
      b. It only took <u>thirty SECONDS</u>⎬ (Not thirty minutes)

These may be compared with [165], where there is no contextual
narrowing:

[165] a. It took only <u>THIRTY SECONDS</u>⎫
      b. It only took <u>THIRTY SECONDS</u>⎬ (Not several minutes)

In speech, [163] is distinguished from [164] and [165] by the place of
the intonation nucleus, and ambiguities of the type illustrated by
[161] above are also removed, more often than not, by the intonation. Thus:

[166] He /only 'asked me for :òne of 'those maga'zines #

will naturally be taken to represent [161.b], with focus on *one*. But
the intonation, too, can be ambiguous. For example:

[167] He /only read 'one of the :tèxtbooks #

could be either [168.a], with exceptive *only*, or [168.b], with limiting
only (preceding context in parentheses):

[168] a. (Did he read up the stencils and lecture-notes? – No.)
         He only <u>read ONE OF THE TEXTBOOKS</u>
      b. (Did he read up the stencils and lecture-notes? – Yes,
         he read all of those. – Then why didn't he pass? –) He
         only read <u>ONE</u> of the textbooks.

Notes

1. Or to the missing constituent, if the relative is omitted in the relative clause; *eg* It was John [∧ I meant].

2. On the theme as a unit in the sequential organization of the clause, see Chapter 2 above.

3. I am using the term 'communicative attitude' to denote all that remains when we have abstracted the propositional content. The communicative attitude therefore subsumes what Lyons (1977:749), following Hare (1970), distinguishes as 'tropic' and 'neustic'. In Leech (1981), the term 'predication' is used for what I am calling propositional content, and 'proposition' corresponds to 'statement': 'The PRE-DICATION ... is ... the common category shared by propositions, questions, commands, *etc.*' (*p*124).

4. On the presuppositional analysis of definite descriptions by logicians, see Kempson (1977:139*ff*) and the references given there.

5. Whether this residual proposition should be regarded as logically entailed in positive declaratives or not depends on one's theory of semantics. But it is clear that whatever analysis we adopt, the special status of the residual proposition is semantically significant, if semantics goes beyond the representation of propositions and the study of the truth-functional relations between them. A good deal of the difficulty with the term 'presupposition' can be avoided if we take the position that declarative sentences assert some propositions and presuppose others, whereas propositions entail propositions, but do not assert or presuppose. I am here using 'presupposition' in the sense of 'conventional implicature' (see 4.2.8). Though the residue of a cleft construction (*ie* the embedded clause) cannot contain an assertion, the focus of the cleft construction frequently does contain presuppositions as well as assertions, since the focal element is typically a definite description.

6. 'Presupposes' is not intended to deny that the proposition is logically entailed (see note 5 above).

7. In Quirk *et al* (1972:953) the construction is called 'virtually impossible'. Jespersen (1909–1949: iii. 90) quotes the following example from Thackeray: '...it is not only bachelors on whom the young ladies confer their affections (= not only on bachelors that ...)'. In Jespersen (1937:78) we find the sentence *It was Joan to whom he wrote the letter* cited as one that is awkward for J's system of symbolization – but without any comment on its acceptability as English.

8. There is no syntactic objection, of course, to *It was red, that wine I asked for*. But this is not a cleft sentence at all: the relative clause here is *I asked for*, not **that wine I asked for*, and the sentence differs only in thematic structure from *That wine I asked for was red*. *That*, unlike *which*, cannot function as a relative determiner.

9. Here too we have a possible counter-example that is only apparent, with *of the shop* in extraposition, as an afterthought: *It's the name that/which I've forgotten, of the shop*. In this sentence the phrase *of the shop* belongs to the matrix, not to the relative clause.

10. See Chapter 3 above. The label 'new' is potentially misleading; hence the gloss.

11. To be precise, only part of the nuclear syllable is intonationally foregrounded in [12.a]. *Was* represents 'assertion' + 'past' + 'be', but only 'assertion' is intonationally foregrounded (see Ch. 3 above).

12. This sentence is ill-formed only if *here* is an adjunct. If *Paul here* is an NP, with *here* as postmodifier, the sentence is syntactically unexceptionable.

13. Or rather, in Halliday's analysis, a single 'cognitive theme'. 'Discourse adjuncts', like *however*, *nevertheless*, and 'modal adjuncts' like *perhaps*, *probably*, can be

followed by thematic cognitive adjuncts, eg *Perhaps tomorrow we can go out* (Halliday 1967–8:3.221). In the present analysis, Halliday's 'discourse adjuncts' and 'modal adjuncts' are not given thematic status at all (see Ch. 2 above).

14. One might similarly use the term 'multiple cognitive theme' for the initial adjunct sequences in [26] and the like. Further evidence for the special syntactic status of groups of adjuncts comes from the possibility of coordination with *and*. Compare §2.3 above, note 13, and also the following examples from the corpus:

(i) It is only afterwards, and in the light of Jesus Christ, that we understand the operation and the person of the Holy Spirit (W.9.2)

(ii) It is only mediately and as a testimony that these acts are the redemptive acts of God (W.9.2)

15. Note, however, that though the cleft construction cannot focus on predications, this option is available with the equated relative ('WH-cleft', 'pseudo-cleft'), which has a similar function; eg *What he did was phone Mary*, with *phone Mary* as focus.

16. The qualifications 'clause-initial' and 'by the subject' are probably unnecessary, as it seems that *only* can focus syntactically only on adjacent items. For the apparent counter-examples, see §4.2.2.

17. It is possible for the givenness of 'phoned' to be shown in the intonation pattern by destressing:

[5.b′] /John ′only phoned Màry #

But this destressing is not obligatory. See §3.1 on the interpretation on non-nuclear accents. The concept of semantic interpretation is here taken to include presuppositions of the type that Karttunen and Peters (1978) call 'conventional implicatures'. The interpretation of the semantics in the light of the context is taken to belong to pragmatics. Professor Bolinger (private communication) maintains similarly that 'the "misplaced" *only* is a figment of the grammarian's imagination, and that *only* modifies [ie, in the terminology of the present study, focuses on] what follows, even when the "point" of what it modifies [ie, in our terms, the "contextual focus"] is not adjacent.'

18. The missing focus is of course coreferential with *a second tunnel*, but the latter cannot itself be the focus, since it stands outside the subordinate clause *also dimly lit with candles*, and is therefore outside the domain of *also*. Note also the following example, with *solely* as the focusing adverb:

(i) Some no longer claim that deep structure is the level on which the characterization of semantic representations is based, or solely based. (Kempson 1977:181)

Here too the focus is a missing element, to be supplied from the preceding clause (*on which...is based*).

19. 'Syntactically ill-formed' does not always mean unacceptable. It seems that a syntactically ill-formed sentence may sometimes pass muster if it differs from a corresponding well-formed one only in the placing of a fairly mobile word and the meaning remains quite clear in the context; eg (with the asterisk indicating syntactic ill-formedness):

(i) *It may have well been the case

for:

(ii) It may well have been the case

This might be called a syntactic spoonerism. Acceptability may also be improved by the existence of a similar but structurally unexceptionable sentence with the same contextual meaning. For example:

(iii) *He compared also the French translation with the English one

Here acceptability is improved by the existence of the alternative construction with *and* (cf *Don Alphonzo, with other gentlemen..., are...*). Furthermore, there is the problem of distinguishing between the constructions in [14]–[21] on the one hand and those with 'multiple focus' *eg* [22.b], [23.b] below on the other. It is possible that the crucial difference is not in syntactic function, as I have suggested above (adjunct as against non-adjunct), but that what matters is whether the elements in question are optional or obligatory. The distinction between optional and obligatory is not always clear-cut, which may contribute something to the 'fuzziness' in this area.

20. The intonation pattern of [22.b] and [23.b] is typical but not obligatory; *cf* the following example from the corpus:

(i) Mr !Wăldo # whom he /knew !only by his :Christian name as :Nŏrman # (S.12.4b.16)

21. Whether the focus does in fact, in a particular case, extend over the whole of such a sequence or only over the first part of it will generally be clear from the intonation; *cf* [22] and [23] above.

22. We are speaking here of ordinary as opposed to narrow focus, and taking 'multiple' as a subtype of 'ordinary'. For the constraint on narrow focus, see §4.2.4.

23. This suggests that a string consisting of an agent phrase and a phrase of time or place should also be a potential thematic focus, and this seems to be so. We must of course make allowance for the fact that agent phrases as themes will generally seem clumsy and pointless, even when no focusing is involved.

24. In the sentence:

(i) In Birmingham, fortunately, it was also discussed

The focus of *also* cannot be *in Birmingham, fortunately*, but it can be *in Birmingham*. This only apparently contradicts the statement in the text above and serves in fact to confirm it: *fortunately* is a disjunct, and disjuncts are never thematic in our analysis (see §2.3).

25. The intonation has been marked to correspond with focus on the theme, which is shown also by the underlining. The normal written forms of [36.a–b] are of course ambiguous between theme focus and predication focus.

26. It is also a single constituent if used as a parenthesis; but this is not relevant here.

27. 'Scalar focus' is required also when *only* has 'local scope'. See §6.1.6.

28. The adjuncts and prepositional objects are perhaps best regarded as two ends of a scale, rather than fully discrete categories. For some of the difficulties involved in separating adjuncts from prepositional objects, see Quirk *et al* (1972:813ff).

29. We must exclude from the category of 'prepositional phrase' instances of *with* introducing a non-finite or verbless clause, *eg*:

(i) With only George to help us, we'll need more time

See also the examples in §6.1.5.2 – The prepositional phrase that contains the narrow focal element is usually an element in clause structure or in the structure of the predication; but it may also be embedded in an NP, as in the following corpus examples:

(ii) ...showed a net gain of only 6 p.c. (W.12.6)
(iii) Bids for only 2150 tons had been received (W.2.2).

'Resistance' to narrow focus on non-scalar items is not uniform, either for different speakers or for different types of item. In particular, as Professor Quirk (private communication) has pointed out, the constraint may not be effective for demonstratives; *eg*:

(iv) They succeeded in only this case

30. The domains of the focusing adjuncts are dealt with in Chapter 5.
31. This looks as if it is connected with the fact that *also* cannot have scalar focus; but the matter is complicated by *even*, which can have narrow focus, but in a different set of contexts from *only*.
32. In this sentence and in [65], *on Sunday* is intended as a postmodifier to *lunch*.
33. This does not mean, of course, that the semantic representations do not contain elements common to both.
34. On the possibility of disambiguation by intonation, see below. What concerns us here is only the possibility of distinguishing syntactically between the two readings.
35. It is interesting to note that this constraint did not exist in earlier English; see the quotations in OED, s.v. *only* adv., I.c, for example: 1721 *The eldest son shall only inherit his father*.
36. This corresponds in essence to Bolinger's and Halliday's views. In speaking of rare occurrences, I am not referring to anomalous utterances due to performance error.
37. The qualification 'textually' serves as a reminder of the fact that the contextual focus on *lavatory* is IN the syntactic focus of *only* but not OF it.
38. Bolinger (private communication) gives the following examples of patterns similarly open to conflicting interpretations:

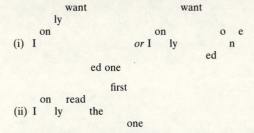

He comments: 'I suspect that it is a combination of intonational pointing and plausibility that makes us see these one way or the other – plausibility in the context...and plausibility in the wider sense of sometimes getting an absurd interpretation on almost any grounds, *eg*:

being interpreted as "All I do with this nickel is have it". My guess is that a majority of "misplaced" *only*'s are rendered harmless by this fact.'

39. Connectives may, but need not, be focus markers; and focus markers may, but need not, be connectives. Thus *moreover* is an additive connective but not a focus marker; *only* and *especially* are focus markers but not connectives; and *too* and *also* are additive connectives and focus markers.

40. An instance of *too* before a marked rheme is cited (without analysis) in *Webster's Third International Dictionary* (1961). There are additional examples, analyzed in terms of focus, in Jacobson (1964:354) and Sopher (1976:64*f*).

41. [103] seems more tolerable than [100], and similarly [110] below seems more tolerable than [109]. An explanation for this is suggested below.

42. The overlapping sets of properties of *only*, *even*, *also*, and *too* exemplify what Bolinger (1961b) has called 'gradience', and more particularly what Quirk (1965) has called a 'serial relationship'. Such serial relationships reflect the dynamic nature of language and help to account for the blurred edges of grammaticality.

43. The vigilant reader will have noticed that the opening sentence of this paragraph is itself an instance of such a pattern, more specifically of the type represented by [115].

44. See the discussion in §4.2.3.

45. We are assuming throughout this section that the scope of *only* or *also* is co-extensive with the sentence. This does not hold good for all sentences that have *only* or *also* as focus markers. See Chapter 6 below.

46. The extent of the focal segment may be further restricted by the presence of a 'negative-polarity item'. See §6.1.1.

Five

Scope without focus: The domain of negation

5.1 THE 'FOCUS' OF NEGATION

In Chapter 1 we introduced the notion of 'domain' (or scope) of a focus marker, loosely defined as its sphere of operation. This notion is akin to the logical concepts 'scope of a connective' and 'scope of a quantifier', which may be defined (for a given occurrence of the connective or quantifier) as 'the shortest propositional function in which it occurs' (Lemmon 1965:143). It is natural, therefore, that we should require the notion of scope, or domain, for the semantic analysis of negation. But whereas the focus markers (as the term implies) have as their defining property the foregrounding of some part of their domain ('the focus') and the correlative backgrounding of the rest of the domain ('the residue'), this does not hold good for the semantic element 'negative' which may be considered to inhere in *not, no, none*, etc. In a cleft construction, or a WH-question, there is a syntactic-semantic focus inherent in the structure of the sentence itself. The same is true (if we provide for varying degrees of ambiguity, see Chapter 4 above) of structures with focusing adverbs. What is sometimes called the focus of negation, on the other hand, is not inherent in the syntactic structure of the sentence, but depends on the interpretation of particular utterances in particular contexts, this interpretation being guided, to a greater or lesser extent, by the intonation. The intonation, as we saw in Chapter 3, highlights selected parts of an utterance and so provides the basis for an assessment of the information contained in it in terms of 'given' and 'new'. Usually, though not always, the negation is interpreted as part of the 'new' information,[1] so that the negative is associated with the focal item or items within its scope (see Akmajian 1970:228ff; Quirk *et al* 1972:382f; Jackendoff 1972:254ff, 352ff). The examples in [1] below will serve to show what is meant:

[1] a. /Jŏhn doesn't love 'Mary #
   b. John /doesn't lŏve 'Mary #
   c. John /doesn't love Măry #

[1.a–c] may be interpreted as conveying something like [2.a–c]:

[2] a. Although some person or persons love Mary, John isn't the one, or isn't one of them
    b. Although there is some relationship between John and Mary, it isn't love, or love is no part of it
    c. Although John loves some person or persons, Mary isn't the one, or isn't one of them

The item bearing the intonation nucleus in utterances like [1.a–c] above is called 'focus of negation' in Quirk *et al*, while in Jackendoff's account the negation is said to 'undergo association with focus'.[2]

[1.a–c] are simple cases, where the whole sentence is within the scope of negation (for the sense of 'scope of negation' here, see §5.2–3), and each utterance contains only one intonation nucleus, which does not fall on the negative item. But other possible relationships between intonation focus and negation must also be taken into account:

1. The utterance of a negative sentence may contain two or more intonation foci representing two or more 'new' items (apart from the negation itself).
2. There may be no accent anywhere except on the negative item itself (*eg* on *not*, *never*, or one of the negative auxiliaries – note that in *isn't*, *doesn't*, etc the negative morpheme *n't* is represented by an unstressed syllable and gets its accent by proxy, as it were).
3. There may be no accent anywhere within the scope of the negation.[3]

The situations described in 1–3 above are exemplified in [3]–[6] below:

[3] /John likes :Mǎry # . but /Mary 'doesn't like :Jòhn #

[4] /Why does Jóan 'like him # – she /dòesn't ('like him) #

[5] /Lòts of 'people 'don't 'like him #

[6] I /tòld you they 'don't 'like him #

The negative clause in [3] can be analyzed on essentially the same lines as [1.a–c] above, though the association of the negative with two focal items (*Mary* and *John*) does rather complicate matters. In quasi-ordinary English, the negative clause in [3] may be said to convey something like [7]:

[7] Although there is at least one pair of sets of persons such that the first member of the pair likes the second member, Mary and John are not such a pair

Or, in semi-logical representation à la Jackendoff:

[8] Presupposition: λ (x,y) [x likes y] is well-formed
Assertion: (Mary, John) $\notin$ λ (x,y) [x likes y]

The second clause in [4] can also be said to contain two propositions, but these are not related to each other in the same way as the presupposition and assertion (or focal proposition) in [1.a–c] or in [3]. The meaning of the second clause in [4], in its context, may be represented roughly as in [9]:

[9] Though you assume that she likes him, the fact is that she doesn't like him

The intonation nucleus on *doesn't* signals the contradiction between the overtly represented proposition 'she doesn't like him' and the covert proposition 'she likes him'. More generally, the meaning may be represented as in [9']:

[9'] a. 'She doesn't like him'
b. '"She...like him" is given; "doesn't (*ie* negative + declarative + non-modal)" is new'.

The representation in [9] is the interpretation of that in [9'] in the context of the utterance [4].

In [5], the scope of negation does not include the item that bears the intonation nucleus (*lots*); for the sentence corresponds to [10.a], not [10.b]:

[10] a. (many (not (like him)))
b. (not (many (like him)))

Or in ordinary English, [5] corresponds to [11.a], not [11.b]:

[11] a. There are many people who don't like him
b. There aren't many people who like him

It follows that although the clause is (in one sense) a negative one, and there is a single intonation nucleus, which does not fall on the negative item, there is no 'focus of negation' here in the sense in which the term was used with reference to [1.a–c] above. Nor is there a 'focus of negation' in [6], though the details of the case are different. In [6] we have a clause (*they don't like him*) which is entirely within the scope of negation – it may be represented as '(not (they like him))' – but as the whole clause is in the 'tail' of the intonation unit, no part of it bears any accent, and so there is no focus for the negation to associate with.

Even the 'simple' cases in [1] above are not as simple as they seem to be at first sight. Consider the following example:

[12] You know /Mary 'isn't a pŏpular 'girl # at /àll # – /Tŏm doesn't 'like her #. /Gĕorge doesn't 'like her #. and /Terry and :Jack can't !stànd her #

The second and third clauses in [12] are syntactically and intonationally like [1.a],[4] but the context makes it reasonable to associate the negation in these clauses not with the focal proposition, as in [1.a], but with the presupposition. We may conclude from all this that 'focus of negation', in the sense that has here been considered, is a tricky notion, to be used with circumspection.

The data considered above can best be accounted for, it seems, if we take the view that the function of intonation is essentially cohesive and attitudinal, and only marginally semantic.[5] Negative sentences, in this view, are vague rather than ambiguous (*cf* Kempson 1975), and the sense of a negative sentence will not be taken to include the pragmatic motivation for the utterance that contains it. This agrees with Leech (1974), who similarly distinguishes between the 'conceptual meaning' of a negation and the 'expectations' that are involved in the production of a negative utterance:

'(i)   a cancelled expectation (which is the corresponding positive assertion . . .)
(ii)   an actual expectation (which is that part of the positive content of the assertion that remains after the negated content has been "subtracted" from it') (*p*319)

The 'actual expectation' in Leech's account derives from the principle that 'when one negates an assertion, it is assumed in most contexts that part of the content under the scope of negation remains positive' (*p*320). 'Expectation relations are not to be found in the abstract logical system of language, but rather in the "pragmatics" of com-

munication, along with thematic ordering, information focus, *etc*'
(*p*322).[6]

Apart from the sense of 'focus of negation' that has been discussed above, and which we exclude from our account of the syntax and semantics of negation, there are other possible uses for
the term which we have not considered so far and which do form an
integral part of the syntax and semantics of the language. Firstly, we
have cleft sentences with negation of the matrix clause: *eg* (with cleft
focus underlined):

[13] It wasn't <u>John</u> who called me yesterday

[14] It wasn't <u>me</u> that John called yesterday

[15] It wasn't <u>yesterday</u> that John called me

In many contexts, there will be pragmatic equivalence between these
sentences and simple negative sentences with the intonation nucleus
on the corresponding elements:

[16] /Jŏhn didn't call me yesterday #

[17] /John didn't call mě yesterday #

[18] /John didn't call me yěsterday #

But syntactically and semantically, the focus in [13]–[15] is cleft focus
(*cf* §4.1), and hence there is no need here for the additional concept
'focus of negation'. All there is to be said about [13]–[15] follows
automatically from the simultaneous choice of cleft focus and matrix
negation.

Secondly, we have sentences with coordination of phrases by
not. . .but. . .; eg:

[19] Not John but Bill called me yesterday

[20] John called not me but my brother yesterday

[21] John called me not yesterday but the day before

Here we are certainly justified in regarding the elements preceded
by *not* as focal. But the semantic representation of each of these
sentences entails both a negative and a corresponding positive proposition, and the contrast involved serves to foreground the positive as well as, and even more than, the negative member of the
pair of coordinated phrases.

Finally, we have sentences with *hardly* or *scarcely*. These words may be used either with or without focus, depending on their position in the sentence. When they precede the (main) verb, there is no semantic focus, so that [22] and [23] below, for example, are truth-conditionally equivalent:

[22] They hardly gave any information to anyone

[23] They hardly gave anyone any information

In the corresponding passive sentences, however, the *hardly* (or *scarcely*) must be initial and must therefore focus on whichever of the arguments has been selected as the subject:

[24] Hardly any information was given to anyone

[25] Hardly anyone was given any information

The syntactic-semantic focusing of *hardly* in [24] and [25] prevents these sentences from being truth-conditionally equivalent. Thus [24] is compatible with [26]:

[26] One piece of information was given to many people (*or* to everyone)

But [26] is not compatible with [25]. On the other hand, [25] is compatible with [27]:

[27] One person was given a lot of information (*or* all the information)

And [27], in turn, is incompatible with [24]. So *hardly* (and similarly *scarcely*) can focus on something that is within their scope. But, as negators, these words are somewhat anomalous. They do indeed turn positive sentences into negative ones (for the criteria, see §5.2.2); but they do not reverse the truth-values of the corresponding propositions, as we can see from [28] and [29], for example:

[28] I know him

[29] I hardly (*or* scarcely) know him

The reason for this anomaly is of course that these words have a semantic complexity that is not reflected in their morphological makeup. The negator that they contain on the semantic plane (a possible gloss would be 'not to a significant degree') is not separately represented on the morphological plane and is therefore not separately removable. These items, therefore, are negators of a very special kind.[7]

We can sum up by saying that in simple sentences negation is in general semantically unfocused.[8]

5.2 SENTENCE NEGATION

5.2.1 Forms and meanings of negative sentences

In logic, negation is a simpler matter than in the grammar of English (or of natural languages in general). For every possible proposition in logical notation, we can have a corresponding negative proposition (obtained by prefixing an instance of the negative operator) such that the whole of the negative proposition constitutes the scope of the negative, and such that its truth-value is the reverse of the truth-value of the proposition without the negative. For example:

[1] a.   F (a)
     b. ~F (a)

If [1.a] is true, [1.b] must be false, and if [1.a] is false, [1.b] must be true.

In English, some sentences cannot be negated in the same way by the mere addition of a negator. The reason may be purely syntactic (the need for 'do-support') and so rather trivial from the present point of view, eg:

[2] a. I know John
     b. *I not know John/ *I know not John

But it may also be semantic, as with [3] below:

[3] a. We must go
     b. We must not go

The truth-value of [3.b] is not the reverse of the truth-value of [3.a]: though they cannot both be true, they can both be false. In other words, [3.a] and [3.b] are contraries but not contradictories. The same holds good for [4], though here the b-sentence is much less likely to occur:

[4] a. No one is ready
     b. No one is not ready

But of course the addition of *not* can, and often does, produce contradictories, *eg*:

[5] a. John is ready
    b. John is not ready

[6] a. Many of us are ready
    b. Not many of us are ready

Here the a-sentences and the b-sentences cannot both be true and they cannot both be false. We must note (i) that the same position of *not* that failed to produce a contradictory in [3] and [4] succeeds in doing so in [5], and (ii) that the contradictory to [6.a] requires a different position for *not* from the contradictory to [5.a]. [6.b] must be distinguished from [6.c] below. The latter is not contradictory to [6.a], since both could be true (though they could not both be false – such pairs might be called 'compatibles'):

[6] c. Many of us are not ready

Sentence [5.b] shows that in some cases the scope of a *not* that follows the auxiliary will include the whole sentence, and [6.c] shows that in some cases it cannot do so (since *many* must be outside the scope of the following *not*).

The examples in [6] above show that there are sentences in which the position of the negator unambiguously determines its scope relationship to a quantifier (here *many*), and so distinguishes between a contradictory and a non-contradictory meaning. But there are also sentences for which this does not hold good, where the same syntactic form (and even two identical utterances of a given syntactic form) may be given two different interpretations, depending on different scope relations between the negative and quantifier. For example:

[7] a. He doesn't know a great deal
      = (not (a great deal (he knows)))
    b. He doesn't know a great deal
      = (a great deal (not (he knows)))

The two sentences in [7] may be disambiguated by their existential paraphrases:[9]

[7'] a. There's not a great deal that he knows
     b. There's a great deal that he doesn't know

The conflation of negatives with other items (as in *no*, *never*, *few*, etc) leads to further complications. On the one hand we have different syntactic structures which are logically equivalent but linguistically distinct nevertheless (see especially Bolinger 1977:38*ff* on the meanings of what is there called 'rightshifting'), and on the other hand we have single syntactic structures with different logical values. These two types of complication are illustrated by [8] and [9] respectively:

[8] a. He didn't say anything
      b. He said nothing

[9] a. I forced him to do nothing
         (= I forced him not to do anything)
      b. I forced him to do nothing
         (= I didn't force him to do anything)[10]

5.2.2 Criteria for sentence negation

When we speak of negative sentences in English, we are not necessarily referring to the linguistic correlates of negative propositions in the sense in which the term was used in the opening paragraph of §5.2.1. Such a logical definition of 'negative sentence' is of course possible, and is in fact the one adopted in Jackendoff (1972), where the following test is used (*p*321):

[10] A sentence $[_S X - neg - Y]$ is an instance of sentence negation if there exists a paraphrase (disregarding presuppositions) It is not so that $[_S X - Y]$

By this criterion, [11.a] is a negative sentence, but [11.b] is not; for only [11.a] is paraphrased by [11.c]:

[11] a. Not many of them went
       b. Many of them did not go
       c. It is not so that many of them went[11]

Other linguists, however, (*eg* Klima 1964; Quirk *et al* 1972; Ross 1973), have worked with a concept of 'negative sentence' which is not so well-defined logically but has a stronger intuitive appeal. In this they have followed a tradition that is well established in teaching-grammars of English (see, for example, Kelly 1947:69*ff*; Eckersley and Eckersley 1960:183) and goes back to Palmer (1924) at least.[12]

The criterion of the teaching-grammars is the reversed-polarity interrogative tag, which the speaker may append to a declarative clause in order to elicit from the hearer a response indicating his agreement or disagreement with the speaker's assertion. For example:

[12]   a.   The house is furnished, isn't it?
       b.   The house isn't furnished, is it?

The tag is sensitive to the difference between *is not furnished* and *is unfurnished*, as is clear from a comparison of [12.b] with [12.c]:

[12]   c.   The house is unfurnished, isn't it?

It is sensitive also to the difference between *almost* and *not*:

[13]   a.   They almost sold it, didn't they?
       b.   They didn't sell it, did they?

The declarative clause in [13.a] is shown to be positive, even though the proposition it asserts entails the negative proposition 'they did not sell it'.

The usual term for the reversed-polarity interrogative tag is simply 'question tag'; but this is not entirely satisfactory, since it fails to distinguish between the tag with reversed polarity and another tag, which is identical in structure, but agrees in polarity with the preceding clause and has a different discourse function from the tag with reversed polarity:

[14]   So you know him, do you?
[15]   He refuses, does he?

After negative clauses this tag is rare, but it does occur (see Quirk *et al* 1972:392); *eg*:

[16]   So you don't know him, don't you?

By adding this tag, the speaker indicates that the preceding declarative clause represents merely a repetition of, or an inference from, what he has just been told. Very often, this tag seems to have hostile overtones. It has been described as potentially 'aggressive, challenging' (Sinclair 1972:79) and as sometimes conveying 'sarcastic suspicion' (Quirk *et al* 1972:392). However, a more neutral use is also possible; 'it is often used to acknowledge statements that cause surprise' and 'it is one of the ways that we *repeat* information so that both parties can be sure that it has been passed correctly' (Sinclair). The two tags may be distinguished, following Sinclair, as the 'checking tag' (reversed polarity) and the 'copy tag' (constant polarity).[13] The copy tag is not normally used as a test for negativeness, but if its existence is not kept in mind, it is liable to cause confusion.

Klima (1964) uses the 'checking tag' and three additional tests:

(i) '*Either*-conjoining' (with focus on the subject)
(ii) The 'negative appositive tag' with *not even*
(iii) The '*neither*-tag'

Their use is illustrated in the following examples:

[17] Publishers will usually reject suggestions, and writers will $\left\{\begin{array}{l}\text{not}\\ \text{scarcely}\\ \textit{etc}\end{array}\right\}$ accept them, either (=Klima's (43))

[18] Writers will $\left\{\begin{array}{l}\text{not}\\ \text{seldom}\\ \textit{etc}\end{array}\right\}$ accept suggestions, not even reasonable ones (=Klima's (48a))[14]

[19] Writers won't be accepting suggestions, and neither will publishers (=Klima's (60)).

The last of these tests, [19] above, is regarded by Klima as a test of 'strong negation', because not all the sentence types that pass the other three tests (*ie* [17], [18], and the 'checking tag') will also pass the test of the 'neither-tag'. From this is it only a short step to the notion that negativity is a cline (or that 'negginess' is a 'squish'), as is argued by Ross (1973, quoted in Tottie 1977). Ross adds two further criteria:

(i) The suitability of *I guess/suppose/reckon/hope* (etc) *not*, as a response indicating agreement
(ii) Collocability with a following *I don't think*

(see Tottie 1977:13–14).

There can be no doubt that such a battery of tests will not give us a sharply-defined category of negative sentences, and even the use of a single test does not produce a clear-cut decision one way or the other over the whole range of sentence types. So whatever our choice of criteria, we must be prepared to deal with an area of apparent indeterminacy between 'undoubtedly negative' and 'undoubtedly positive'. For example, there is evidence that sentences like [20]:

[20] Few people like him

are not universally treated as negative, either according to the checking-tag or according to the *neither*-tag (Langendoen 1970:17*f*; Tottie 1977:19). Furthermore, the place of the negative item in the sentence has been shown to be significant. [20] above, with *few* used initially, in the subject, shows a higher proportion of 'negative' responses than [21], where *few* occurs later in the sentence, in the object (Tottie 1977:13, 19, 23):

[21] I see few people these days

This untidiness in the data creates a serious problem for our semantic representation, a problem for which no fully explicit solution seems to have been proposed so far (and none will be attempted here). In principle, there are two ways of accounting for this 'fuzzy' negation, with radically different implications for semantic theory:

(i) Fuzziness as inherent gradience
(ii) Fuzziness as indeterminacy of semantic structure (with gradience as an epiphenomenon)

If we adopt the 'inherent gradience' interpretation, we must abandon truth-conditional semantics altogether. If, on the other hand, we take the fuzziness to be due to indeterminacy of structure, we must find alternative semantic representations for certain syntactic structures containing negatives. In each of these structures, at least one of the semantic representations will have to have the negation embedded in such a way as to leave the sentence positive. The morphological items that apparently call for this double analysis include *few*, *little*, *seldom*, *rarely*, *hardly*, and even *nothing* and *no one*. Just as we can have truth-conditional equivalence with syntactic non-equivalence between [22] and [12]:

[22] He didn't tell us anything
[23] He told us nothing

so we would have, by the account here suggested, pragmatic equivalence with semantic non-equivalence between the declarative clauses in [24]:

    [24] a. We see few people these days (don't we?)
          b. We see few people these days (do we?)

In other words, the declarative clause pattern in [24] would have at least two semantic forms: one corresponding to its own syntactic form,[15] and one corresponding to the syntactic form of [25]:

    [25] We don't see many people these days

For some items, eg *nowhere*, *nobody*, there is a third option, interpretation as a proper name, which makes possible the trick played on Polyphemus by Odysseus, and also the following exchange between Alice and the King in *Through the Looking-Glass*[16].

    'I see nobody on the road,' said Alice.
    'I only wish *I* had such eyes,' the King remarked in a fretful tone. 'To be able to see Nobody! And at that distance too! Why, it's as much as I can do to see real people, by this light!'

To return to the range of criteria for negativity, it may seem that the first of the two added by Ross is radically different from all those used by Klima, in that Ross's test clearly relates to discourse structure, while Klima's relate to syntax. But this impression is deceptive. It is true, of course, that Klima's criteria were all regarded by himself and others as syntactic, at the time they were proposed. But that was a time when grammar, at least in the school of thought to which Klima belonged, concerned itself exclusively with the generation of sentences. And as long as discourse was regarded as being, by definition, beyond the scope of linguistic enquiry proper, it was natural for linguists to be rather expansionist in drawing the boundaries of the sentence: it was the only way of bringing various interesting phenomena within the legitimate bounds of their field of study. Hence the 'annexation' of question-tags by sentence grammar, which is implied in Klima (1964), and is made explicit in Burt (1971) and in Sinclair (1972) (though the latter is not transformational). Of course traditional punctuation helped, by camouflaging the tags as sentence parts (together with other types of elliptical sentences). But Hudson (1973) shows the feasibility of analyzing the declarative clause with question-tag as a sequence of sentences; and it is quite possible that the traditional account will not long survive the establishment of 'discourse grammar' as a linguistically respectable part of language study. The 'elliptical sentence' analysis is no less plausible for the *neither*-tag, and it is possible also for the tag with *not even*, which leaves '*either*-conjoining' as the only one of Klima's tests whose narrowly grammatical status is unlikely to be challenged.

If the sentential status of the tags is accepted, we shall have to choose between two options:

(i) We can rely on *either*-conjoining as a test for sentence negativity, possibly in conjunction with Ross's second test

(ii) We can give full and open recognition to the relevance of discourse structure

If the second alternative is chosen, there are further tests that can be added, *eg*:

(i) The polar interrogative tag with changed subject
(ii) The *why*-interrogative with changed subject
(iii) The confirmation
(iv) The denial
(v) The hostile response

These are illustrated below:

[26] a. I like it. Don't you?
     b. I don't like it. Do you?

[27] a. They've done it. Why don't you?
     b. They didn't do it. Why should you?

[26] and [27] represent types (i) and (ii) above. They both convey the idea that it would be reasonable for the fact stated in the declarative clause to be paralleled by another fact, which is suggested by the interrogative clause. [28], [29], and [30] represent types (iii), (iv), and (v):

[28] a. It's important. – Yes (it is)
     b. It's not important. – No (it isn't)

[29] a. It's important. – (No) it isn't
     b. It's not important. – (Yes) it is

[30] a. It's important. – (Oh) is it (indeed)!
     b. It's not important. – (Oh) isn't it (just)!

If negativity is to be studied as a gradience phenomenon (whatever the theoretical explanation may be), it would seem reasonable to include some of these utterance types in the set of criteria for the negativity matrix.

But whether we restrict the criteria for sentence negativity to intrasentential features, or use a combination of intrasentential and discourse features, the result will be significantly different in either case from what we would obtain by the application of Jackendoff's logically based criterion. In Jackendoff's negative sentences, everything is within the scope of negation. In negative sentences as determined by purely linguistic criteria, this is not necessarily so. In the following section we shall examine the varying scope of negation in negative sentences, in the widest sense.

5.2.3 The scope of the negative in sentence negation

5.2.3.1 Introductory

We saw in §5.2.2 that certain sentence forms with negative quantifiers may be regarded as either intermediate or ambiguous between positive and negative sentences, *eg*:

[31] a. We see few people these days (don't we?) (=[24.a] above)
       b. We see few people these days (do we?) (=[24.b] above)

If we choose to analyse in terms of ambiguity rather than inherent gradience, then, in such a case as [31], it seems possible to correlate the status 'positive sentence' with a semantic interpretation in which the scope of the negation is limited to a part of the sentence, and the status 'negative sentence' with a semantic interpretation in which the negation is all-inclusive; perhaps as in the following paraphrases in semi-English:

[31'] a. We see a number of people that is not large (positive sentence)
        b. We don't see a number of people that is large (negative sentence)

So the occurrence of markers of positiveness as well as markers of negativeness could be reconciled in such cases with the definition of 'negative sentence' as 'a sentence wholly within the scope of negation'. But such a solution will not account for all sentence types. There is no way of giving a sentence like:

[32] Sometimes they don't understand

a semantic interpretation with all-inclusive negation, as represented by:

[33] NEG [sometimes they understand], *ie* 'It is not so that sometimes they understand'

For [32] is logically compatible with:

[34] Sometimes they understand

whereas [33] contradicts [34]. Yet though the negation in [32] cannot be all-inclusive, the sentence is syntactically (or textually) compatible with at least some of the criteria for sentence negation, *eg*:

[35] a. Sometimes <u>they</u> don't understand, either (with the focus of *either* on *they*)
     b. Sometimes they don't understand, do they? (checking-tag)

We therefore have to ask the following questions about the scope of negation in negative sentences:

(a) What must be inside?
(b) What can be inside or outside?
(c) What must be outside?

There is no doubt about one element – the main verb. This must always be within the scope of negation; otherwise the sentence is positive, as we can see from:

[36] No water means no life, doesn't it? – Yes, it does

The following categories of items are problematic in various ways:

(i)   Quantifiers
(ii)   Conjunctions and disjunctions
(iii) Adverbial elements in sentence structure
(iv)   Auxiliary verbs

Before we begin our examination of the categories listed in (i)–(iv) above, there are two technical points that require attention. First, a matter of terminology. In speaking of scope relations, it is convenient to have a less clumsy way of saying 'A has B within its scope' or 'A takes wide scope with respect to B'. I shall be using the verb 'dominate' in this sense:

'A dominates B' = (by definition) 'B is within the scope (or domain) of'

On the analogy of this use of 'dominate', I shall also be using 'domain' as a synonym for 'scope'.[17] 'Dominate' and 'domain', as used here, are purely semantic terms and involve no reference to syntactic configurations. In the terminology of transformational-generative grammar, of course, 'dominate' is used in a totally different way, to denote a phrase-structure relationship. Ideally, one would like to avoid such conflicts of terminology, but the supply of suitable words is limited. There are similar difficulties with the word 'scope', which I am using in the sense it normally has in logic. Lasnik (1972) uses 'scope' in the sense of 'focus' (see note 2), and Jackendoff (1972) uses it to denote a particular syntactic relationship between a so-called 'modal operator' and another item; he uses the term 'dependent on' for the semantic relationship that I am calling 'dominated by' or 'within the scope (or domain) of'.[18]

The second point concerns the notation. The scope (or domain) of the negative will be marked by angle-brackets, as follows:

[37] a. ⌞He doesn't know a great deal⌟ ('There isn't a great deal that he knows')
b. ⌞He doesn't know⌟ a great deal ('There's a great deal that he doesn't know')

In most cases it will be unnecessary to mark the domain of quantifiers or other items when the domain of negation is marked.

5.2.3.2 *Quantifiers*

The English quantifier-words can be divided into three sets:

(i) Negative quantifiers: *no*, *neither*, *few*; *seldom*; *hardly*; *never*, etc
(ii) Non-negatives containing a universal quantifier: *all*, *every*, *both*; *always*; 'free choice' *any*, 'free choice' *either*; etc
(iii) Non-negatives containing an existential quantifier: *some*; *any*,[19] *either*;[19] *one*, *two*, *three*, *many*; *often*; *ever*, etc

The negative quantifiers (except for *hardly*) may be regarded as the semantic equivalents of the simple negator *not* dominating one of the existential quantifiers: *no = not any*; *neither = not either*; *few = not many*; etc. It remains to describe the scope relations between sentence negation and quantifiers belonging to groups (ii) and (iii).

The universals are usually dominated and preceded by the negative. For example:

[38] ⌐Not all the boys were invited⌐

[39] ⌐They didn't invite all the boys⌐ (=[38])

The pattern with the universal preceding the negative is marked[20]:

[40] a. ⌐All the boys were not invited⌐
     b. All the boys ⌐were not invited⌐

In [40], the negative may dominate the universal or vice versa, or in other words, [40] may be equivalent to [38] – the reading of [40.a] – or to:

[41] ⌐None of the boys were invited⌐

– which is the reading of [40.b]. *Every*, *each*, and *always*, it seems, never dominate the sentence negation.

The existentials can be divided into three groups:

(a) *Some* and its compounds, *several*, etc
(b) *Any* and its compounds, *either*, and *ever*
(c) The cardinal numerals, *many*, etc

Some and the others in its group always dominate the negative, regardless of sequence – *eg*:

[42] Some of the boys ⌐were not invited⌐

[43] ⌐They didn't invite⌐some of the boys (=[42])

– unless the sentence is intended as a denial of the corresponding assertion, or the negative is in the matrix of the clause that contains the quantifier[21]:

[44] ⌐I didn't know that they had invited some of the boys⌐

Sentence [44] may be truth-conditionally equivalent to:

[45] ⌐I didn't know that they had invited any of the boys⌐

Any and the others in its group are always dominated by the negative.[22] For example:

[46] ↓They didn't invite any of the boys↓

The negative may be in the matrix of the clause that contains the quantifier (see [45] above). Existential quantifiers of the *any*-group cannot precede the negative unless it is in the matrix. Compare [47] with [48]:

[47] *↓Any of the boys were not invited↓ (impossible as equivalent to [46] above)

[48] ↓That they had invited any of the boys I did not know↓

The behaviour of group (c) (the numerals, *many*, etc) is more complicated than that of (a) or (b). When the negative precedes the quantifier, the negative usually has wider scope, but the converse interpretation is also possible:

[49] They didn't invite five boys

can be taken to correspond either to:

[50] ↓There weren't five boys that they invited↓

– where *not* dominates *five* – or to:

[51] There were five boys ↓that they didn't invite↓

– Where *five* dominates *not*. Similarly with *many* in:

[52] They didn't invite many boys

When the quantifier precedes the negative, the quantifier has wider scope:

[53] Five boys ↓were not invited↓ (=[51], not =[50])

[54] Many boys ↓were not invited↓

There are counterexamples to the rule that a group (c) quantifier dominates a following negative, but they all seem to involve either 'generic' or 'potential' contexts; *eg*:

[55] ↓One swallow doesn't make a summer↓

[56] ↓Two beers can't do you any harm↓

The negative dominates the numeral in both [55] and [56], so that they are equivalent (apart from the coordination) to [57] and [58]:

[57] ↓Nor does one swallow make a summer↑

[58] ↓Nor can two beers do you any harm↑

But [55] is not equivalent to [59], where the negative also has wide scope:

[59] a. ? ↓Not one swallow makes a summer↑
     b. ? ↓No swallow makes a summer↑

One might try to explain the difference between [55] and [57] on the one hand and [59.a,b] on the other by suggesting that the former should be interpreted as having a verbless clause as its subject (*one swallow* – 'the appearance of one swallow'). But no such expedient will help with the example given by Ladusaw (1980:60):

[60] One TA can't always grade all of the homework assigned

Yet here, too, the meaning of *one…n't* is quite different from the meaning of *no* or *not one*; cf:

[61] a. ↓Not one TA can always grade all of the homework assigned↑
     b. ↓No TA can always grade all of the homework assigned↑

The difference between [60] and [61] can be made clearer by the following crude representations of the scope relations:

[62] It is not (always (possible (for one TA to grade all the homework))) (=[60])

[63] There is not (one TA (who can (always grade all the homework))) (=[61])

To show the difference between [55] and [59] above in the same way, we would have to allow the generic element in the meaning of these sentences to 'materialize':

[64] It is not (generally the case (that one swallow makes it summer))

[65] There is not (one swallow (that generally makes it summer))

[64] corresponds to [55], and [65] to [59]. We can now qualify our rule as follows: the negative of the auxiliary may dominate a preceding numeral only on condition that a modality (overt or covert) intervenes in the logical structure.[23]

5.2.3.3 Conjunctions and disjunctions

It has been observed (McCawley 1972; Horn 1972) that conjunctions and disjunctions of phrases (eg (*both Harry and John*, (*either*) *Harry or John*) are linguistically parallel in some ways to universally and existentially quantified phrases (eg *both of the boys*, *one of the boys*). This is not surprising, of course, in view of the well-known logical relationship between conjunction and universal quantification on the one hand and disjunction and existential quantification on the other. Instead of writing:

[66] Fa & Fb, *ie* 'The individual *a* has the property *F* and the individual *b* has the property *F*'

we can always write:

[67] ∀x   Fx, *ie* 'It holds good for all individual members
     x{a,b}
     of the class *x* (complete list of members: *a,b*) that they have the property *F*'

And similarly, instead of writing:

[68] Fa v Fb, *ie* 'The individual *a* has the property *F*, or the individual *b* has the property *F*, or both of them have it'

we can always write:

[69] ∃x   Fx, *ie* 'It holds good for at least one individual
     x{a,b}
     member of the class *x* (complete list of members: *a,b*) that he has the property *F*'

However, the semantics of English (or of any natural language) cannot be identified with logic. Just as we have noted how the individual quantifiers differ from one another in their scope behaviour, so also we must note the individual characteristics of the co-ordinators that function as syntactic markers of conjunction and disjunction[24]:

(i)   a. ...*and*...
    b. *both*...*and*...
(ii) a. ...*or*...
    b. *either*...*or*...

The simple co-ordinator *and* normally dominates a following negative:

[70] Bob and Harry ˌwere not invitedˌ

When the negative comes first, both readings are normal:

[71] a. ˌThey didn't invite Bob and Harryˌ *ie* 'At least one of them was not invited'
     b. ˌThey didn't inviteˌ Bob and Harry *ie* 'Neither was invited'

The correlative co-ordinators *both*...*and*...normally stand after the negative and in its domain:

[72] ˌThey didn't invite both Bob and Harryˌ

The converse, with the negative following the co-ordinators and dominated by them, is highly marked:

[73] Both Bob and Harry ˌwere not invitedˌ

The simple *or* does not normally precede the negation unless the context is modal – in which case the *or* does not dominate the negative:

[74] ?Bob or Harry was not invited
[75] ˌBob or Harry would not have been invitedˌ

[74] is odd in the sense of 'One of them was not invited', and quite impossible in the sense of 'Neither was invited'. [75] is equivalent in truth-value to:

[76] ˌNeither Bob nor Harry would have been invitedˌ[25]

Compare [55] and [60] above and the analyses in [62] and [64]. An *or* that follows the negative comes within its domain:

[77] ˌThey didn't invite Bob or Harryˌ

The correlative co-ordinators *either...or...* dominate a following negative[26] and are usually dominated by a preceding negative:

[78] a. Either Bob or Harry ˌwas not invitedˌ
      b. *ˌEither Bob or Harry was not invitedˌ

[79] a. ˌThey didn't invite either Bob or Harryˌ (unmarked)
      b. ˌThey didn't inviteˌ either Bob or Harry (marked)[27]

5.2.3.4 *Adverbial elements in sentence structure*

The adverbial elements in sentence structure are divided by Quirk *et al*: (1972:420*ff*) into two major classes:
(i) Those that are 'integrated to some extent into the structure of the clause'
(ii) Those that are 'peripheral to clause structure'

The distinction is based on a set of criteria that includes syntactic, semantic, and intonational elements, but it seems that practically the same division can be made on a purely semantic basis: we can define as 'peripheral' those elements that are compatible with sentence negation but cannot be included in its domain.[28] For example, with *however* and *fortunately* as peripheral adverbials:

[80] However, ˌthey didn't notice anythingˌ

[81] Fortunately, ˌit didn't last longˌ

Most peripheral adverbials may stand in two or more different positions in the sentence. For example:

[82] a. ˌThey,ˌ however, ˌdidn't notice anythingˌ
      b. ˌThey didn't,ˌ however, ˌnotice anythingˌ
      c. ˌThey didn't notice anything,ˌ however

Some adverbial items must be regarded as pairs of homonyms, one member of the pair being 'peripheral' and one being 'integrated'. For example:

[83] ˌHeˌ clearly ˌcould not explain itˌ, *ie* 'It is clear that he could not explain it' (peripheral)

[84] ˌHe could not explain it clearlyˌ, *ie* 'He could not give a clear explanation' (integrated)

The redefinition of 'peripheral adverbials' in terms of negative scope suggests the following general classification of adverbial elements (excluding 'polarity-sentive items'[29] and negative adverbials):

[85] (i) 'Nuclear' adverbials, *ie* items that must always be inside the domain of sentence negation

(ii) 'Intermediate' adverbials, *ie* items that may be inside or outside the domain of sentence negation

(iii) 'Peripheral' adverbials, *ie* items that must always be outside the domain of sentence negation

Class (i) includes 'intensifiers' (Quirk *et al* 1972:438*ff*)[30] 'process' adverbials, *ie* adverbials of manner, means or instrument (*pp*459*ff*) direction adverbials (*pp*427*ff*), and adverbials denoting location in time or space (*pp*483*ff*, 472*ff*).

Class (ii) includes adverbials denoting extent over time or space (see *pp*486*ff* for adverbials of duration and frequency; extent over space is denoted by *throughout the country*, *in many countries*, *in England and* (*in*) *France*, and the like), adverbials of cause, reason, or motive (*p*321, also *pp*752 and 753),[31] or volition (*pp*466*ff*), and conditional clauses introduced by *if*.[32]

Class (iii) includes conditional clauses introduced by *unless*, *provided that*, *on condition that*, or *if and only if* (*p*746), 'disjuncts' (*pp*507*ff*) and 'conjuncts' (*pp*520*ff*).[33]

The question now arises how we can derive from the classification in [85] above a more comprehensive scheme that will include polarity-sensitive items (henceforth PSI's) and negative adverbials, and will delimit a class of 'sentential adverbials', these being distinct from 'verb-modifiers' on the one hand and from 'suprasentential adverbials' on the other.

The affirmative-polarity items (henceforth API's) are easily dealt with. All of them can be dominated by sentence negation in denials and in questions, and in addition we find them in the scope of negation in negative clauses that are embedded in negative sentences or in *only*-sentences (as pointed out by Baker 1970). But while some of them (eg *sometimes*, *somewhere*) can also dominate the negation, others (eg *rather*, somewhat, *a little*) cannot do so. For example:

[86] ↗Doesn't he sometimes get drunk?↘

[87] No, ↗he doesn't sometimes get drunk↘

[88] ₎You can't convince me that ₎he doesn't sometimes get
      drunk₍₍

[89] a. Sometimes ₎he doesn't get drunk₍
      b. ₍He₍ sometimes ₎doesn't get drunk₍

[90] ₎Don't you rather like George?₍

[91] No, ₍I don't rather like George₍

[92] You must be the only one ₍who doesn't rather like George₍

[93] *₍I₍ rather ₎don't like George₍

[94] I rather dislike George

The evidence of [86]–[94] suggests that API's like *sometimes* can be
added to Class (ii), while the *rather*-group can be added to Class (i).

We now come to the negative-polarity items (NPI's). These can be
divided between Class (i) and Class (ii) on the basis of the suppletive
relationship between sets of API's and NPI's: *at all, in the least, in the
slightest* are complementary to *rather, somewhat, a little; ever* is
complementary to *sometimes; anywhere* to *somewhere*.

The negative adverbials *never, nowhere, seldom* can be assigned to
Class (ii) on the basis of their equivalence to *not ever, not anywhere,*
and *not often*.[34]

It follows from the definitions of Classes (i)–(iii) that only the
'intermediate' adverbials (Class (ii)) can give rise to ambiguity of
negative scope. Such ambiguity may occur when the intermediate
adverbial stands in final position; *eg:*

[95] a. ₍I didn't lock the door deliberately₍
      b. ₍I didn't lock the door₍ deliberately

[96] a. ₍Jean didn't put salt in the porridge to annoy Bob₍
      b. ₍Jean didn't put salt in the porridge₍ to annoy Bob

[97] a. ₍Susan hasn't been here for three days₍
      b. ₍Susan hasn't been here₍ for three days

The meanings of [95.a] and [95.b] can be unambiguously represented
by [98.a] and [98.b]:

[98] a. ₍I didn't deliberately lock the door₍
      b. ₍I₍ deliberately ₎didn't lock the door₍

The meaning of [96.b] can be unambiguously represented by:

[99] To annoy Bob, ⌐Jean didn't put salt in the porridge⌐

And the meaning of [97.b] can be unambiguously represented by:

[100] For three days, ⌐Susan hasn't been here⌐

Ambiguity of scope may be eliminated not only by the position of the adverbial, as in [98]–[100], but also by the aspectual character of the predicate[35]; eg:

[101] a. *⌐Jean hasn't written a letter for three days⌐
b. ⌐Jean hasn't written a letter⌐ for three days

or by a polarity-sensitive item, eg:

[102] a. ⌐Susan hasn't been here yet⌐
b. *⌐Susan hasn't been here⌐ yet

In sentences with conditional clauses introduced by if, the interpretation of the scope relations is determined pragmatically. Such sentences can be represented (if they are positive) by the formula

'if p, then q'

or, more explicitly,

'the truth of p is sufficient to ensure the truth of q'.

If they are negative, they can be interpreted either as

'not (if p, then q)'

that is

'the truth of p is not sufficient to ensure the truth of q'

or as

'if p, then not-q'

that is

'the truth of p is sufficient to ensure the truth of not-q'.

The first interpretation is appropriate for

They won't ring the police if you're late

and the second for

They won't let you in if you're late.

In the absence of pragmatic clues, we have ambiguity, as in

They won't be angry if you leave at once.

This can be interpreted either as 'Your leaving at once won't make them angry' or as 'By leaving at once you can see to it that they won't be angry'.

In Quirk *et al* (1972) there is no division of the 'integrated' adverbials that corresponds to the division between 'nuclear' and 'intermediate'. Thomason and Stalnaker (1973) suggest a different division – based on a set of four semantic criteria – between 'predicate modifiers' (roughly = 'nuclear') and 'sentence modifiers' (the rest); but they do not separate the 'intermediate' adverbials from the 'peripheral' ones. The taxonomy outlined above has the advantage of separating the three classes and doing so by means of a small and homogeneous set of criteria.[36]

It remains to be seen what bearing the options for the scope of negation may have on the analysis of sentences in terms of syntactic constituency. The same applies to other semantic phenomena, such as the coreference options investigated by Reinhart (1976, 1981).

5.2.3.5 *Auxiliary verbs*

A number of auxiliary verbs seem to be normally outside the domain of sentence negation in declarative sentences and WH-interrogatives. The clearest cases are *must* and *should*. For example:

[103] Mary mustn't find out
[104] He shouldn't tell her

That [103] and [104] are negative sentences is clear from:

[105] Mary mustn't find out either, must she? – No, she mustn't

[106] He shouldn't tell her either, should he? – No, he shouldn't

Yet the meanings of [103] and [104] cannot be represented by:

[107] *$_{\downarrow}$Mary mustn't find out$_{\downarrow}$, *ie* not (necessary (Mary find out))

[108] *$_{\downarrow}$He shouldn't tell her$_{\downarrow}$, *ie* not (incumbent (he tell her))

They must be represented rather by:

[109] $_\lrcorner$Mary$_\llcorner$ must $_\lrcorner$n't find out$_\llcorner$, *ie* necessary (not (Mary find out))

[110] $_\lrcorner$He$_\llcorner$ should $_\lrcorner$n't tell her$_\llcorner$, *ie* incumbent (not (he tell her))[37]

Sentences with the *may* of possibility require the same analysis, though this item differs from *must* and *should* (and also from the *may* of permission) in two respects: (i) it cannot be followed by the contracted form of the negative *n't*; and (ii) the negative declarative *may not* is not normally followed by a positive checking-tag.[38] However, the barring of the contracted negative need not have any semantic significance; we have *aren't*, *isn't*, but not **amn't*; and the lack of a positive checking-tag follows from a general avoidance of inverted forms with this auxiliary; *eg*:

[111] *May Mary have found out?

The negative status of sentences with *may not* is sufficiently clear from the *either*-test:

[112] <u>Mary</u> may not be going, either

We therefore analyze:

[113] $_\lrcorner$Mary$_\llcorner$ may $_\lrcorner$not be going$_\llcorner$ *ie* possible (not (Mary be going))

– like [109] and [110] – as a negative sentence dominated by a positive auxiliary.[39]

The *may* of permission falls within the domain of sentence negation:

[114] $_\lrcorner$You may no go out$_\llcorner$, *ie* not (permitted (you go out))

When the *may* of permission is outside the scope of negation, the negation is not sentential (see 5.3.3).

The complex modal auxiliary *have got to* – like its synonym, the 'catenative' verb *have to*, and unlike *must* – falls within the domain of sentence negation in most varieties of Standard English, so that:

[115] You haven't got to tell him / You've not got to tell him

is contradictory, not contrary, to:

[116] You have got to tell him

There are, however, varieties of English in which *have not got to* is ambiguous (Hughes and Trudgill 1979:23), so that [115] may be either (115′.a] or [115′.b]:

[115′] a. ˌYou have not got to tell himˌ
b. ˌYouˌ have ˌnotˌ got ˌto tell himˌ

[115′.a] is contradictory to [116], and [115′.b] is contrary to [116].

5.3 CONSTITUENT NEGATION

5.3.1 Constituent negation and lexical negation

We shall distinguish constituent negation from sentential negation on the one hand and from lexical negation on the other. Constituent negation and lexical negation are alike in leaving the polarity of the sentence unaffected. They differ in that constituent negation uses negators that can also produce sentential negation, such as *not*, *no*, *never*, whereas lexical negation uses negators that never produce sentential negation, such as *un-*, *in-*, *dis-*. For example:

[1] <u>The other flat</u> is furnished too, ˌisn't it?ˌ

[2] <u>The other flat</u> is ˌunfurnishedˌ too, ˌisn't it?ˌ

[3] ˌThe other flat isn't furnished eitherˌ, is it?

[4] <u>You</u> can say something too, ˌcan't you?ˌ

[5] <u>You</u> can ˌsay nothingˌ too, ˌcan't you?ˌ

[6] ˌYou can say nothing eitherˌ, can you?

If we look at the first sentence (*ie* the 'sentence' without the tag) in each of these examples, we see that there is no negation in [1] and [4], sentential negation in [3] and [6], lexical negation in [2], and constituent negation in [5].

It might be suggested that we can distinguish lexical negation from all other kinds simply by the 'rank' of the negator: words for sentential or constituent negation as against affixes for lexical negation. But this is not really satisfactory. A word like *never* can be regarded as a lexical item that contains a negative prefix (*ie* as *n + ever*), yet the scope of this prefix may encompass a whole sentence. Moreover, the word *not* is reduced to an affix in the negative auxiliaries, but unlike *-less* in a word like *harmless*, the suffix *-n't* produces sentence negation.

The scope of the lexical negation in [2] above is confined to the word *unfurnished*, whereas the constituent negation in [5] dominates the phrase *say nothing*; but though lexical and constituent negation differ in the nature of their domains, something more is involved than the number of words in the constituents or their rank. Consider, for example [7] and [8]:

[7] He was unable to give us any information
[8] Something is better than nothing

On the one hand, the occurrence of *any* in [7] suggests that the domain of the *un-* extends over the whole phrase *unable to give us any information*. On the other hand, although the negation in [8] does not extend beyond the single word *nothing*, one would hardly want to dissociate the analysis of [8] from that of [9] and [10]:

[9] Half a loaf is better than ˩no bread˩
[10] Something for everyone is better than everything for one and ˩nothing for anybody else˩

In what follows, we shall not be concerned with lexical negation, except incidentally (see §5.3.4.6).[40]

Constituent negation can be divided into different types, according to the part of the sentence that is affected. The negative domain may be confined to:

(a) a subordinate clause (finite, non-finite, or verbless)
(b) a predication
(c) one of a set of 'lower-ranking' structures

Classes (a), (b), and (c) will be referred to as 'clausal', 'predicational', and 'local' negation respectively. The domain of constituent negation need not encompass the whole of the affected constituent, just as sentence negation does not always encompass the whole sentence (see §5.2.3).

5.3.2. Clausal negation

5.3.2.1 Finite clauses

Finite subordinate clauses use the same range of negatives as independent sentences, except for initial *neither*, and *nor*. Ambiguity between finite-clause negation and sentence negation is rare; but it does occur, as has been pointed out by Bolinger (1977:40):

[11] You told John you would help him. – I didn't tell John I would do any such thing (Bolinger's (38))

[12] I told John I would do no such thing (Bolinger's (39))

It is possible to substitute [12] for the second sentence in [11], *ie* to use it merely as denying that the speaker made a certain kind of statement, rather than as asserting that he made a negative statement. The usual tests for sentence negation are textually inappropriate here (see §5.2.2), but we can distinguish between the two readings of [12] by the choice between these two continuations:

[13] Honestly (truly, really) I didn't

[14] Honestly (truly, really) I did

If the appropriate continuation to [12] is [13], we have a case of sentence negation with 'rightshifting' of the negative into the subordinate clause;[41] if the appropriate continuation is [14], we can regard [12] as a positive sentence with constituent negation. Ambiguity of this kind is avoided, of course, by auxiliary negation; *eg*:

[15] I told John that I wouldn't do any such thing

Here the matrix clause must be read as positive.

5.3.2.2 *Non-finite clauses*

The options for negation in non-finite clauses are similar, but ambiguity between constituent negation and sentence negation is commoner.[42] For example:

[16] a. I advised him ↓to do nothing illegal↳, didn't I?
     b. ↓I advised him to do nothing illegal↳, did I?

[17] a. I suggested ↓doing nothing controversial↳, didn't I?
     b. ↓I suggested doing nothing controversial↳, did I?

The use of *not* before the verb serves to disambiguate such sentences:

[16] c. I advised him ↓not to do anything illegal↳
[17] c. I suggested ↓not doing anything controversial↳

5.3.2.3 *Verbless clauses*

When the clause is verbless, the negative has to be located in a non-verbal element, normally in the initial nominal phrase; *eg* (with square brackets enclosing the verbless clauses):

[18] [↓No news↓] is good news

[19] [Half a loaf] is better than [↓no bread↓]

[20] [↓Nothing↓] agrees with me more than [oysters] (Quirk *et al* 1972:381)

[21] I promise you [↓no punishment↓] (Bolinger 1977:43)

[22] The colonists' demand was [↓no taxation without representation↓]

[23] I suggest [↓no more coffee for any of us tonight↓] – we've had more than is good for us already

[24] The doctor advised [↓no cigarettes at all↓ for a month]

The analysis of [24] above shows that the domain of negation in verbless clauses (as in other kinds of subordinate clauses and in sentences) need not be co-extensive with the whole unit. (For the potential ambiguity of duration adverbials in relation to negatives, see [97.a,b] in §5.2.3.4).

The analysis of the bracketed sequences as clauses is based on semantic considerations. These may be supported by syntax when the verbless clause has subject function and consists of a plural nominal phrase; *eg*:

[25] [↓No sweets↓] is better than [too many]

Here the apparent lack of subject-verb agreement points to the clausal analysis for *no sweets*. But even in such cases we can have an alternative form camouflaging the clausal status of the subject:

[26] [↓No sweets↓] are better than [too many][43]

5.3.3 Predicational negation[44]

Predicational negation is usually referred to as 'main-verb negation' (see for instance Quirk *et al* 1972:383*ff*), but this term fails to distinguish two quite different patterns, *viz*:

(i) A type of sentence negation that excludes the first auxiliary verb from its domain

(ii) A type of constituent negation from which the subject as well as the first auxiliary are excluded

The first of these was dealt with in §5.2.3.5, and may be represented by:

[27] ⌊Mary⌊ must ⌊n't find out⌊ (=[103] above)

This is a negative sentence dominated by a positive modal auxiliary (*must*). The second pattern may be represented by:

[28] You may ⌊not take the exam today⌊

– *ie* 'You have the option of not taking the exam today'. In [28] – as marked – the sentence is positive; but the same sequence of words can of course be given a different reading, which is in fact commoner, *viz*:

[29] ⌊You may not take the exam today⌊

–*ie* 'You are not allowed to take the exam today'. The reading of [28] is forced on us, however, if a parenthetic element is inserted before the *not*, eg:

[30] You may, of course, ⌊not take the exam today⌊

The same set of options exists with *can*, when it is used to denote permission or ability (as distinct from possibility, where it joins *may* as the second member of a suppletive pair). For example:

[31] You can (simply) ⌊not go to the meeting⌊

[32] ⌊You cannot go to the meeting⌊

The exclusion of the subject from the scope of negation in the pattern of [28], [30], and [31], as opposed to its inclusion in the patterns of [27] – with the auxiliary excluded – and [29], [32] – with the auxiliary included – is reflected also in the contrast between [33] below on the one hand and [34], [35] on the other:

[33] a. The teachers may ⌊set no exams⌊, *ie* 'The teachers are free to set no exams' (predicational negation)

b. *⌊No exams⌊ may ⌊be set⌊ by the teachers (passive of a.)

[34] a. ⌐The teachers⌐ may ⌐set no exams⌐, *ie* 'It is possible that the teachers will set no exams' (sentential negation)

b. ⌐No exams⌐ may ⌐be set by the teachers⌐ (passive of a.)

[35] a. ⌐The teachers may set no exams⌐, *ie* 'The teachers are not allowed to set exams' (sentential negation)

b. ⌐No exams may be set by the teachers⌐ (passive of a.)

The passive corresponding to [33.a] is ill-formed, unlike the passives corresponding to [34.a] and [35.a], because the passive in such cases brings the negation into the subject. Only in sentences with the *may* of possibility can the subject be negated without negating the auxiliary as well. Compare also [36.a,b]:

[36] a. The accused may give no evidence
b. No evidence may be given by the accused

[36.a] is three ways ambiguous (corresponding to the readings of the active sentences in [33]–[35]). [36.b], on the other hand, has only two readings, corresponding to the passive sentences in [34] and [35].

Predicational negation is also possible with non-modal auxiliary verbs, *eg*:

[37] a. He has, on occasion, ⌐not said anything about it⌐, hasn't he?

b. He has, on occasion, ⌐said nothing about it⌐, hasn't he?

[38] She does sometimes ⌐eat nothing at all for breakfast⌐, doesn't she?

It is possible even without an auxiliary verb altogether, *eg*:

[39] She sometimes ⌐eats nothing at all for breakfast⌐, doesn't she?

5.3.4 Local negation[45]

Little more will be needed here than to list the subtypes and give examples of each.

5.3.4.1 *Prepositional phrases with adverbial function*

[40] They will deliver your order ⌐at no extra charge⌐

[41] He managed to cross over ⌐with no great difficulty⌐[46]

[42] I can find the way ˌwith no guide except the starsˌ

[43] The arrangements were made quietly and efficiently, ˌwith no fussˌ

[44] Then all of a sudden, ˌfor no good reason that any of us could seeˌ, the whole thing was off

[45] Soon after that, ˌto nobody's regretˌ, he left for good

It is not obvious what is the precise nature of the semantic relations between the verb and the adverbial that are required to 'licence' the local negation. The adverbials are of all the three types distinguished in 5.2.3.4 – nuclear [40]–[43], intermediate [44], and peripheral [45]. Initial placement of the negative phrase (*eg* [44] and [45]) fails to induce subject-operator inversion (*cf* also §5.3.4.3 and §5.3.4.6).

5.3.4.2 *Prepositional phrases with postmodifying function*

[46] We saw a cat ˌwith no tailˌ[47]

[47] Various matters ˌof no real importanceˌ have been allowed to hold up the proceedings

5.3.4.3 *Quantifiers in adverbials of spatial or temporal distance*

[48] ˌNot farˌ away, he had a cottage

[49] ˌNot longˌ after, we left for Ireland

[50] ˌNot many yearsˌ later, they built this house

[51] ˌNot an hourˌ ago, they were happy and carefree

As noted by Klima (1964:306), such adverbials do not induce subject-operator inversion when placed initially, unlike negative adverbials with sentential scope, such as *never before, never after, never since, not once, not for a moment, not often*. For example:

[52] ˌNever before had they been so happyˌ

Compare also §5.3.4.1 and §5.3.4.6.

5.3.4.4 *Inherently negative quantifiers*

[53] We have overcome ˌnot a fewˏ difficulties

[54] I sensed ˌnot a littleˏ malice in his words

[55] Your behaviour has caused us ˌno littleˏ distress

[56] The news afforded her ˌno smallˏ satisfaction

The use of *small* as a quantifier, as in [56] above, does not seem to have been noticed by grammars. It is normally found only with a particular set of abstract nouns, mainly nouns denoting feelings (eg *It was small consolation that others had fared no better*). *Small* in such contexts can be glossed 'not much'.

The stylistic effect of this type of negation is formal and somewhat literary.

5.3.4.5 *Degree markers*

[57] He's been managing ˌnot tooˏ badly

[58] She was asked a number of ˌnot veryˏ difficult questions

[59] This ˌnot entirelyˏ altruistic offer was welcome nevertheless

The following examples (from Langendoen and Bever 1973:405) are semantically similar but involve the negation of prefixes:

[60] Harry's ˌnot overˏdeveloped muscles were not up to the task

[61] We worship a ˌnot allˏ-powerful deity

5.3.4.6 *Contrary-negative prefixes*
(of adjectives or adverbs)

[62] In encounters of this sort, he had learnt to manoeuvre ˌnot unˏskilfully

[63] The child seems ˌnot unˏintelligent

[64] We have now collected a ˌnot inˏconsiderable sum of money

[65] In this way he sometimes achieves a ˌnot disˌpleasing effect

[66] ˌNot inˌfrequently, crop yields are severely reduced by drought

As with other instances of local negation (see §5.3.4.1 and §5.3.4.4), initial placement does not induce subject-operator inversion. Contrast [66] above with [67]:

[67] ˌNot often has the crop. been a total lossˌ

It seems that for an adjective or adverb to permit this sort of double negation, it must be gradable in its positive form, and the positive and negative forms must denote contrary opposites.[48] The negative member of the pair may also be gradable (eg unintelligent(ly), infrequent-(ly), but it may not be (eg inconsiderable). The adjectives in [68] and [69] below do not meet these specifications, and the sentences are consequently ill-formed:

[68] *We rented a ˌnot unˌfurnished flat

[69] *He had a ˌnot unˌeasy feeling that everything would be all right

[68] is ill-formed because furnished is not gradable: [69] is ill-formed because even though easy is gradable, it is not the opposite of uneasy.

It is a moot point whether the requirement stated above should be regarded as something dictated by a semantic rule or as following from a general pragmatic principle ('Avoid pure redundancy'). However the rule is formulated, the result is that the use of not un-, not in-, etc with local scope for not serves to denote a point or a 'stretch' that is located somewhere between the two extremities of a scale. Pragmatically, it must of course be described as a form of understatement – like the type of local negation in §5.3.4.4.

5.4 'RAISED' NEGATION

We have already noted (§5.2.1) that the two sentences repeated here as [1.a] and [1.b]:

[1] a. We must go
    b. We mustn't go

serve to express two contrary, but not contradictory, statements, *ie* that though they could not both be simultaneously true, they could both be simultaneously false. In this they differ from 'normal' pairs of positive and negative sentences, *eg*:

[2] a. We can go
    b. We can't go

[3] a. Harry has gone
    b. Harry hasn't gone

We accounted for the anomaly of [1.b] by an analysis (§5.2.3.5) that involved excluding the auxiliary verb (*must*) from the scope of the negator (*n't*) which is attached to it syntactically. Linguists using the theoretical framework of transformational-generative syntax have usually achieved the same effect by syntactic derivations which place the negative in an embedded clause at an early stage (in 'underlying structure') and 'raise' it into its position in the matrix clause by a transformation. The verbs that seem to call for this kind of transformational analysis are accordingly referred to as 'neg-raising' verbs.

The following pairs of sentences (among others) pose similar problems:

[4] a. We should go
    b. We shouldn't go

[5] a. We're supposed to go
    b. We're not supposed to go

[6] a. They may have gone
    b. They may not have gone

[7] a. I want you to go
    b. I don't want you to go

[8] a. I thought you were going
    b. I didn't think you were going

[4.b] and [5.b] resemble [1.b] in that they normally represent the contraries of the corresponding a-sentences; [6.b] is neither a contrary nor a contradictory negation of [6.a] but rather a compatible one – [6.a] and [6.b] cannot both be false, but they can both be true; and [7.b] and [8.b] could each be said to have two readings, one contrary and one contradictory to the reading of the a-sentence, the contrary reading being the commoner one.

All the anomalous (*ie* non-contradictory) negations in these sentences are naturally accounted for by the same kind of analysis as has been used above for [1.b], if we make the following assumptions:

(i)   The anomalous verb (auxiliary or main) has the same sense in the positive and in the negative sentence; *eg* we do not interpret *must* in [1.b] as having the sense 'be permitted'

(ii) The negator (*not/n't*) has the same sense in these anomalous negations as elsewhere, *viz* the sense of contradictory negation

(iii) The pragmatic import of these sentences corresponds to their semantic meaning, in the sense that the 'anomalous' readings are not simply the result of interpreting the negative sentences as understatements; *eg I don't want you to go* in its contrary reading is not merely the substitution of a weaker statement for *I want you not to go*, but is truth-conditionally equivalent to the latter

However, any of these assumptions could be, and in fact all of them have been, challenged. Furthermore, one might wish to maintain all three assumptions in some cases, but reject one of them in others. The subject is very complex, and not to be summarily disposed of. The most comprehensive and thorough treatment is to be found in Horn (1978).

Notes

1. Even, in some contexts, when the negative item is unaccented (see Ch. 3, §2, note 13). Jackendoff (1972:352*ff*) tries to formulate a rule for the association of negation with intonation focus. But he ignores the accentuation potential of non-nuclear stresses, and even where no non-nuclear accents are involved (in utterances like *Frĕd didn't see John* and *Frèd didn't see John*) his analysis oversimplifies the relations between prosody and context.

2. Akmajian (*loc cit*) uses the term 'scope of the negative' for the focal item in such utterances. This must be understood in the context of his semantic analysis in terms of 'presupposition' and 'focal proposition'. Such an analysis would give us the following representation for [1.a]

    [x loves Mary],
    NEG [John = x]

    The term 'scope of negation' is still a misnomer, of course, since 'scope of negation' applies, in the terminology of logic, to the whole of the formula 'NEG [John = x]'.

Both Akmajian and Jackendoff regard the information structure ('presupposition-focus' structure) as part of the structure of the sentence and so include their interpretation of the prosody in their semantic analysis. Quirk *et al* are not explicit on this point.

3. This is of course incompatible with the statement (Quirk *et al* 1972:382) that 'the scope must include the focus'. The focus is clearly outside the scope of negation in [5] and [6].

4. It remains to be seen whether the fall-rise patterns starting on *Tom* and *George* in this example are distinct in any way from those in utterances that associate the negative with the focus (as in the interpretation of [1.a] above).

5. The disambiguation of such a sentence pattern as *John also phoned* (cf §4.2.5) would be regarded as a semantic function in the present account.

6. On the pragmatics of negation, see also Givón (1978).

7. The possibility of focusing *hardly* on different sentence elements (though not described in these terms) is noted by Stockwell, Schachter, and Partee (1968, repr. 1973:237) as a problem for their analysis of negation.

8. For the special case of *not only*, see Chapter 7 below.

9. It is sometimes claimed that the intonation can be relied on to disambiguate such sentences. Compare Lasnik (1972:40, 42*f*). But the relationship between intonation and scope relations, like the relationship between intonation and syntax, is far from simple.

10. For the syntactic conditions under which *not...any* and *no* may be logically equivalent, see Klima (1964), Labov (1972), and Bolinger (1977:Ch. 3.)

11. The difference between [11.b] and [11.c] becomes clear when we consider that [11.b] is compatible with:

Many of them went

whereas [11.c] is not.

12. It is suprising to find that Jespersen's study of negation (Jespersen 1917) does not distinguish consistently between sentential and non-sentential negation, either on a logical or on a grammatical basis. Though his 'nexal' negation does seem to be always grammatically sentential, the converse does not hold good; witness his listing of *never* (1917, repr. 1962:42) and of sentences like *Not many of us wanted the war* (*p*44) as examples of 'special' negation.

13. The 'copy tag' is called 'echo tag' by Horn (1972:189).

14. The *not even* test indicates clausal negation, but not necessarily negation of the sentence.

15. That is with the scope of negation encompassing only the NP *few people*. In the case of *They were eating nothing*, we can distinguish two semantic forms that yield positive sentences: (i) *nothing* = 'something non-existent' (imaginary, pretended)', *ie* the 'Barmecide feast' reading (Bolinger 1977:58); (ii) the scope of negation encompasses *eating nothing* but excludes *They were*.

16. The example from Carroll is more complex than the Homeric one, since it plays also with the possibility of interpreting *nobody* as denoting an imaginary person – a mime or a madman may talk earnestly to nobody in this sense (*cf* also note 15 above).

17. Huddleston (1971) also uses 'domain' in this sense.

18. Jackendoff's 'dependent on' does not in fact correspond exactly to our 'dominated by'. For example, *All* in *All the men didn't go* (cf [40] below) cannot be 'dependent on' negation (1972:352–3), since dependence is possible only within the 'scope' of negation (in Jackendoff's sense of 'scope', which 'consists of everything commanded by the negative morpheme and to its right' (*p*349)).

Jackendoff tries to overcome this difficulty by using the concept of 'association with focus' (352*ff*) – a dubious expedient, both empirically and logically.

19. I am assuming that there are two pairs of homonyms: any_1 and any_2, and $either_1$ and $either_2$. See Appendix.

20. On the sequence *all...not*, see Carden (1970). Although this paper deals with dialectal variation, it is not made clear precisely how or from whom the data were elicited. For some salutary caveats in such matters, see Greenbaum (1973). In this context, as elsewhere, different intonation patterns tend to favour different scope readings. There are many possibilities, and only a thorough study of utterances in context could do justice to the complexity of this aspect of language use. On Jackendoff's difficulty with [40.a], see note 18.

21. See also Baker (1970: 169–186) and Ladusaw (1980: Ch. 7).

22. I am here dealing only with *any*, etc 'triggered' by negation. On other triggers, see Quirk *et al* (1972: 225*f* and 380, note *b*). For a general analysis of *any*-triggers in terms of entailment relations, see Ladusaw (1980: Ch. 6), – Groups (a) and (b) are often referred to as 'affirmative-polarity items' (API's) and 'negative-polarity items' (NPI's) respectively.

23. Ladusaw's statement (*p*60) implies a general license for auxiliary *not* to dominate preceding numerals, which seems to go too far.

24. There is an unfortunate clash between syntax and logic in the use of the word 'conjunction'. Logical conjunction and logical disjunction are both indicated by syntactic items classified as 'coordinating conjunctions.' It is therefore better to avoid the use of the syntactic term 'conjunction' in this context and speak simply of 'coordinators'.

25. *Neither...nor...* contains two negative morphemes, but is equivalent to a single negative dominating a disjunction: ⟩ *not..either...or...* ⟨. This seems to be the one and only redundant double negative in present-day Standard English. Contrast the following:

(i) They didn't invite Bob or Harry (*Bob nor Harry)
(ii) They invited neither Bob nor Harry (*Bob or Harry)

26. There is no option corresponding to [75] above, with simple *or*.

27. This option does not seem to exist with simple *or*.

28. The coordinators (*and, or, but, neither, nor*), which must also be regarded as peripheral to clause structure, are not included in the class of adverbial elements. If they were, the definition of 'peripheral adverbial' would have to be amended, since *neither* and *nor* are themselves markers of sentence negation when they are used as sentence co-ordinators, and are then necessarily within the domain of sentence negation.

29. Polarity-sensitive items are either 'affirmative-polarity items' (eg *sometimes, already*) or 'negative-polarity items' (eg *ever, yet*). Compare the (a) and (b) groups of existential quantifiers distinguished in §5.2.3.2. For studies of polarity-sensitive items, see Lakoff, R. (1969), Baker (1970), Borkin (1971), Fauconnier (1975), and Ladusaw (1980).

30. All further page references in this and the two following paragrahs are to Quirk *et al* (1972).

31. Some adverbials of cause, however, are peripheral; *eg* clauses with *as* and *since*.

32. Unless they are 'style disjuncts' (see Quirk *et al* 1972: 746, note *a*), in which case they belong to Class (iii). For example:

(i) She and I are just friends, if you follow me.

Viewpoint adverbials (*ibid.* 429*f*) can also dominate negation, provided that they contain quantifiers or consist of items co-ordinated by *and*. For example:

(ii) From some points of view, none of this matters very much
(iii) Socially and politically, there has been no change.

33. The terms 'conjunct' and 'disjunct' for classes of adverbial elements (420*ff*) have nothing to do with the logical terms 'conjunction' and 'disjunction'. – A number of items classified as adjuncts (*ie* as 'integrated') by Quirk *et al* are 'peripheral' in accordance with the definition of Class (iii) in [85] above. For example *honestly*, as in I *honestly don't know what he means*; *just*, as in I *just can't understand it*; *obviously*, as in *They obviously don't want it*; *simply*, as in I *simply don't believe it* (p440). The adverbials in Group A of Quirk *et al's* 'subject adjuncts' (465*ff*) are somewhat problematic, since it is hard to find negative sentences that can follow them, but they can probably all be accommodated in Class (iii). For example:

(i) Proudly, he wouldn't accept the reward
(ii) Manfully, they did not complain

34. We can adduce a further reason for including the negative adverbials in Class (ii). There is a subset of Class (ii) adverbials (those denoting extent over time or space) that can either dominate a quantified subject or be dominated by it, thus giving rise to semantically distinct readings. Compare:

(i) Frequently, someone got drunk
(ii) Someone frequently got drunk

While in (i) *frequently* must dominate *someone*, (ii) is ambiguous between a reading identical with (i) and a reading with someone dominating *frequently* (Thomason and Stalnaker 1973:203). This property is shared by *never*, *nowhere*, and *seldom* – and also, of course, by *not*. For example:

(iii) Many people had never listened to him before
(iv) Never before had many people listened to him

In (iii), *many* dominates *never*, whereas (iv) is ambiguous between a reading with *never* dominating *many* and a reading with *many* dominating *never*.

35. On 'aspectual character' or 'Aktionsart', see Lyons (1977:705*ff*). See also Karttunen (1974) on the analysis of (*not*) *until*.

36. Of Thomason and Stalnaker's four criteria, Nos. 1–3 are not claimed to be decisive. No. 4, they say, 'comes close to being a 'necessary and sufficient condition' for establishing an adverb as a 'sentence modifier', but it is based on paraphrase, to which (as they themselves say earlier in the same paper) 'there is a general methodological objection' (*p*198). It is not even necessary, therefore, to examine the criteria and their application in detail in order to see that Thomason and Stalnaker's theory of adverbs, for all the technical sophistication of its formalism, is open to criticism. Quirk *et al's* criteria for 'peripheral' adverbials produce a class of items that has, in general, a strong intuitive appeal; but the heterogeneity of the set of criteria (which includes intonational as well as syntactic and semantic ones) gives rise to a suspicion that there ought to be a more satisfactory basis for the classification. And the criteria proposed in the text above do indeed seem to be preferable.

37. Sentences like [109] or [110] are often said to have 'main-verb negation', but this term is also applied to something different, *viz* what is dealt with below under the heading of 'predicational negation' (§5.3.3). In the terminology of Huddleston

(1980:68*f*), auxiliaries like *must* are within the 'syntactic scope of *not*' but outside its semantic scope.

38. Langendoen (1970:12*ff*) reports an elicitation experiment in the course of which 21 out of 46 subjects produced negative checking-tags with *may* (*may I not*: 11; *mayn't I*: 10) and a further 5 produced negative tags with *might*; and in the same experiment 32 out of 46 produced the positive checking-tag *may I*. But these data are less impressive than they seem at first sight, for the following reasons:

    (i)   It is not clear whether all the subjects interpreted the stimulus sentences (*I may (not) see you tomorrow*) as containing the *may* of possibility rather than the *may* of permission

    (ii) The procedure was such as to put strong pressure on the subjects to follow the regular tag pattern: the same task – to supply a checking-tag – had to be performed on a total of 90 items (the test was administrated as a homework exercise)

    (iii) There was no judgement test

    On elicitation techniques, see Greenbaum and Quirk (1970).

39. Huddleston (1971:297*ff*) distinguishes between the *may* of uncertainty (or possibility) and three other 'epistemic' uses of *may*. One of these, the *may* of 'exhaustive disjunction', is within the domain of a following *not*:

    (i)   The anemones may not be blue or dull green

                                                              (H's (6'), *p*299)

    Here '*not* cannot negate *be blue or dull green* to the exclusion of *may*' (*p*299). Palmer (1974) includes Huddleston's 'exhaustive disjunction' under the heading of 'generalization'. He considers 'auxiliary negation' to be merely the preferred interpretation, in the presence of the disjunction, the probability being reversed otherwise (*pp*119–120). The *may* of uncertainty can be in the scope of negation in the sort of context studied by Baker (1970); *eg*:

    (ii) You can't convince me that he may not sometimes make a mistake

    Compare [88] in §5.2.3.4.

40. On the factors determining the choice between lexical and non-lexical negation, see Tottie (1980).

41. The term 'rightshifting' (adopted from Bolinger) is not intended to imply a transformational analysis.

42. The type of ambiguity represented by [16.a,b] was noted (and accounted for transformationally) by Klima (1964).

43. Compare Quirk *et al* (1972:743):

    (i)   Wall to wall carpets in every room is the housewife's dream
    (ii) Are fast cars wise in cities?

44. 'Predication' is used here in the sense of Quirk *et al* (1972:35). For the analysis of this constituent as a non-finite clause, see Pullum and Wilson (1977).

45. The term 'local negation' is adopted from Quirk *et al* (1972:381*f*), but the principal example given there been analyzed here as negation of a verbless clause (see [20] in §5.3.2).

46. For 'with no great difficulty', 'with no guide', 'with no fuss' one could substitute 'without (any) great difficulty', 'without any guide', 'without (any) fuss'. According to the definition of §5.3.1, this would be lexical negation.

47. Or 'without a tail'. See note 46.

48. For a slightly different formulation of essentially the same constraint, but relating to adjectives only, see Langendoen and Bever (1973:396*f*).

Six

Scope and focus: The domains of the focusing adverbs

6.1 THE DOMAIN OF *ONLY*

6.1.1 Unrestricted and restricted domains

In §4.2.8 we saw that a sentence with focusing *only* may be analyzed semantically as including two propositions: one containing the focus and the residue and one containing the anti-focus and the residue, as shown in [1]–[1']:

[1] Only <u>John</u> watched the game

[1'] '(A) <u>John</u> watched the game &
(B) <u>No one else</u> watched the game'

Analyses of this sort (or with the modification of the (B)-proposition that is needed for 'limiting *only*': see §4.2.9) are adequate only for those cases in which the domain (or scope) of the focus marker is unrestricted, *ie* in which it includes the whole of the sentence. In this chapter we shall extend our analysis to take in sentences in which the domain of the focus marker is restricted in some way, so that the two complementary propositions (A) and (B) do not account for the whole of the sentence. We shall distinguish, as with negation, between sentential, clausal, predicational, and local scope, dealing first with those categories of items that were found to be sometimes outside the scope of negation, *viz* quantifiers, conjunctions, *etc*. We shall see that the interaction of such items with *only* is similar to, but not identical with, their interaction with negation.

6.1.2 Quantifiers, conjunctions, and disjunctions

We are not concerned here with quantifiers that are part of the focal segment, as in [2] or [3]:

[2] What did you do in Tel Aviv? – We only <u>visited some friends of ours</u>

[3] Was it you that ate all the chocolates? – No, I only took <u>one</u>

Some in [2] and *one* in [3], being within the focus of *only*, are of course necessarily within its domain. What we shall be examining here is the non-focal quantifiers.

Existential quantifiers are normally outside the domain of *only* if they precede the *only*. In [4] below, for example, *some* cannot be within the domain of *only*, since [5] is not equivalent in meaning:

[4] Some of the men spoke only <u>English</u>

[5] '(A) Some of the men spoke <u>English</u> &
(B) None of the men spoke <u>anything but English</u>' (=Neg [some of the men spoke some other language])

For though [5] entails [4], [4] does not entail [5], or more specifically the (B)-proposition in [5]. We therefore represent the meaning of [4] as [6]:

[6] 'Some of the men $\begin{cases} \text{(A) spoke } \underline{\text{English}}' \\ \qquad \& \\ \text{(B) didn't speak } \underline{\text{anything but English}}' \end{cases}$

Or in logical notation (using 'R' for the residual predicate and 'f' for the focal argument, as in §4.2.8)[1]:

[7] $\exists x \qquad (R(x,f) \ \& \sim \exists y \quad R(x,y))$
$\quad x\{\text{the men}\} \qquad\qquad\qquad y \neq f$

If we wish to indicate the scope of *only* directly, without rewriting, we can do so by means of a bracketing device, as follows:

[8] Some of the men °⁻spoke only <u>English</u>⁻°

Unlike (A) and (B) in [1'] above, the (A)- and (B)-components in [6] – which correspond to 'R(x,f)' and '~∃y R(x,y)' respectively in [7] – are not propositions but propositional functions, or open sentences, since they contain a covert free variable (represented by 'x' in [7]). This variable is bound by the existential quantifier 'some', which is thus outside the scope of *only* (represented by the conjunction of the (A)-and (B)-components).

But the scope of the initial existential may be narrowed if a modal verb follows. Consider, for example, the ambiguity of:

[9] One taxi could only take <u>five</u> passengers

Here the scope ambiguity between *could* and *one* gives rise to a corresponding scope ambiguity between *only* and *one*, so that [9] may be read as either [10] or [11][2]:

[10] One taxi °⁻could only take <u>five</u> passengers⁻° (It was licensed only for five)

[11] °⁻One taxi could only take <u>five</u> passengers⁻° (That was the law)

When *only* is preceded by *all* or another universal quantifier, such as *every*, *each*, or *both*, the quantifier seems to be always outside the domain of *only*.[3] Thus:

[12] All the men spoke only <u>English</u>

is represented by:

[12′] 'All the men $\begin{cases} \text{(A) spoke } \underline{\text{English}} \\ \qquad \& \\ \text{(B) didn't speak } \underline{\text{anything but English}}.' \end{cases}$

Or in logical notation:

$$[12''] \quad \forall x \qquad (R(x,f) \ \& \ {\sim}\exists y \qquad R(x,y))$$
$$x\{\text{the men}\} \qquad\qquad y{\neq}f$$

When an existential quantifier follows *only*, there is ambiguity of scope. For example:

[13] °⁻Only <u>English</u> was spoken by⁻° some of the men

[14] °⁻Only <u>English</u> was spoken by some of the men⁻°

[13] is truth-conditionally equivalent to [4] above, while [14] is truth-conditionally equivalent to [15]:

[15] °⁻Only <u>English</u> was spoken by any of the men⁻°

In [15] the use of the 'negative-polarity item' *any* (see §5.2.3.2, note 22, and §5.2.3.4) forces the reading with unrestricted scope for *only*. [15] is much commoner than [14]. The ambiguity shown in [13]–[14] is found also with *several*, *a few*, *many*, *a lot*, and the cardinal numerals. For example:

[16] °⁻Only <u>George</u> knew a lot of these places⁻° (The others knew only a few)

[17] $^{\circ-}$Only <u>George</u> knew$^{-\circ}$ a lot of these places (There were a lot that only George knew)

When *only* is followed by universal quantifiers, it always seems to have wide scope. For example:

[18] $^{\circ-}$Only <u>George</u> knew all the answers$^{-\circ}$

[19] $^{\circ-}$Only <u>George</u> knew everything$^{-\circ}$

Although *only* resembles negation in its ambivalent relationship with quantifiers, there is an important difference: The existential quantifier dominating the negation is logically equivalent to the negation dominating the universal quantifier, as is shown by the equivalence in truth-value between [20] and [21] below; and the negation dominating the existential is logically equivalent to the universal dominating the negation, as is shown by the equivalence in truth-value between [22] and [23]:

[20] Some of these facts ⌞were known to none of the others⌟ (=[21])

[21] ⌞None of the others knew all of these facts⌟

[22] ⌞None of the others knew any of these facts⌟ (=[23])

[23] All of these facts ⌞were known to none of the others⌟

Since an *only*-sentence has a positive as well as a negative semantic component, neither of these equivalences hold good for *only*-sentences. So corresponding to the two distinct propositions represented by [20]–[23], we have four distinct propositions in [24]–[27], as shown by [24′]–[27′]:

[24] Some of these facts $^{\circ-}$were known only <u>to George</u>$^{-\circ}$

[24′] 'Some of these facts $\begin{cases} \text{(A) were known } \underline{\text{to George}} \\ \qquad\qquad \& \\ \text{(B) ⌞were known } \underline{\text{to no one else}}⌟\text{'} \end{cases}$

[25] $^{\circ-}$Only <u>George</u> knew all these facts$^{-\circ}$

[25′] '(A) <u>George</u> knew all these facts &
      (B) ⌞<u>No one else</u> knew all these facts⌟'

[26] $^{\circ-}$Only <u>George</u> knew any of these facts$^{-\circ}$

[26'] '(A) George knew some of these facts &
(B) ↓No one else knew any of these facts↓'

[27] All these facts °⁻were known only to George⁻°

[27'] 'All these facts ⎰(A) were known to George
          ⎱   &
           (B) ↓were known to no one else↓'

The following entailment relation holds between [24]–[27]: [27] →
[25] → [26] → [24].

The behaviour of disjunctions and conjunctions is similar, as
expected, to the behaviour of quantifiers. Thus [28]–[31], for example, represent four distinct propositions:

[28] Either Joan or Susan °⁻answered only one question⁻°

[29] °⁻Only one question was answered either by Joan or by
Susan⁻°

[30] Both Joan and Susan °⁻answered only one question⁻°

[31] °⁻Only one question was answered both by Joan and by
Susan⁻°

We have seen that the existential quantifier *some* can occur

(i)   in the focus of *only* – as in [2]
(ii) outside the domain of *only* – as in [13]
(iii) (less often than (i) or (ii)) in the residue, *ie* inside the domain of
      only but outside the focus – as in [14]

Existential *any*, on the other hand, and negative-polarity items
generally, can occur only in the residue of the *only*-domain, as in [15]
above, or in:

[32] °⁻Only in California had he ever seen anything like it⁻°

In a sentence like:

[33] °⁻They only ever went anywhere at weekends⁻°

the items *ever* and *anywhere* serve to mark *ever went anywhere* as
outside the syntactic-semantic focus of *only*. Contrast:

[34] °⁻She only met him occasionally in town⁻°

where the focus of *only* extends over the whole predication.

6.1.3 Adverbial elements

In Chapter 5 we divided adverbial elements into three major classes on the basis of their relationship to the scope of negation (see §5.2.3.4):

(i)   Nuclear (always within the scope of negation)
(ii) Intermediate (inside or outside)
(iii) Peripheral (always outside)

Not surprisingly, the scope relationships with *only* yield the same division. Thus intensifiers and manner adverbials must be within the scope of *only*. For example:

[35] $^{o-}$Only the youngest had forgotten us completely^{-o}

[36] $^{o-}$Only one of them spoke his lines both clearly and intelligently^{-o}

The same applies to adverbials denoting a point (or something treated as a point) in time or space. For example:

[37] $^{o-}$Only Peter was here that day^{-o}

[38] $^{o-}$They play only soccer in Hungary^{-o}

But adverbials denoting extent over time or space may be inside or outside the domain of *only*:

[39] $^{o-}$Only Peter was here the whole of that day^{-o} (No one else stayed so long)

[40] a. $^{o-}$Only Peter was here^{-o} the whole of that day (=b)
b. The whole of that day, $^{o-}$only Peter was here^{-o}

[41] $^{o-}$Only soccer is played in a lot of countries^{-o} (The other kinds of football are not so widespread)

[42] a. $^{o-}$Only soccer is played^{-o} in a lot of countries (=b)
b. In a lot of countries, $^{o-}$only soccer is played^{-o}

[43] $^{o-}$They see only neighbours very often^{-o} (They see others less frequently)

[44] a. $^{o-}$They see only neighbours^{-o} very often (=b)
b. Very often, $^{o-}$they see only neighbours^{-o}

[45] °⁻Only <u>Spanish</u> is spoken throughout the city⁻° (Other languages are spoken only in certain neighbourhoods)

[46] a. °⁻Only <u>Spanish</u> is spoken⁻° throughout the city (=b)
b. Throughout the city, °⁻only <u>Spanish</u> is spoken⁻°

[47] °⁻Only <u>one</u> shop was open both on Saturday and on Sunday⁻° (The others closed on at least one of these days)

[48] a. °⁻Only <u>one</u> shop was open⁻° both on Saturday and on Sunday (=b)
b. Both on Saturday and on Sunday, °⁻only <u>one</u> shop was open⁻°

The 'intermediate' adverbials in [39]–[48] all contain a quantificational component in semantic structure (if we use 'quantification' in a broad sense to subsume the conjunction in [47]–[48]), and it is this quantifier component that must be outside the scope of *only* in the even-numbered examples. But no quantification is involved in the ambivalence of adverbials of cause or reason, as in [49]–[50]:

[49] °⁻Only <u>Edith</u> stayed on account of the meeting⁻°

[50] a. °⁻Only Edith <u>stayed</u>⁻°, on account of the meeting (=b)
b. On account of the meeting, °⁻only <u>Edith</u> stayed⁻°

Peripheral adverbials are always outside the scope of *only*. For example:

[51] °⁻I told only <u>Robert</u>⁻°, honestly

[52] °⁻Robert told only <u>Mary</u>,⁻° fortunately

[53] °⁻Mary told only <u>Peter</u>,⁻° wisely

[54] In short, °⁻only <u>the four of us</u> know about it⁻°

6.1.4 Auxiliaries: Sentential and predicational *only*

The domain of *only*, like the domain of negation, regularly excludes certain auxiliaries, viz *may* (possibility), *must*, *should*, *ought* (cf §5.2.3.5). For example:

[55] °⁻His reply⁻° may °⁻only <u>have made things worse</u>⁻°

[55']'It is possible that $\begin{cases} \text{(A) his reply } \underline{\text{made things worse}} \\ \qquad\qquad\qquad \& \\ \text{(B) his reply } \underline{\text{did nothing else}} \end{cases}$'

And in logical notation (with symbols as in §4.2.8, plus '$\Diamond$' for the possibility operator):

[55''] $\Diamond \ (\text{F}r \ \& \sim \exists \Phi \quad \Phi r)$
$\qquad\qquad\qquad\quad \Phi \neq \text{F}$

[56] $^{\circ -}$You$^{-\circ}$ should $^{\circ -}$use this number only $\underline{\text{in an emergency}}^{-\circ}$

[56'] 'It is requested that $\begin{cases} \text{(A) you use this number } \underline{\text{in an emer-}} \\ \underline{\text{gency}} \\ \qquad\qquad\qquad \& \\ \text{(B) you not use this number } \underline{\text{other-}} \\ \underline{\text{wise}} \end{cases}$'

Unlike the *may* of logical possibility, the *can* of logical possibility is regularly included within the domain of *only*, so that the two auxiliaries make a complementary set. Compare [55] with [57]:

[57] $^{\circ -}$His reply can only $\underline{\text{have made things worse}}^{-\circ}$

[57'] '(A) It is possible that his reply $\underline{\text{made things worse}}$ &
(B) It is not possible that his reply $\underline{\text{did anything else}}$'

The *can* and *may* of logical possibility must be distinguished from the *can* of ability, potential, or option[4] and the *may* of permission. The latter come within the scope of sentence negation, but may also occur in positive sentences with predicational negation (*cf* §5.3.3). Their options with *only* correspond to their options with negation. For example:

[58] $^{\circ -}$You may take only $\underline{\text{the diploma course}}^{-\circ}$ (You are not eligible for any other)

[59] You may $^{\circ -}$take only $\underline{\text{the diploma course}}^{-\circ}$ (You are not obliged to take any other)

[60] $^{\circ -}$The disease can affect only $\underline{\text{part of the population}}^{-\circ}$ (It never affects the whole population)

[61] The disease can $^{\circ -}$affect only $\underline{\text{part of the population}}^{-\circ}$ (Sometimes it affects only part of the population)

[62] °⁻You can have only <u>what we're all having</u>⁻° (You don't have the option of choosing anything else)

[63] You can °⁻have only <u>what we're all having</u> ⁻° (You have the option of not choosing anything else)

6.1.5 Complex sentences: Clausal and sentential *only*

6.1.5.1 *Finite and infinitive clauses*

When *only* occurs in a subordinate clause, there may be ambiguity between clausal and sentential scope. For example:

[64] I knew °⁻he had learnt only <u>Spanish</u>⁻° (I knew he hadn't learnt any other language)

[65] °⁻I knew he had learnt only <u>Spanish</u>⁻° (I didn't know he had learnt any other language)

[66] They were advised °⁻to learn only <u>Spanish</u>⁻° (They were advised not to learn any other language)

[67] °⁻They were advised to learn only <u>Spanish</u>⁻° (They were not advised to learn any other language)

[68] I knew °⁻he had missed only <u>one</u> lecture⁻° (I knew he had not missed more than one)

[69] °⁻I knew he had missed only <u>one</u> lecture⁻° (I did not know he had missed more than one)

[70] I managed °⁻to miss only <u>one</u> lecture⁻° (I managed not to miss more than one)

[71] °⁻I managed to miss only <u>one</u> lecture⁻° (I did not manage to miss more than one)

The scope ambiguities illustrated above can be avoided by shifting the *only* as in [72] or [73]; but such a change creates another kind of indeterminacy (as shown by the underlining of the focus):

[72] I knew °⁻he had only <u>learnt Spanish</u>⁻°

[73] °⁻They were only <u>advised to learn Spanish</u>⁻°

It is ironic that a writer who prefers [64] to [72], or [67] to [73], in order to avoid the 'misplacing' of *only* (assuming that the contextual focus intended is *Spanish* in both cases), merely exchanges one kind of indeterminacy for another. But judgements about clarity can be usefully made only in context.

For *only* with sentential scope, we have an alternative option with marked theme and subject-operator inversion:

[74] °‾Only <u>once</u> was he asked to ring‾° (They did not ask him to ring more than once)

When the scope is clausal, there is no inversion.

[75] °‾Only <u>once</u>‾° he was asked °‾to ring‾° ('Ring only once', they told him)

6.1.5.2 *Non-finite or verbless clauses introduced by* with

In sentences containing clauses introduced by *with*, the position of *only* indicates whether its domain is the *with*-clause or the superordinate clause (or sentence). There is also a corresponding difference in focus. For example:

[76] She talked to him °‾with only <u>a guard</u> present in the room‾°

[77] °‾She talked to him only <u>with a guard present in the room</u>‾°

[78] He managed it °‾with only <u>George</u> helping him‾° *or* °‾with only <u>George</u> to help him‾°)

[79] °‾He managed it only <u>with George helping him</u>‾° *or* only <u>with George to help him</u>‾°

Even though the *with* that introduces such clauses is historically derived from the preposition *with*, the sequence *with* + subject in sentences such as the above does not count as a prepositional phrase for the purpose of the rule that restricts *only* within prepositional phrases to cases with scalar focus (see §4.2.4).[5]

6.1.6 Local domains

6.1.6.1 *Types of local domains*

We may distinguish the following types of local domains for *only*:

(i) Elements with adverbial function in the clause or sentence
    a. Prepositional phrases
    b. Adverbial phrases (*ie* phrases with adverbs as heads)

(ii) Elements with modifying function in the nominal phrase
 a. Prepositional phrases
 b. Adjectival phrases (*ie* phrases with adjectives as heads)

In all these domains a scalar item is required as focus of *only*.[6] [80] below is an example of (i.a):

[80] °⁻After only <u>a quarter of an hour</u>,⁻° half the audience were asleep

[80′] 'When
{
(A) <u>a quarter of an hour</u>
 had passed &

(B) not <u>more than a quarter
 of an hour</u> had passed
}
half the audience
were asleep'

We may contrast [80] with the ill-formed example [81], where a non-scalar item has been substituted as focus:

[81] *°⁻After only <u>the chairman's introduction</u>,°⁻ half the audience were asleep

[82] is an example of (i.b):

[82] °⁻Only <u>two days</u> later,⁻° he was as fit as a fiddle

[82′] 'When
{
(A) <u>two days</u> had passed
 &
(B) not <u>more than two days</u> had passed
}
he was fit
as a fiddle'

(ii.a) may be represented by:

[83] We saw a horrible giant °⁻with only <u>one eye</u>⁻°

[83′] 'We saw a horrible giant
{
(A) that had <u>one</u> eye
 &
(B) that did not have <u>more than</u>
 one eye'

And (ii.b) may be represented by:

[84] We have an °⁻only <u>slightly</u> shopsoiled⁻° copy

[84′] 'We have a copy
{
(A) that is <u>slightly</u> shopsoiled
 &
(B) that is not <u>more than slightly</u> shop-
 soiled'

[84] contrasts with the ill-formed [85], which lacks a scalar focus:

[85] *We have an °⁻only <u>shopsoiled</u>⁻° copy

Both in [81] above and in [85], the awkwardness is linguistic, not logical, since the ill-formed sentences can be understood perfectly well. Witness [86], for example, where the adjectival phrase of [85] is expanded into a clause, but the sense is unchanged:

[86] We have a copy °⁻that is only <u>shopshoiled</u>⁻°
(a copy that has nothing else <u>wrong</u> with it)

6.1.6.2 Local and sentential domains

A sentence that begins with a 'local *only* domain' has normal subject-verb order, whereas 'sentential *only*' focusing on an initial sentence element induces subject-operator inversion. Compare [87], with local *only*, and [88], with sentential *only*:

[87] °⁻After only <u>two hours,</u>⁻° they received the telegram
(Expected reaction: 'That was quick!')

[88] °⁻Only <u>after two hours</u> did they receive the telegram⁻°
(Expected reaction: 'That was slow!')

[89] °⁻For only <u>£100,</u>⁻° he acquired the drawing
(They didn't know its real value)

[90] °⁻Only for <u>£100</u> did he acquire the drawing⁻°
(They drove a hard bargain)

Here the position of *only* also differentiates between the two structures, so that the distinction remains overt when the time adjunct is final and the difference in subject-verb ordering disappears. For example:

[91] They received the telegram °⁻after only <u>two hours</u>⁻°

[92] °⁻They received the telegram only <u>after two hours.</u>⁻°

The next set of examples shows that the scope difference does not always involve a difference in the position of *only*:

[93] °⁻Only <u>two hours</u> later,⁻° they received the telegram

[94] °⁻Only <u>two hours later</u> did they receive the telegram⁻°

[95] °⁻Only <u>a week</u> after this quarrel,⁻° he resigned

[96] °⁻Only <u>a week after this quarrel</u> did he resign⁻°

In [91]–[96] the examples with local scope differ from those with sentential scope in the extent and nature of the focal segment. Compare [97]–[102]:

[97] *They received the telegram °⁻after only <u>that</u>⁻°

[98] °⁻They received the telegram only <u>after that</u>⁻° (/...only <u>afterwards</u>⁻°)

[99] *°⁻Only <u>later</u>,⁻° they received the telegram

[100] °⁻Only <u>later</u> did they receive the telegram⁻°

[101] *°⁻Only <u>after this quarrel</u>,⁻° he resigned

[102] °⁻Only <u>after this quarrel</u> did he resign⁻°

When [93] or [96] are replaced by the corresponding structures with final adverbials, there is no overt syntactic difference to distinguish between sentential and local scope, but the covert difference in focus remains:

[103] They received the telegram °⁻only <u>two hours</u> later⁻°

[104] °⁻They received the telegram only <u>two hours later</u>⁻°

[105] He resigned °⁻only <u>a week</u> after this quarrel⁻°

[106] °⁻He resigned only <u>a week after this quarrel</u>⁻°

We can disambiguate [104] from [103], and [106] from [105], by 'misplacing' <u>only</u>:

[107] °⁻They only received the telegram <u>two hours later</u>⁻°

[108] °⁻He only resigned <u>a week after this quarrel</u>⁻°

The following sentences show that there can be a contrast between sentential and local scope without a corresponding difference in focus (*cf* [64]–[67] in §6.1.5, for contrast between sentential and clausal scope with no difference in focus):

[109] °⁻Only <u>last Monday</u>,⁻° the machine was (still) in working order

[110] °⁻Only last <u>Monday</u> was the machine in working order (again)⁻°

[111] °⁻Only <u>yesterday</u>,⁻° we had a phone-call from her (as recently as that)

[112] °⁻Only <u>yesterday</u> did we have a phone-call from her⁻° (at last)

Again, placing the time adjunct in final position produces ambiguity:

[113] We heard from her °⁻only <u>yesterday</u>⁻° (So we're not worried)

[114] °⁻We heard from her only <u>yesterday</u>⁻° (You can imagine how worried we were by that time).[7]

Finally, we may observe that the difference between sentential and local scope gives rise also to a difference in the use of polarity-sensitive items, since negative-polarity items are licenced in the residue of an *only*-domain, but not outside the domain (*cf* 6.1.2):

[115] °⁻After only <u>two hours</u>,⁻° we had some (*any) more news

[116] °⁻Only <u>after two hours</u> did we have any (some) more news⁻°

[117] °⁻Only <u>yesterday</u>,⁻° someone (*anyone) called

[118] °⁻Only <u>yesterday</u> did anyone (someone) call⁻°

6.2 THE DOMAIN OF *ALSO*

6.2.1 Sentential and other domains

The domain of *also*, like that of *only*, may be sentential, clausal, or predicational; but unlike that of *only*, it cannot be local. This restriction is brought out by the following set of examples (with ᵃ⁻ ⁻ᵃ marking the domain (scope) of *also*):

[1] a. Efficiency is important, of course. But if possible, we want a person ᵃ⁻who's also <u>polite</u>⁻ᵃ
  b. ...*But if possible, we want an ᵃ⁻also <u>polite</u>⁻ᵃ person

[2] a. We shall discuss this matter ᵃ⁻when <u>John</u> is also present⁻ᵃ
  b. *We shall discuss this matter

> (i)   [a]−in the presence of also John−[a]
> (ii) [a]−in the presence also of John−[a]
> (iii) [a]−in John's also presence−[a]

In [1.a] and [2.a] *also* has clausal scope and the sentences are well-formed. In [1.b] and [2.b], which are intended as equivalents to the (a)-examples, *also* has local scope and the sentences are ill-formed. This restriction on the use of *also* is parallel to the restriction on the use of 'exceptive *only*'. As we saw in §6.1.6.1, only 'limiting *only*' can have a local domain.

The fact that *also*-sentences contain two positive propositions, as against one positive and one negative for *only*-sentences (see §4.2.8), means that the ambiguities between sentential and predicational scope, or between sentential and clausal scope, yield some relatively subtle sense differences. For example:

[3] I've ordered tea; but [a]−you can also have coffee−[a]

[4] I've ordered only the dessert; but you can [a]−also have coffee−[a]

[3'] '(A) You can have coffee &
      (B) you can have something else'[8]

[4'] ...'You can {
      (A) have coffee
           &
      (B) have something else'
}

In [3] coffee is offered as an alternative; in [4] it is offered as an addition. Here the ambiguity is between sentential scope in [3] and predicational scope in [4]. In [5] and [6] below, we have ambiguity between sentential and clausal scope.

[5] Of course I'm anxious to hear John's version; but [a]−I'm anxious to hear also what Peter has to say−[a]

[6] What John told us may be true; but I'm anxious [a]−to hear also what Peter has to say−[a]

[5'] ...'(A) I'm anxious to hear what Peter has to say &
       (B) I'm anxious to hear something else'

[6'] ...'I am anxious {
       (A) to hear what Peter has to say
            &
       (B) to hear something else'
}

We may compare [58]–[63] in §6.1.4 for similar ambiguities with *only*.

The ambiguity exhibited in [3]–[4] above is possible also with *may* in the 'permission' sense (*cf* [29]–[32] in §5.3.3 and [58]–[63] in §6.1.4 on the parallelism between *can* and *may* in some of their uses). The *may* of logical possibility differs semantically and syntactically from the *may* of permission (compare, for example, [33]–[35] in §5.3.3), but like the latter it may be either included in or excluded from the scope of *also*. Since the *may* of logical possibility is a one-place predicate, its apparent subject must be taken in the semantic representation with the content of the predication (*They may know* – 'It may be that they know'), but apart from this difference the scope ambiguity with *also* in [7]–[8] below is essentially like that in [3]–[4].

[7] Of course it may be all right, but [a]it may also <u>be a trick</u>[a]

[8] I know he is a poet, but [a]he[a] may [a]also be a painter[a]

[7′] ...'(A) It is possible that it is a trick &
(B) It is possible that it is something else'

[8′] ...'It is possible that $\begin{cases} \text{(A) he is a painter} \\ \qquad\qquad \& \\ \text{(B) he is something else'} \end{cases}$

The *also*-sentence in [7] asserts two possibilities 'A' and 'B' which need not be mutually compatible, and which, in the context of [7], will be interpreted as incompatible. The *also* sentence in [8], on the other hand, asserts the possibility of a conjunction 'A & B', and this entails the possible compatibility of the conjoined propositions with one another.[9] Compare [9], where *also* dominates 'possible', as in [7], and [10], where 'possible' dominates *also*, as in [8]:

[9] It is also possible that it is a trick

[10] It is possible that he is also a painter

6.2.2 Quantifiers, conjunctions, and disjunctions

Also, like *only*, may either dominate or be dominated by existential quantifiers; and the distinction is clearly significant. For example:

[11] Some of these poems [a]were translated also <u>by Ezra Pound</u>[a]

[12] a. [a-]Ezra Pound also translated some of these poems[-a]
  b. [a-]Ezra Pound also translated[-a] some of these poems
      (=[11])

Sentences [11] and [12.b] may be represented as in [13]:

[13] 'Some of these poems $\begin{cases} \text{(A) were translated by Ezra Pound} \\ \qquad\qquad \& \\ \text{(B) were translated by someone else'} \end{cases}$

Or in logical notation (with 'f' for the focal argument and 'R' for the residual predicate):

[14] $\exists x \qquad\qquad (R(f,x) \;\&\; \exists y \quad R(y,x))$
  $x\{\text{these poems}\} \qquad\qquad\quad y \neq f$

[12.a], on the other hand, may be represented as in [15]:

[15] '(A) Ezra Pound translated some of these poems &
   (B) Someone else translated some of these poems'

Or in logical notation:

[16] $\exists x \qquad\qquad R(f,x) \;\&\; \exists x \qquad\qquad \exists y \quad R(y,x)$
  $x\{\text{these poems}\} \qquad\qquad x\{\text{these poems}\} \quad y \neq f$

The reading indicated by [13]–[14] means that some of the poems were translated at least twice; the reading of [15]–[16], on the other hand, makes no such claim. In the logical formulae, this follows from the fact that the 'x' in the first function $(R(f,x))$ and the 'x' in the second function $(R(y,x))$ are bound by the same instance of the existential quantifier in [14] but by two different instances in [16], which means that the two instances of 'x' necessarily represent the same poems in [14] but that nothing is said about their identity or non-identity in [16].

Disjunctions yield the same two logical possibilities as existential quantifiers. For example [17]–[18], with focus of *also* on *(by) the Hereford choir*:

[17] Either 'Men of Harlech' or 'Pop Goes the Weasel' [a-]will be sung also by the Hereford choir[-a]

[18] [a-]The Hereford choir will also sing 'Men of Harlech' or 'Pop Goes the Weasel'[-a]

Sentence [17] implies that one of the two songs will be sung at least twice; [18] has no such implication. [17] entails [18], just as [11] – or [12.b] – entails [12.a].

With universal quantifiers or conjunctions in the residue, we also find a distinction that depends on the order of the elements. Compare [19] with [20], and [21] with [22]:

[19] Every one of these poems ^{a−}was translated also <u>by Ezra Pound</u>^{−a}

[20] ^{a−}<u>Ezra Pound</u> also translated every one of these poems^{−a}

[21] 'Men of Harlech' and 'Pop Goes the Weasel' ^{a−}will be sung also <u>by the Hereford choir</u>^{−a}

[22] ^{a−}<u>The Hereford choir</u> will also sing both 'Men of Harlech' and 'Pop Goes the Weasel'^{−a}

The logical difference is brought out by [23] and [24], the former corresponding to [19] and [21], and the latter to [20] and [22]:

[23] $\forall x \quad (R(f,x) \ \& \ \exists y \quad R(y,x))$
$ x\{\ldots\} y \neq f$

[24] $\exists y \quad \forall x \quad (R(f,x) \ \& \ R(y,x))$
$ y \neq f \ \ x\{\ldots\}$

What is crucial here is the relative ordering of the existential and universal quantifiers (cf *Every boy loved some girl* and *Some girl was loved by all the boys*). The change of order can make a difference to the well-formedness of a discourse. Compare [25] and [26]:

[25] In Jean's school they taught French and German. In Batsheva's school they taught English and Arabic. French and English ^{a−}were taught also <u>in Anneke's school</u>^{−a}

[26] *In Ian's school they taught French. In Yigal's school they taught English. ^{a−}<u>In Willem's school</u> they also taught French and English^{−a}

The sequence of sentences in [26] can be tolerated as a discourse only to the extent that we are willing to read the last sentence not as it is marked, but rather as '^{a−}In Willem's school they also taught^{−a} French and English', *ie* as equivalent in semantic structure to the last sentence in [25]. Otherwise, *ie* on the normal reading of the sentence, we are presupposing the previous mention of a place where both French and English were taught. Contrast the last sentence in [25], where we are presupposing only the previous mention of a place where French was taught and the previous mention of a place where English was taught (not necessarily the same place).

The direction of entailment in *also*-sentences with universals or conjunctions in the residue is the opposite to the direction in *also*-sentences with existentials or disjunctions in the residue. In the latter set, a sentence with narrow scope for *also* entails the corresponding sentence in which *also* has wide scope, *eg* [17] entails [18]; in the former, a sentence with wide scope for *also* entails the corresponding sentence in which *also* has narrow scope, *eg* [22] entails [21].

6.2.3 Adverbial elements

The division of adverbial elements into nuclear, intermediate, and peripheral, on the basis of their interaction with negation (see §5.2.3.4), was found to be highly relevant to the grammar of *only* (see §6.1.3). It is relevant, too, to the grammar of *also*; but the situation is complicated here by an additional option, which we did not find with *only* (see [33]–[39] below).

Nuclear adverbials can be taken as relating to each of the conjoined propositions (or functions) of the *also*-sentence, but no contrast is possible between this reading and a reading that takes the adverbial as applying to the conjunction of the two propositions (or functions). For example:

[27] <u>Joan</u> also resented it deeply

can be interpreted as:

[28] '(A) Joan resented it deeply &
     (B) Someone else resented it deeply'

and this cannot contrast with:

[29] *(A) Joan resented it   ⎫
          &   ⎬ deeply'
     (B) Someone else resented it ⎭

Hence we take *deeply* as included in the domain of *also*. Similarly with [30]–[32]:

[30] [a]<u>Robert</u> was also arguing very persuasively[-a]

[31] $^{a-}$Peter also studied medicine at Glasgow^{-a}

[32] $^{a-}$Susan also called the following day^{-a10}

But though we cannot justify a distinct reading in which the adverbial dominates the conjunction of the two propositions, we do find nevertheless that an additional relationship is possible between *also* and the adverbial. This is illustrated by the following:

[33] $^{a-}$Joan also resented it^{-a} – deeply

[34] $^{a-}$Peter also studied medicine^{-a} – at Glasgow

[35] $^{a-}$Susan also called^{-a} – the following day

The final adverbial in sentences like [33]–[35] is taken solely with the asserted component of the *also*-sentence (*eg* 'Joan resented it'), to the exclusion of the implicature (*eg* 'Someone else resented it'); and corresponding to the contrast in semantics and punctuation we have a clear contrast in intonation: *eg*:

[36] /Susan !àlso 'called the 'following 'day #

[37] /Susan !àlso 'called # – the /fòllowing 'day #

[36] corresponds to [32], and [37] to [35]. The final adverbial in [33]–[35] can be regarded as the sole constituent of a following elliptical sentence, and this analysis is supported by the possibility of making various additions which do not fit into the preceding sentence, *eg*:

[38] $^{a-}$Joan also resented it^{-a} – even more deeply than Mary

[39] $^{a-}$Susan also called^{-a} – but not till the following day

We may refer to such final adverbials, therefore, as 'appended sentences'.[11]

Intermediate adverbials yield the same kind of contrast depending on scope as we found with *only*:

[40] Quite often, $^{a-}$John also watched the games^{-a}

[41] a. $^{a-}$John also watched the games quite often^{-a}
     b. $^{a-}$John also watched the games^{-a} quite often

[42] In many schools, $^{a-}$French is also taught^{-a}

[43] a. [a]‾<u>French</u> is also taught in many schools‾[a]
     b. [a]‾<u>French</u> is also taught‾[a] in many schools

Peripheral adverbials are always semantically superordinate to the
sentence in which they occur, and therefore relate to the conjunction
of the two component propositions of the *also*-sentence. For example:

[44] Fortunately, [a]‾there is also <u>another way</u>‾[a]

[45] [a]‾There is‾[a] probably [a]‾also <u>a bus</u>‾[a]

At first sight it may seem as if *fortunately* and *probably* relate only to
the assertion component ('There is another way' in [44], 'There is a
bus' in [45]), but such an analysis gets into difficulties. Compare the
following:

[46] They certainly learnt Spanish and they probably also learnt
     French

[47] *They probably learnt Spanish and they certainly also learnt
     French

Of these two examples, only [46] is well-formed.[12] The difference in
well-formedness between [46] and [47] is explained automatically if
we take the adverbs in the *also*-sentence as assigning a probability to
the conjunction of the two propositions:

(i) The assertion – 'They learnt French'
(ii) The implicature – 'They did something else', interpreted in this
     context as 'They learnt Spanish'

For the combined probability of two propositions 'p' and 'q' (the
probability of the conjunction 'p & q') can be less than the probability
of either of them separately, but it cannot be greater. Hence the
normality of [46], where the combined probability is less ('certainly' –
'probably'), and the anomaly of [47], where the combined probability
is greater ('probably' – 'certainly'). If the adverb relates only to the
assertion component, this explanation is unavailable – and no other
seems to suggest itself.

     Similar arguments can be constructed for other types of disjuncts.
Returning to [44], with the adverb *fortunately*, we see that it may be
the case, in a particular context, that a speaker's reason for expressing satisfaction is the content of the asserted component alone

('There is another way'), but this is not the meaning of the construction as such. Or in other words, it may be the meaning of the utterance of the sentence, but it is not the meaning of the sentence. A satisfactory analysis of the sentence-meaning must account for the fact that a speaker's expression of satisfaction or dissatisfaction may be inappropriate for the asserted component taken separately, but appropriate for the conjunction of the two components. Thus one might say:

> [48] I had hoped either to speak to Bill myself, or if he was out to leave a message with his wife; but unfortunately ^{a⁻}<u>his wife</u> was also out^{⁻a}

In this context, it is clear that what the speaker regrets is not the asserted component ('His wife was out') in isolation, but the conjunction of this with the implicature, which is here naturally interpreted as conveying 'Bill was out'.

We may conclude that the semantic relationship between a peripheral adverbial and the remainder of an *also*-sentence is analogous to the relationship between a peripheral adverbial and the remainder of an *only*-sentence, and distinct from the relationship between *also*-sentences and final adverbs functioning as 'appended sentences' (see [33]–[39] above).

Notes:

1. Strictly speaking, of course, the existential quantifier is not equivalent to English *some*, but this does not affect the point at issue.
2. Compare [60] in §5.2.3.2. This option for inclusion in the scope of a following modal seems to be confined to numerals.
3. Contrast the ambiguity of the sequence *all...not* (see §5.2.3.2).
4. It is not easy to determine whether 'ability', 'potential', and 'option' are all different facets of one sense or more senses than one, and if more than one, how many (see Palmer 1974 and 1979).
5. Note the following examples from the corpus:

    (i) .../yàwning gap thére # be/tween extra còver . and gúlly # with /only !Còrling # /on the 'deep :pòint [/L bòundary #]# (S. 10. 1. 46)
    (ii) ...the Customs people were very dubious about how I had got into the country with only a Maidngwi [*sic*] stamp on my passport! (W. 7. 2. 33)

6. On scalar focal items, see §4.2.8.
7. [114] has been interpreted as containing 'limiting *only*'. See [143] in §4.2.8 on ambiguity between 'limiting' and 'exceptive' *only*. Quirk *et al* (1972:434) mention *only yesterday* in the sense of 'as recently as *yesterday*', but do not consider the possibility of 'not until yesterday'.

8. Both here and in the following representations, the (A)-component is the assertion and the (B)-component the implicature.
9. There is no similar ambiguity with *only*, owing to the suppletive relationship between *may* (possibility) and *can* (possibility) (see [55] and [57] in §6.1.4).
10. There is a semantic difference between [27] and [30] on the one hand and [31] and [32] on the other. With adverbials of intensity and manner, as in [27] and [30], the 'joint' reading makes no sense. With points of time and place (as in [31] and [32]), the 'joint' reading is not nonsensical, but the distinction between 'joint' and 'separate' is vacuous.
11. On the analogy of 'appended clause', as used by Quirk *et al* (1972:544).
12. [47] becomes well-formed if *also* is dropped, or is taken, somewhat oddly, as harking back to the previous mention of a third language. This latter option is blocked if we take [46] and [47] as possible answers to the question 'What foreign languages did they learn?'

Seven

Overlapping domains and convergence of focusing

7.1 OVERLAPPING DOMAINS

7.1.1 Kinds of overlap

'Overlapping' is used here to denote any of the following relationships between domains:

(i)   Intersection
(ii) Inclusion
(iii) Co-extensiveness

If we use parentheses to indicate the beginning and end of a domain, and distinguish between two overlapping domains by raising one pair of parentheses and lowering the other pair, we can represent these relationships as follows:

(i′) $\begin{pmatrix} & & \\ A & B & C \\ & & \end{pmatrix}$ A B C

(ii′) A B C

(iii) A B C

All three relationships are found to obtain between intonational and syntactic focusing domains; *eg*:

[1] (#) But °⁻the /ŏthers # were /only pre!tènding⁻° of 'course #

[2] (#) But °⁻the /others were 'only pre:tènding⁻° of 'course #

[3] (#) The /others were 'only pre:tènding#

The relationship between the domain of a sequential focus (of marked theme or marked rheme) and the domain of negation or of a syntactic-semantic focus marker (cleft, *only*, *also*, etc) may be coextensiveness or inclusion;[1] *eg* (with ⌐T⁻...⁻T marking the domain of marked theme and '___' for the marked theme itself):

[4] T⁻These he had not seen before⁻T

[5] T⁻Some of them ₎he had not seen before⁻T

[6] ₒT⁻These he had seen only once⁻ₒT

[7] T⁻Some of them ᵒ⁻he had seen only once⁻ₒT

Between the domains of the syntactic-semantic focus markers, or between any of their domains and the domain of negation (which is also syntactic-semantic), only the relation of proper inclusion is possible.[2] For example:

[8] ᶜ⁻It was John ₎who didn't answer₍⁻ᶜ

[9] ₎ᶜ⁻It was ⁻ᶜn't ᶜ⁻John who answered⁻ᶜ₍[3]

The existence of the three types of relationship between intonational domains and syntactic-semantic domains is due to the fact that the domains belong to different levels of linguistic organization and so do not interact directly. Even when one domain seems to be included in the other, there is no part-whole relation between them. Sequential focus, like intonational focus, is essentially non-semantic, and so in [5] and [7] also there are no part-whole relations between the domains. However, since sequential focus depends on the interaction of linear and hierarchical ordering, its domain is less free than the domain of intonation.

7.1.2 Focusing adverbs and negation

The focusing adverbs differ from one another in the ways their domains may overlap with the domain of negation. *Only* dominates a following negator, and normally the converse also holds good. For example:

[10] ᵒ⁻Only ₎George wasn't invited₍⁻ᵒ *(only* before *n't)*

[11] ₎ᵒ⁻They did⁻ᵒn't ᵒ⁻invite only George⁻ᵒ₍ *(n't* before *only)*[4]

Also is generally avoided in negative sentences. Thus the meaning of:

[12] ˌᵃ⁻You need⁻ᵃn't ᵃ⁻also <u>put on your raincoat</u>⁻ᵃˌ (in addition to taking an umbrella)

– which may be compared to:

[13] ˌYou don't need an umbrella AND a raincoatˌ

– is generally expressed rather by:

[14] ˌᵃ⁻You need⁻ᵃn't ᵃ⁻<u>put on your raincoat</u> as well⁻ᵃˌ

For the opposite scope relationship, we use the disjunctive focus marker *either* within the negative domain instead of putting the negation within the domain of *also*. Thus rather than the ill-formed:

[15] *ᵃ⁻ˌYou needn't <u>put on your raincoat</u>ˌ also⁻ᵃ

– which is analogous (if interpreted as marked) to:

[16] An umbrella and a raincoat are both unnecessary

in that the conjunction dominates the negation in both – we use:

[17] ˌⁱ⁻You need⁻ⁱn't ⁱ⁻<u>put on your raincoat</u> either⁻ⁱˌ

– which is analogous to:

[18] ˌYou don't need an umbrella OR a raincoatˌ

Even differs from *also* in being freely used with sentence negation, like *only*. A further resemblance to *only* is that *even* may be preceded by initial *not*, as in [19]:

[19] Not even George was invited –

In appearance, this is parallel to [20], with *not only*:

[20] Not only George was invited

But the similarity does not extend to the semantics: in [19], the negation has narrow scope (excluding *even*), whereas in [20] the negation has wide scope (including *only*).

7.1.3 Overlap between domains of focusing adverbs

When a sentence contains two focusing adverbs with overlapping domains, the scope relations normally depend on the linear order of the focal items. Compare [21] and [22]:

[21] $^{o-}$Only $^{a-}$Paul can also speak Mohawk^{-a-o}

[22] $^{a-o-}$Mohawk^{-o} also $^{o-}$is spoken only by Paul^{-o-a}

Sentence [21] implies that there is something other than speaking Mohawk which Paul can do (or more specifically, if 'speak' is given, that there is at least one language other than Mohawk which Paul can speak); but it does not imply that there is no one else with the same additional accomplishment (or if 'speak' is given, that there is no one else who speaks the same additional language). [22] goes beyond [21] in implying that there is some specific language other than Mohawk which is spoken by no one but Paul.[5]

We have similar pairs of options with *only* and *even*:

[23] $^{o-}$Only $^{e-}$Paul speaks even Mohawk^{-e-o}

[24] $^{e-}$Even $^{o-}$Mohawk is spoken only by Paul^{-o-e}

In this case we have a further complication, which is due to the 'scalar implicature' of *even*.[6] According to [23], it is relatively unlikely for a person to speak Mohawk, while according to [24] it is relatively unlikely for a person NOT to do so. The reading of [23] represents the more likely scope relationship for its linear sequence, but the converse reading (corresponding to the scope relation in [24]) is also possible. It can be forced by means of a suitable lexical bias; *eg*:

[25] $^{e-o-}$Only Paul is studying^{-o} even such a fascinating language as Mohawk^{-e}

Sentences with two *only*'s are generally felt to be stylistically objectionable, and harder to take in than sentences with one *only*; but (*pace* Kuroda 1969) they are well-formed syntactically and semantically and are not intolerably difficult to interpret (see Horn 1969). As pointed out by Horn, the first of the two *only*'s must be outermost. Compare [26] and [27]:

[26] $^{o1-}$Only $^{o2-}$John ate only rice^{-o2-o1}

[27] $^{o1-}$Only $^{o2-}$rice was eaten only by John^{-o2-o1}

Both [26] and [27] entail 'John ate rice'; but [26] entails also 'John ate nothing else' – which does not follow from [27] – and [27] entails 'No one else ate rice' – which does not follow from [26]. If we substitute *nothing but* for the second *only* in [26], the semantic structure is unchanged but the sentence becomes more acceptable; and the same holds good for the replacement of the first *only* in [26] by *no one but*:

[28] Only John ate nothing but rice

[29] No one but John ate only rice

7.2 CONVERGENCE OF FOCUSING

We shall use the term 'convergence of focusing' to denote the situation where the focus of one marker coincides wholly or in part with the focus of another marker. We shall be considering syntactic markers in relation to intonation, syntactic markers in relation to sequential focusing, and syntactic markers in relation to one another.

7.2.1 Syntax and intonation

7.2.1.1 *The cleft construction*

The focus of the cleft construction (or part of it) usually receives nuclear prominence, as in [1] and [2] (cleft focus underlined):

[1] How did you find out? – It was /Dìck who 'told us #

[2] Did you take the station wagon? – /Nò # it was /Jòhn's 'car that we 'used #

But the cleft focus may receive a non-nuclear accent, with the principal intonation prominence falling within the residue of the cleft construction; *eg*:

[3] How do you know that Harry will agree? – It was /he who sug!gèsted it #

It is also possible for the whole of the cleft construction to be intonationally backgrounded (treated as given), *eg*:

[4] What makes you think it was Tom's fault? – It's /àlways 'Tom that 'starts these 'quarrels #

7.2.1.2 *The focusing adverbs*

With the focusing adverbs, as with the cleft construction, various relationships are possible, and since there is a range of syntactic options too, the total number of possibilities is very large. There are, however, for each focusing adverb, patterns that may be regarded as typical.

Only. The marker usually precedes its focus, and the focus (or part of it) receives nuclear prominence; *eg* (with adverbial focus underlined):

[5] /Only Jòhn 'wrote to her #

[6] /John only :wròte to her #

[7] /John only 'wrote to :hèr #

[8] /John wrote 'only to :hèr #

When *only* follows its focus and stands in sentence-final position, the focus receives a non-nuclear accent and the nucleus falls on *only*; *eg*:

[9] There'll be /two ònly #

Also. The typical position is medial (after the operator). If the focus precedes *also*, the focus usually has a non-nuclear accent and *also* has a nuclear accent. For example:

[10] /John has àlso 'written 'to her #

If the focus follows *also*, the focus receives a nuclear accent, and *also* – usually – a non-nuclear accent; *eg*:

[11] /John has 'also :wrìtten 'to her #

[12] /John has 'also 'written to :hèr #

Not infrequently, *also* stands in prefinal position and focuses on the final element. In such a case the focus must receive a nuclear accent and there is usually an additional nuclear ·accent on *also*. For example:

[13] He has /written àlso # to the /Ministry of Làbour #

It is possible for a focus that precedes *also* to be totally unstressed. This is regularly the case where the focus is a relative pronoun; *eg*:

[14] She /had a :frìend # who was /àlso 'studying 'medicine #

Too. The typical position is sentence-final, and the accentuation in this position is always nuclear. The focus may have nuclear or non-nuclear prominence. For example:

[15] /Ì think so # /tòo #

[16] /I think so :tòo #

[17] I /phòned her # /tòo #

[18] I /phoned her !tòo #

When the focus of *too* is the initial element in the sentence, *too* may follow directly, as a rule with nuclear prominence (and with a non-nuclear accent on the focus); *eg*:

[19] /Here tòo we 'made a mi'stake #

[20] /That tòo was a mi'stake #

When the focus of *too* is the final element in the sentence, the focus must have a nuclear accent and there is an additional accent (not necessarily nuclear) on *too*; *eg*:

[21] We /saw tóo # that there /wasn't much tìme #

We may sum up by saying that the adverbial focus constructions normally converge, at least in part, with intonational focusing. As a rule, there is nuclear prominence either on the focal element itself, or on the marker, or on both, with greater prominence (where there is a difference) on whichever follows the other.

7.2.2 Adverbial and sequential focusing

In general, the combination of adverbial focusing with marked theme or marked rheme is characteristic of the more formal varieties of English. For example (with continuous underlining for adverbial focus and a broken line marking sequential focus)

[22] Only in England is the system still used

A less formal style would use clefting instead of marked theme: *It's only in England that the system is still used.*
   The adverbial focus marker may itself serve to create the marked sequence by separating the subject or the final element from the remainder of the sentence; *eg*, with *also* shifted to the left:

[23] This question also will be dealt with by the committee

Here the interposition of *also* between subject and operator turns the subject into a marked theme. The corresponding sentence with *also* after *will* is less marked stylistically: *This question will also be dealt with by the committee.* In [24] below, we have *also* shifted to the right:

[24] He has written also to the Ministry of Labour

Here the placing of *also* between the verb and the prepositional phrase makes the latter into a marked rheme. Again, the version with *also* in medial position is likely to be preferred in less formal varieties: *He has also written to the Ministry of Labour.*

Too, like *also*, can have the double function of focusing adverb and 'partition' in the theme-rheme structure:

[25] They, too, had left

[26] She remembered, too, their meeting in Florence

The following structure is typical of the style of newspaper reporting:

[27] Also present at the reception were Mr and Mrs Discobbolos

Here it is the end-placement of the subject that produces the marked rheme. In this kind of inverted sentence the initial *also* cannot focus on anything but the subject. Similarly with *too*:

[28] Present, too, at the ceremony was the Akond of Swat

7.2.3 Convergence of syntactic markers

The use of cleft focus, or of the adverbial focus markers, always has direct semantic implications; and it is therefore natural that some syntactic convergences should be barred for purely logical reasons. Horn (1969:106) notes the following contrast in well-formedness:

[29] It's $\begin{Bmatrix} \text{only} \\ \text{*even} \\ \text{*also} \end{Bmatrix}$ Muriel who . . .   (Horn's (59))

He comments: 'As pointed out by Bruce Fraser...the natural explanation for the facts of (59) is that clefting, like *only*, specifies uniqueness, while *even* and *also* presuppose non-uniqueness and thus cannot be clefted.' There is an apparent contradiction between the position represented by Horn and Fraser and the following statement by Quirk *et al* (1972:438): 'Focusing adjuncts can appear within the focal clause of a cleft sentence to focus on an item:

$$\text{It was} \left\{ \begin{array}{l} only \\ particularly \\ also \\ even \end{array} \right\} \text{John who protested.'}$$

If all the adverbs in this example are intended to focus on *John*, the sentences with *also* and *even* are very odd indeed. But *also* and *even* can be taken (unlike *only* and *particularly*) to focus on the relative clause, making the sense equivalent to:

$$\text{John was} \left\{ \begin{array}{l} also \\ even \end{array} \right\} \underline{\text{the one who protested.}}$$

In this interpretation, the sentences with *also* and *even* may both be regarded as well-formed, though *even* is much less likely to occur in this structure than *also*. But in such a case, of course, there is no convergence between the cleft construction and an additive focus marker, as shown in [30]:

[30] It was also John who protested.

The cleft focus is *John* and the focus of *also* is *who protested*. Compare also:

[31] It was Edison, too, who invented the phonograph

This can only be interpreted as indicated, *ie* as approximately equivalent to:

[32] Edison was also the inventor of the phonograph[7]

The constraint is strictly linguistic, of course, and would continue to hold even if we believed that the phonograph was invented independently by two or more people.

When the focus of the cleft construction denotes a cause or reason, convergence with *also* is possible; *eg*:

[33] It was also <u>because of the children</u> that they decided to move[8]

The reason for the admissibility of [33] seems to be the feeling that causal explanations are typically partial rather than exhaustive; compare:

[34] It was partly because of the children that they decided to move

Notes

1. Although the term 'inclusion' has been used both for the relationship in [5] and [7] and that in [8] and [9] below, the cases are not really the same, as is hinted by the placement of the markers denoting the ends of the domains, simultaneous in [5] and [7], but in sequence in [8] and [9]. The simultaneous endings in [5] and [7] are made possible by the fact that the boundaries are on different levels (see below).
2. The same holds good, of course, for the overlapping between negation and the quantifiers, and between the focusing adverbs and the quantifiers, which have been dealt with in Chapters 5 and 6 respectively.
3. The domain of the cleft construction is marked by '^{c}⁻...⁻^{c}'. The cleft construction in [9] is discontinuous (being interrupted by the negator $n't$), and so needs two pairs of boundary markers.
4. With $not\ only$ directly preceding a nominal or adverbial focus, eg in:

    (i) ↓Not °⁻only <u>George</u> made this mistake⁻°↓
    (ii) ↓Not °⁻only <u>in this</u> was he mistaken⁻°↓

    the negation focuses obligatorily on the negative component in the meaning of the $only$-construction.
5. Compare [25] and [26] in §6.2.2.
6. The term is due to Karttunen and Peters (1978:33), but the property to which it refers has often been noticed; see the references $ibid$, p29.
7. The corpus contains the following examples of the pattern in [31]:

    (i) If no man comes to the Father but by Jesus Christ, it is also Jesus Christ who sends that other Comforter who testifies of Jesus Christ and makes possible His abiding presence (W.9.2.135–4)
    (ii) The Southeast Neolithic ... pottery stamped with repeated geometric designs ... a link with Southeast Asia, where the tradition ... has continued ... It was also under the influence of this technique that the Southeastern craftsmen decorated bronzes of the Chou period in a style quite unlike that of North China. (W.11.6.4a)

8. I owe this observation to Hilary Glassman.

Eight

Only, *also*, *too*, and *as well*: Data from the corpus

8.1 THE CORPUS AND ITS PARTS

The main object of this chapter is to note the frequencies of various patterns with the focusing adverbs listed in the heading. Wherever practicable, we shall compare speech and writing, and 'private' with 'public' speech. We shall also note incidentally certain other uses of the same words.

The data used are drawn from a total of 156 samples of text, each containing *ca* 5000 words, from the Survey of English Usage at University College London. Of these samples, 88 are transcriptions of recordings of spoken English and 68 have their origin in writing. The Survey classification of these texts is as follows:

Speech:

Conversation:	Surreptitious:	Intimates:	14
Conversation:	Surreptitious:	Equals:	14
Conversation:	Surreptitious:	Disparates:	6
Conversation:	Non-surrept.:	Intimates:	7
Conversation:	Non-surrept.:	Equals:	11
Conversation:	Non-surrept.:	Disparates:	6
Conversation:	Telephone:	Intimates:	3
Conversation:	Telephone:	Equals:	4
Conversation:	Telephone:	Disparates:	3
Spontaneous Commentary:	Sport:		4
Spontaneous Commentary:	Non-sport		5
Spontaneous	Oration:		5
Prepared	Oration:		6

The class of non-surreptitiously recorded conversation between equals consists of two subclasses:

(a) public – containing radio discussion programmes, *eg* 'Brains Trust', 'Any Questions?', and

(b) private

The breakdown of the text samples with origin in writing is as follows:

A. Written for spoken delivery (transcription of recordings):
    Talks: 4
    News: 3
    Stories: 1
    Speeches: 2
    Drama: 3

B. Non-printed (handwritten or typed):
    Letters: Social: 5
    Letters: Non-social: 7
    Diaries: 3
    Exam scripts: 3

C. Printed:
    Learned arts: 4
    Learned sciences: 4
    Instructional: 3
    General non-fiction: 6
    Press: 6
    Administrative: 2
    Statutory: 1
    Persuasive: 4
    Fiction: 7

The spoken texts may be divided in accordance with the type of speech situation they represent into two sets:

(a) 'Private' speech, *ie* private conversation between intimates or equals (46 samples, or 230,000 words of text)
(b) 'Non-private' speech, *ie* conversation between disparates, or public discussion, or broadcast commentary, or oration (42 samples, 210,000 words of text)

The samples of writing may be grouped into the following sets:

(a) 'Private' writing, *ie* social letters and diaries (eight samples)
(b) Written dialogue in drama (three samples)
(c) Fiction – a mixed category containing both dialogue and other writing (eight samples)
(d) Miscellaneous non-private writing, including writing for spoken delivery (49 samples)

We shall set up a category of non-private writing, made up of (d) and the non-dialogue parts of (c).[1] The set of samples in this category gives us approximately 270,000 words of text.

As one would expect, these three major sets of samples, grouped by context of utterance, differ from one another in various linguistic characteristics, including the uses of the focusing adverbs, with 'private' speech and 'non-private' writing at the two extremes of a number of scales, and 'non-private' speech in the middle. If there had been more samples representing fiction, it would have been interesting to compare the dialogue-narrative contrast in fiction with the contrast between speech and non-private writing in the rest of the corpus; but with only eight samples of fiction in all, the amount of data was insufficient for this purpose. (See however note 10.)

8.2 ONLY

8.2.1 The uses of *only*: Speech and writing

We shall distinguish first of all between the following distinct uses of *only*:

(i) *Only₁*, the focusing adverb, *eg*:

    [1] He was /only :twenty fíve # (S.12.2.9)

(ii) *Only₂*, part of the complex phrase coordinator *not only ... but (also)* ..., *eg*:

    [2] He was very conscientious not only in preparing a great variety of work but also in getting to know his students, devoting time and energy to them (W.7.6.10)

    [3] In the course of developing her argument Miss X deploys her very wide reading, not only in literary history, but in the history of art and of ideas (W.7.6.92)

(iii) *Only₃*, part of the anticipatory clause connective *not only ... (but)* ..., *eg*:

    [4] Not only did it secure a clear majority, but no fewer than 13 cabinet ministers went into the lobby to support it (W.11.2.3)

    [5] Not only did the Tories fail to take preventive measures; throughout the previous year they were busily feeding the pre-Election boom (W.15.3b.4–3)

(iv) *Only₄*, the 'conjunct' (Quirk *et al*, *GCE* (1972) 8.89), *eg*:

> [6] /Ànybody could prodúce # at /least !two test tèams # of /Ènglish wríters # . who /would be !"much better worth celebráting # . /than Búrns # only be/cause we're so :cònstipated about ˙national ˙celebrations in Éngland # we /don't dò it # (S.5.1.29)

(v) *Only₅*, part of the combination *if only, if . . . only* (see GCE 11.31, note), *eg*:

> [7] Now the /Liberal Party "!càn [pro/Ldùce #] # – /this effective opposítion # if /only people will "vóte # in suf/fìcient númbers # to /put !more Liberals !bàck # (S.5.5.26)

> [8] Now /if you could !only get :thǎt on to 'tape # /that would be !very ìnteresting # (S.2.5a.12)

(vi) *Only₆*, the 'restrictive adjective' (GCE 5.32), *eg*:

> [9] /Gold 'shares pro:vided the !only :brìght 'spot in Nmárkets # (W.2.2e.6)

We are chiefly concerned here with *only₁*, and we shall start by considering *only₁* with clausal scope, in clauses[2] with subject and finite verb. The instances that come under this heading amount to 561 in all, 344 from speech (sample: 440,000 words) and 217 from non-private writing (sample: 270,000 words). The overall frequency is therefore *ca* eight per 10,000 words of text, both in speech and in writing.

The syntactic categories that we shall distinguish in the first place are defined by the focus and position of *only* as follows:

(a) Focusing on a pre-subject element (with consequent subject-operator inversion), *eg*:

> [10] Some 16 years ago Stone's installed their first electric furnace and experience gained since that time indicates to them that only with electric melting could the high standard of casting be achieved (W.15.4b.11)

(b) Focusing on the subject, *eg*:

> [11] At length only the three dinner guests remained (W.16.5. 23–3)

(c) In medial position, adjacent to the (contextual) focus, *eg*:

[12] /One can 'only 'keep one's 'fingers ,Ncròssed # (W.1.5a.4)

[13] I've /only 'just been e:lècted # (S.3.3.6)

[14] I was only joking (W.16.5.18–4)

(d) In medial position, separated from the (contextual) focus, *eg*:

[15] My /wife is a par:ticularly good :còok # . but /Gòd [/knòws #] [/what she'd !gìve me #] # if I /only gave her :three pound :ten a :wèek # (S.5.4.37)

[16] You can . /only dis:tìnguish 'these of 'course # . in /dàylight # . be/cause at !nìght'time you 'can't sèe # (S.2.4a.90)

[17] The calculation of the multiplying constant *A* can only be carried out in simple types of assembly (W.9.9.33–2)

(e) In postmedial position, *eg*:

[18] The person convicted was fined only a pound (W.12.2.45)

[19] ...and similarly, the decomposition in benzene of a symmetrical disubstituted peroxide yields only the monosubstituted diaryl (W.9.10.34–5)

[20] I /saw you :only at 'week'ĕnds # when /I was a!way from !schòol # (S.6.4a.21)

The distribution of these categories for the combined sample of speech and writing (710,000 words) is as follows:

a	b	c	d	e	total
13	52	197	204	95	561

In percentages:

a	b	c	d	e	total
2.3	9.3	35.1	36.4	16.9	100

Dividing the sample into speech and writing, we obtain, as expected, two very different distributions:

	a	b	c	d	e	total
Speech:	1	18	129	163	33	344
Writing:	12	34	68	41	62	217

Or in percentages:

	a	b	c	d	e	total
Speech:	0.3	5.2	37.5	47.4	9.6	100
Writing:	5.5	15.7	31.3	18.9	28.6	100

The difference in the proportions between adjacent and non-adjacent focus clearly reflects the greater influence on the written form of the prescriptive maxim that *only* should be placed 'near the word it modifies' (*ie* next to its focus). The relevant figures here are those for column (d) (medial, non-adjacent) and column (e) (postmedial, adjacent), since column (c) (medial, adjacent) represents the cases where there is no choice.

The other points of interest are the frequencies of categories (a) and (b). Category (b) – *only* focusing on the subject – is relatively infrequent for the corpus as a whole, amounting to just over nine per cent; but in addition there is a considerable difference between speech and writing: 5.2 per cent as against 15.7 per cent. These facts are probably to be associated with what has already been noted (GCE 13.76) for the relationship between noun phrase structure and syntactic function, *viz* the general preference for simple NP's in subject position and the difference between different types of text in the strength of the association of simple with subject (greatest for informal speech, least for scientific writing).

The even greater rarity of category (a) – *only* focusing on a pre-subject element – and the almost total avoidance of this structure in speech[3] are no doubt similarly connected with the preference for simple elements in initial position. But there is presumably an additional factor – the concomitant subject-operator inversion, a syntactic feature which (apart from its use in interrogatives) is historically on the wane and gradually becoming archaic.

The use of *only* with local scope (see §6.1.6) is comparatively rare, with only 18 instances in 710,000 words of speech and writing. Since the use of 'local *only*' is a feature making for compression – complexity being pushed down from clausal to phrasal rank – we naturally expect it to occur in writing more often than in speech. And the figures for the corpus, though small, agree with this expectation: 12 for 270,000 words of writing, as against six for 440,000 words of speech; *ie* local *only* occurs three times as often in writing as in speech.

The difference is not only a matter of numbers. Here are the instances:

[21] /These figures come :òut of # – the re/port of the Advisory Commíttee # and were sub/mitted to me "":bỳ the Home Sécretary # /only forty eight hours a:gò # (S.5.3.22)

[22] /Lord Párker # [. . .]/made a par!ticularly ""!pòwerful cáse # for /what I am ádvocating # /only a few weeks a!gò # (S.5.3.51)

[23] And er /one's !Nsèen # – oh /only !rècently # – the . ""/Gèrman [/Socialist LNPàrty #] [for e/LNxàmple #] – er re/fòrming itsélf # (S.5.5.33)

[24] because /only !rècently # . /lîterally # I /mean a ˙few ˙days a!gò # /the of:fícials # of the /comp'troller and 'auditor géneral # . /left the :còllege # (S.11.2.33)

[25] er /only – erm . a ""!Wyèar a'go # – as /recently as a :year agò # [. . .] er we /pùt up our númbers # (S.3.2b.12)

[26] In /fact 'only the 'other !nìght # I /had a !strànge 'dream # (S.6.5.34)

[27] In this case the metastable phase could, ideally, persist until conditions are changed so much that the free energy 'hump' YZX (fig. 3(a)) drops to nearly zero, at which stage only a very small fluctuation is sufficient to promote the transition (W.9.9.28–1)

[28] If the original conception was of an epic of twelve books each one illustrating one of the Aristotelian virtues, then the production of only half the amount must leave an epic story which is a hopeless failure, in that it is half complete (W.6.1.8)

[29] There was a possibility of errors, and only seconds after the start England made one (W.12.5c.2)

[30] Dougan did, in fact, glance a free kick from Bailey a foot wide of the far post after only two minutes (W.12.5e.4)

[31] Last week he shook a Hamburg crowd of 64,000 by putting Cardiff ahead after only five minutes (W.12.5f.4)

[32] It /seemed im!pòssible # that /only twò of them # could /make so much :nóise # (W.3.1b.6)

[33] . . . and /stopped his èars # to/ [shut òut] the :sìlence # – the /rīch # /pêrfect ˙silence # – that he'd been /drinking like :rare wìne # /only an !hòur ago # (W.3.1b.23)

[34] /This was desNcríbed # as /still [ònly] mòderately áctive # (W.2.2e.7)

[35] And the /Rùssian 'army's # /Nmòbilised # . /just a'cross the ,fróntier # /only 'twenty 'minutes' !wàlk a'way # (W.1.3a.30)

[36] "/I can re:Nmĕmber # as if it had /been !only Nyèsterday # the /look on 'Mr 'Kuerton's ,fāce # (W.1.3a.36)

[37] After only three months, two of the undergraduates were commenting perceptively on The Battle of Maldon, the Wanderer and the Seafarer, and even the Dream of the Rood (W.7.6.72)

[38] After only two years research, any conclusions must be provisional and inconclusive (W.7.8.46)

The instances from speech are all essentially of one type, *viz* phrases meaning 'only a short time earlier', whereas the instances from writing exhibit considerable variety, two being of the type 'only a short time earlier', five having other kinds of time phrases as their domains, one occurring in a locative phrase, one in an adjectival phrase, and three in a nominal phrase functioning as subject.

It is noteworthy that the examples of local scope in the spoken corpus do not contain a single instance of *only* following a preposition, whereas the written corpus contains six instances. If we look beyond the category of 'local *only*', we find 13 further examples of *only* after a preposition[4] – all except two in the written corpus. Since the placing of clausal *only* after a preposition represents as a rule a striving for clarity of expression, the object being to get as close as possible to the intended focus, the association of this feature with writing is natural.[5] Of the two instances from the spoken corpus, one seems to be a result of non-fluency rather than stylistic choice:

[39] /This is a – !nèw deNpártment # /ìsn't it # it's been /going for –– ((only)) :two yèars # (S.6.1c.5)

The other, by contrast, is a clear instance of style being affected by context and subject matter:

[40] We re/lȳ # to /only a 'very 'small ex,*N*tènt # –/on !fŭnds
    # — /stemming from the 'uni'versity 'grants com*N*mìttee #

It is interesting to note also the distribution of two other types of *only*, viz *only*$_2$ and *only*$_4$. *Only*$_2$ (*not only* ... *but* (*also*) ...) occurs 17 times in speech as against 33 times in writing, *ie* (in relation to the length of the samples) three times as often in writing as in speech. Since the construction is more likely to be found in planned and elaborate than in impromptu and casual language, the greater frequency in writing is natural.[6]

Only$_4$, the conjunct (= *but*) is definitely informal in character. This is reflected in its total absence from the non-private written texts, contrasting with 14 occurrences in speech (plus three in the dialogue of one of the novels).

8.2.2 *Only* in 'private' and 'non-private' speech

We can now consider the differences between the two parts of the spoken corpus: 'private' and 'non-private' speech (see §8.1 above for the sense in which these terms are being used). It is natural that non-private speech should tend to be more formal and more carefully planned than private speech, and thus intermediate in style between private speech and non-private writing; and this is indeed reflected in the distributions of the features we have examined, insofar as the small numbers of occurrences make it possible to draw any conclusions. First, here are categories (a)–(e), as distinguished in §8.2.1. above (the figures for writing are added for comparison):

	a	b	c	d	e	total
Private speech:	–	4	75	96	10	185
Non-private speech:	1	14	54	67	23	159
Non-private writing:	12	34	68	41	62	217

And in percentages:

	a	b	c	d	e	total
Private speech:	–	2.2	40.5	51.9	5.4	100
Non-private speech:	0.6	8.8	34.0	42.1	14.5	100
Non-private writing:	5.5	15.7	31.3	18.9	28.6	100

The corpus of private speech contains no instances of *only* with local scope or *only* inside a prepositional phrase and one solitary instance of *only$_2$* (*not only...but...*) as against six, two, and 16 instances respectively for non-private speech. On the other hand, private speech contains most of the instances of *only$_4$* (=but): 11 out of 14. Though some of the figures are very small, they agree in placing non-private speech in an intermediate position. The contrasts are very clear for the ratios between columns (d) and (e) (medial, non-adjacent and postmedial, adjacent). The figures are equivalent to 9.6:1, 2.9:1, and 0.7:1; and the numbers of instances involved are not negligible: 106 in private speech, 90 in non-private speech, and 103 in non-private writing.

We see, therefore, that the grouping of the text samples into our three sets, which is based on context of utterance, is meaningful also in purely linguistic terms.

8.3 *ALSO*, *TOO*, AND *AS WELL* IN DIFFERENT CONTEXTS OF UTTERANCE

We are here concerned with *also*, *too*, and *as well* as focusing adjuncts. This excludes the following other items:

(i) *Also* as part of the complex coordinators *and also*, *but also*
(ii) *Also* as a reinforcing conjunct (*GCE* 8.89, 94; 10.21) – usually preceded by *and* or *but*
(iii) *Too* as a degree marker ('intensifier', *GCE* 5.68)
(iv) *Too* as a reinforcement of *and* (*and...too* 'and also')
(v) *Too* as a reinforcing conjunct
(vi) *As well* in the sense of 'no less well'
(vii) *As well* in *may as well* or *might as well*
(viii) *As well* in the compound preposition *as well as*

The conjunct *also*, which is characteristic of the spoken language, particularly private speech, is distinguished by its initial position from focusing *also*, and is usually preceded by *and* or *but*; eg:

[1] /I just got !bòred # with /Llistening to the Wstòries # [as /wèll #]# and /and . and /ǎlso # he was /sort of !desperately 'desperately :kèen # and /that . that/always . puts me óff # (S.2.7.84)

The conjunct *too* is very rarely initial (there is no instance in the corpus), and it must therefore be distinguished from the focus marker by interpretation (in context) of the sentence in which it occurs. It can usually be glossed 'moreover', or 'what's more', or 'not only that'.[7] Conjunct *too* often occurs in elliptical clauses, *eg*:

[2] IF the Prime Minister appeared on television to-night to appeal for homes for a thousand stray dogs, the response would be enormous. And quite right too. (W.15.1.47–2)

[3] I can't think what's possessed Jasper to go flying off to Heligoland of all places at this moment. In term too. I particularly wanted his help in compiling the editorial rules. (W.16.6.168–1)

But of course occurrences in complete finite clauses are also found. For example:

[4] I can /use that library bétter than I can ˙use !thìs ˙one # – /áctually # . and /they've got a ![blòody ˙sight] more :ìn it . [/Ntòo #]# (S.1b.6a.–7)

[5] Goodrich had become much more manageable to his imagination: he was not the mystery man he had been.
    A man, too, ought to earn his living. Goodrich did not do this and apparently could not. (W.16.5.21–3)

If we compare the occurrences of the focusing adverbs *also*, *too*, and *as well* in complete finite clauses, we find that the different parts of our corpus correlate very clearly with different relative frequencies for these items. The figures are:

	also	*too*	*as well*	Total
Private speech:	55	48	43	146
Non-private speech:	91	49	19	159
Non-private writing:	320	45	4	369
Total:	466	142	66	674

In percentages:

	also	*too*	*as well*	Total
Private speech:	37.7	32.9	29.5	100.1
Non-private speech:	57.2	30.8	11.9	99.9
Non-private writing:	86.7	12.2	1.1	100
Total:	69.1	21.1	9.8	100

As regards position in the sentence, *also* is predominantly medial, of course (between operator and main verb if both are present). Deviations are relatively few. Of the 466 instances of focusing *also* in finite clauses, only 15 are shifted to the right so as to adjoin and precede the contextual focus – nine in non-private writing, six in non-private speech, and none in private speech – and four more are shifted to the end to adjoin and follow the contextual focus (all in writing).[8] Of the final elements that are preceded by *also*, five are clauses, *eg*:

> [6] I thought also that on that occasion, and at our previous interviews, I had asked you to restrict your drawings as far as possible (W.7.9.6)

six are prepositional phrases, *eg*:

> [7] It ap/plies *N*álso # to the /use of !còlour # (W.1.1A.18)

three are nominal phrases, *eg*:

> [8] But he /sáw # . "/álso # . the be/ginnings of a ríse # . of /*H*smáll # insig/[*H*nìficant] :tòwns # – /like !Lìverpool # (S.12.2.31)

and one is an instance of multiple focus:

> [9] I /don't just :*N*sèe in them # /Lawrence as a mán #. /I re'gard them *N*ǎlso # /as they ,áre # as . /standing 'on their ówn # . as /nóvels # . as /stories of "!pěople # (S.3.1c.24)

There is one example of final *also* in the spoken part of the corpus, but it belongs to a different category. Here the focus is on the subject, not on the element immediately preceding *also*:

> [10] /This I think :[Òscar] feels àlso #

There are two similar examples in the written part:

> [11] The first floor houses the real heart of the store – the hi-fi departments – but there is much else here also (W.15.4c.9)

> [12] Loudspeaker systems are here also (W.15.4c.10).

[10]–[12] are rare instances of *also* used in a manner more typical of *too*.

Another minor category is *also* in sentences with subject-verb inversion (with focus on the subject). The corpus contains eight instances, six from the written part and two from a broadcast commentary. For example:

[13] This way also lies the best chance of Britain helping the developing countries (W.153c.7–2)

[14] /HHere àlso # . to Saint /Pàul's # /came "!Marlborough's :duchess Sàrah # (S.10.5.18)

Of the other type of inversion, with initial *also* + predication followed by *be* + subject (and with focus on the subject), there are only three instances, two of them, surprisingly, in private speech:

[15] /Also Nt ỳpical of the ˙German ˙system # /was that ˙Luden- dorff :issued ʹorders di:rēct # . to the com/mand . to /ði: comʹmanders of di:vìsions # (S.2.3.84)

[16] Well and /àlso very ʹinteresting # is /how as it Nwère # – al/though people :write all these :pàpers # . you /realise how !little [lòts of it] is a!grēed with # (S.2.8b.20)

In these cases the combination of academic speaker and academic subject probably helps to account for the choice of syntactic form.

For the focusing adverb *too* we shall distinguish four different constructions:

(a) *Too* in final position, with focus on subject or predicate; *eg*:

[17] Ger"/màine's # going on /Thùrsday # I /don't know whether ʹJake's going :tòo # (S.4.2.58)

[18] ... /very ʹlike :WFrànz #[...] and he "/lòoks like ʹFranz [/tòo #]# (S.7.1a.20)

(b) *Too* following and focusing on the initial element; *eg*:

[19] Russell, too, used this metaphor (W.9.1.152–4)

[20] /HHere ,tóo # his /versaʹtility and :flexiʹbility :proved invàluable # (W.4.2a.52)

(c) *Too* preceding and focusing on the final element;[9] *eg*:

[21] It is clear, too, that Colonel Nasser, clutching at any available straws, is hoping to use the impending change at the White House as a means of renewing a dialogue with the US (W.12.3b.5)

[22] It is useful too for the analysis of complex passages (W.9.4.56–2)

(d) *Too* in inverted clauses, following the initial element and focusing on the final element (*ie* the subject); *eg*:

[23] Of /Lsmall 'comfort !tŏo # is the re/flection that it's 'now 'too !làte # for /any pre:cautionary !Wàfterthoughts # (W.1.5a.4)

[24] /HHere Ntòo # is a/[nòther] . if "!slìghter # /Chur˙chillian lìnk # (S.10.5.18)

The figures for these categories are as follows:

	a	b	c	d	Total
Private speech:	45	1	1	1	48
Non-private speech:	30	12	4	3	49
Non-private writing:	18	15	8	3	44
Total:	93	28	13	7	141

There is one instance which belongs to none of these categories:

[25] There are scenes, too, which impress themselves on the mind (focus on *scenes*) (W.6.2a.15)

The differences between the three contextual varieties are very considerable. The favourite position for *too* in the corpus as a whole is of course the final one. But whereas this accounts for 94 per cent of the instances in private speech, the proportion is only 61 per cent in non-private speech, and as little as 41 per cent in non-private writing.

For *as well*, there is to all intents and purposes only one place, the end of the clause; but the frequency of this marker in relation to that of the other two additives varies considerably with context of utterance, as appears from the table on *p*185 above – the proportions being 30 per cent, 12 per cent, and one per cent of the combined occurrences of *also*, *too*, and *as well* as focusing adverbs.

The data here assembled are far from doing justice to the full complexity of this part of the language system, but they do suffice to show (i) that each focus marker has its own grammar, and (ii) that the contexts of utterance we have distinguished are strongly differentiated from one another in their preferences among the options available to the language as a whole.[10]

Notes

1. There is a slight anomaly here, since the non-dialogue parts of the fiction contain a proportion of 'free indirect speech', or 'erlebte Rede', which is often more akin, stylistically, to dialogue than to narrative or description. But it is not always easy to draw the line between free indirect speech and the surrounding text, and in any case the proportion is a small one (less than 10 per cent of the non-dialogue parts of the fiction).

2. 'Clause' and 'clausal' is here taken to include 'sentence' and 'sentential'.

3. The solitary example in the spoken corpus comes from a broadcast discussion and the speaker is an academic.

4. This excludes instances of *only* in clauses introduced by the subordinator *with* (see §6.1.5.2).

5. The instances from the written corpus are: *of only moderate comfort* (W.1.5a.4), *bids for only 2,150 tons* (W.2.2c.10), *with only small net gains* (W.2.2c.12), *in only one literature course* (W.7.7.22), *with only a part of the whole situation* (W.9.4.61–3), *for only the simplest reflex arcs* (W.9.7.97–4), *results in only a very small and irregular solvent effect* (W.9.10.33–2), *in only one nucleus* (W.9.10.34–5), *in only one instance* (W.9.10.36–5), *for only two reasons* (W.12.2.51), *a gain of only 6 p.c.* (W.12.6a.9).

6. Not all kinds of writing, of course, seem equally prone to indulge in such correlative constructions. Some varieties lay more stress on economy, while others favour balanced structures at the cost of some increase in redundancy. In the nine text samples representing news broadcasts, written journalism, administration, and law, we have no more than two instances; whereas in the 13 samples representing scripted speeches, non-social letters, and printed persuasive writing, the number of instances comes to 17. The difference in frequency is almost 1:6, and though the totals are small, the distribution can hardly be accidental.

7. The conjunct uses of *too* and *also* can best be interpreted as expressing what Halliday and Hasan (1976:238*ff*) have called 'internal' conjunctive relations. The distinction between 'internal' and 'external' in this context is explained as follows:

    '[External conjunction] has to be interpreted in terms of the EXPERIENTIAL function of language; it is a relation between meanings in the sense of representations of 'contents', (our experience of) external reality. [Internal conjunction] has to be interpreted in terms of the INTERPERSONAL function of language; it is a relation between meanings in the sense of representations of the speaker's own 'stamp' on the situation – his choice of speech role and rhetorical channel, his attitudes, his judgments and the like.' (*p*240)

8. In two instances, *also* stands to the right of the mid position but is separated from its focus by a parenthesis:

    (i)   I think also, in view of the continued excesses which there have been on your account, that even though you were selling the car this too should have gone in reduction of your indebtedness (W.7.9.28)

    (ii)   What holds for items of List II holds also, if we follow Frege, for items of List IV (W.9.1.153–2).

    There is one instance of *also* standing to the right of the mid position and before a non-final focal item:

    (iii) She contributed also to the teaching of General Studies in the 6th Form in a very helpful and informative way (W.17.2.22)

For the status of the final element in this sentence (*in...way*), see the discussion of [33]–[39] in §6.2.3. Compare also the following example with *too*:

(iv) This process, too, has recently been subjected to investigation, by Rondes-vedt and Vogl (1955, 1956) and by Kochi (1955, 1956) (W.9.10.28–4)

The domain of the focus marker ends with *6th Form* in (iii) and with *investigation* in (iv).

9. In constructions (b) and (c) the focusing adverb functions as a 'partition' in theme-rheme structure, so that the focus is also marked theme in (b) and marked rheme in (c) (see §2.3.4 and §4.2.7).

10. The data used for this study are inadequate for a comparison between fictional dialogue and fictional narrative, but these two varieties are well represented in Jacobson (1964), where the following types of style are distinguished in a study of adverbial positions:

(i) Conversation (*ie* fictional dialogue)
(ii) Narrative (fictional)
(iii) Non-fiction

The figures given for the placement of *only* and *too* (*p*200) show differences between conversation and narrative which are quite similar to the differences between speech and (non-private) writing in the Survey corpus.

Appendix

A problem in the analysis of scope in English: One *any* or two?

1. The behaviour of *any* and its compounds is one of the most interesting and puzzling problems in English grammar. Many of the relevant observations have long been available (see, for example, OED s.v. *any*, Jespersen 1933:181*f*), and there is a systematic account in Quirk *et al* (1972: §4.127, 7.44–48). But as regards the analysis in terms of the logical concept of quantification there are two sharply differing viewpoints, and the issue remains undecided. The two solutions that have been proposed may be conveniently referred to as the two-*any* and the one-*any* analysis.

According to the two-*any* analysis, most of the occurrences of *any* represent an existential-type quantifier[1] that can occur only within the scope of certain logical operators, of which the most important is the negative. Compare the following:

[1] a. John said something just now
     b. *John said anything just now

[2] a. John didn't say anything just now
     b. !John didn't say something just now

Some, and the existential *any* that is posited for negative contexts (*inter alia*), are regarded as a pair of items with a common semantic core, though not semantically identical, and with overlapping but non-identical privileges of occurrence. The ill-formedness of [1.b] reflects a syntactic constraint on *any* that does not apply to *some*. The pragmatic improbability of an utterance like [2.b] is a different matter. [2.b] could represent either of two syntactically and semantically well-formed sentences, depending on whether the scope of the negation is taken to include *something* or not. [2.b.i], with *something* within the scope of the negation, is possible as a denial. Truth-conditionally, it is equivalent to [2.a]. [2.b.ii], on the other hand, with *something* outside the scope of the negation, is truth-conditionally distinct from [2.a] and is equivalent to [3]:

[3] There is something that John didn't say just now

Such a reading of 'negative' + *something* might even be forced on us in some cases, eg *John didn't say just now something that he could easily have said.*

Apart from 'negative', either 'interrogative' or 'conditional' can trigger the occurrence of *any*, though parallel sentences with *some* are also well-formed:

[4] a. Did John say anything?
     b. Did John say something?

[5] a. If John said anything. . .
     b. If John said something. . .

Here the differences between the sentences with *any* and those with *some* depend on the speaker's attitude to the content (see R. Lakoff 1969). Quantificationally, however, the *any*- and the *some*-sentences are equivalent, and it is this, together with the relationships between the sentences in [1] and [2] above, that makes it possible to regard *any*, like *some*, as an existential-type quantifier.

But of course the existential interpretation of *any* will not do for all its occurrences. Consider, for instance, [6] and [7]:

[6] Anyone might say that

[7] Someone might say that

These are not related to one another as [4.a] is related to [4.b], or [5.a] to [5.b]. [6] entails [7], but [7] does not entail [6]. *Any* in [6] can only be interpreted as a universal-type quantifier. The difference between [6] and [8]:

[8] Everyone might say that

which also has a universal-type quantifier, can be accounted for, on the reading which we shall refer to as [8.a], by a difference in scope relationships: *any* in [6] has *might* within its scope, whereas *every* in [8.a] does not. In logical notation:

[6'] $\forall x$: poss (say (x, that))

[8.a'] poss ($\forall x$: say (x, that))

The other reading of [8], which we may refer to as [8.b], is truth-conditionally equivalent to [6], and its logical representation is therefore identical with [6']. There remains, however, an attitudinal difference between [8.b] and [6] (*cf* the attitudinal difference between existential *any* and *some*).[2]

It is now possible to say when *any* is existential and when it is universal (in the version of the two-*any* analysis that is being put forward here). It is existential (i) when a sentence containing *any* is truth-conditionally equivalent to a corresponding sentence containing *some* instead of *any*, *eg* in [4] and [5] above, or (ii) when an utterance containing *any* and a corresponding utterance containing *some* instead of *any* will represent truth-conditionally distinct sentences only if *some* is taken to be outside the scope of the negation, *eg* in [2] above. Should it turn out to be the case that there are types of *any*-sentences where the substitution of *some* would result not merely in improbability but in actual ill-formedness, then (i) above would have to be widened to take in these sentences as well. Everywhere else *any* is universal. The chief contexts for universal *any* are the modals *may*, *might*, *can*, *could*, *will*, *would*. Another is the non-modal verb used generically (*eg They eat anything*). Comparative clauses are problematic. If we compare [9]–[11]:

[9]   John is older than any of us

[10] John is older than all of us

[11] John is older than some of us

We see that [9] entails both [10] and [11], [10] entails both [9] and [11], and [11] entails neither [9] nor [10]. These relationships could be accounted for by regarding *any* in [9] as universal. But if we accept the view that comparative constructions contain an implicit negative (see Mittwoch 1974 and the references there), we have an alternative account that makes *any* in [9] existential and places it within the scope of the implicit negative, as opposed to *all* in [10] and *some* in [11], which are placed outside the scope of the negative. (See below, *p202* for historical evidence associating *any* after comparatives with *any* in negative, interrogative, and conditional contexts.) It is possible that sentences like [9] have two conflicting analyses, both existing within the speaker's linguistic competence. Implicit negatives, like the one here assumed for comparative constructions, have to be admitted into our theory in any case to cope with sentences containing *only*, *hardly*, *seldom*, *few*, *without*, *before*, *reluctant*, *surprised*, etc as well as for constructions with adjectives and adverbs modified by *too*, and NP's with *the first*, *the only*, *the best*, etc.

We could use the terms 'existentially *any*' and 'universal *any*' for the two items that we are here distinguishing, but this is undesirable when it is the very existence of existential *any* that is in dispute. We need a pair of theory-neutral terms. I shall use 'non-assertive *any*' (abbreviated any_1) and 'assertive *any*' (abbreviated any_2). The assertiveness of the second *any* if of course purely superficial, as is pointed out by Quirk *et al* (1972:224), but the term is convenient.

A two-*any* analysis, representing non-assertive *any* as existential and assertive *any* as universal, is assumed by Klima (1964), Stockwell, Schachter and Partee (1968), G. Lakoff (1970b), and Jackendoff (1971b). A logical analysis of the various possible relationships of *any* and *every* with modal operators and negation is given by Horn (1972:136–7).[3] [12]–[15] below correspond to Horn's (320.a–c):

[12] neg ($\forall$x) pos (M (j, x))
  John can't marry (just) anyone (=he must be selective)

[13] neg poss ($\forall$x) (M (j, x))
  John can't marry everyone (=he can't practise omnigamy)

[14] neg ($\exists$x) poss (M (j, x))
  John can't marry anyone, there isn't anyone John can marry
  (= he must remain a bachelor)

[15] ($\forall$x) neg poss (M (j, x)) ≡ [14] above

[14] and [15] correspond to Horn's (320.c). The two-*any* theory chooses the formula in [14] as the linguistically appropriate representation.

2. The logical equivalence of the formulae in [14] and [15] above has prompted certain logicians and linguists (Reichenbach 1947, Quine 1960, Horn 1972, Lasnik 1972, and Kroch 1975) to propose that *any* should be regarded as a universal quantifier in all its occurrences, and that the differences between *any* and *every/all* should be accounted for in terms of different scope relationships between the operators represented by these terms and other logical operators. For example:

[16] a. I didn't solve all of the problems
     b. Not for all x (x is a problem → I solved x)

[17] a. I didn't solve any of the problems
     b. For all x (x is a problem → I didn't solve x)

These examples and analyses are Lasnik's, and are quoted from him by Kroch (1975:71). Kroch sums up by saying (*ibid*:73–74):

'We find Lasnik's analysis of *any* to be extremely convincing, though some linguists would argue that *any* corresponds to the existential quantifier in negative contexts and to the universal quantifier only in modal and some conditional contexts[4] (Karttunen, personal communication). *We know of no factual grounds for choosing between these analyses* [My emphasis. J. T.] and it may be that there can be none since the scope order of operators required by Lasnik's analysis, A~, is logically equivalent to the scope order required by the existential quantifier analysis, ~E. Under these circumstances *the analysis which treats* any *in a unitary way would seem to win out on grounds of simplicity.* [My emphasis. J. T.] Furthermore, as was mentioned earlier, the universal quantifier analysis of *any* begins to explain why that lexical item exists. It is simply a marked variant of *all* or *every* that takes wide scope with respect to operators that these quantifiers tend to have narrow scope with respect to.'[5]

3.1 It is not clear how the universal-quantifier analysis can be said to 'explain' the existence of *any* better than the two-*any* analysis, since they produce equivalent results. But the argument from simplicity is undoubtedly attractive, and it would even be sufficient (other things being equal) if it could be shown that there was indeed an *overall* gain in simplicity. It may very well be the case, however, that the increase in simplicity represented by the elimination of existential *any* is offset, or even outweighed, by the increase in complication in the rules that are needed under the unitary analysis of *any*. In the following subsections I shall analyze a number of phenomena that seem to point in this direction.

3.2 In many contexts the English language permits an existential quantifier to dominate a negative (*ie* to have a negative within its scope; see note 5). This can happen even when the negative precedes the quantifier. Consider the following examples:

[18] a. ˌHe didn't noticeˌ one error (He overlooked one)
　　b. ˌHe didn't notice one errorˌ (He noticed none, or more than one)

[19] a. ˌHe didn't noticeˌ many errors
　　b. ˌHe didn't notice many errorsˌ

In [18] and [19] above, the quantifier dominates the negative in the a-sentences, and the negative dominates the quantifier in the b-sentences. Corresponding to such sentences, we have others (with or without negation) that have universal instead of existential quantifiers (here the negative normally dominates the quantifier):

[20] a. He noticed all (the) errors
　　b. He didn't notice all (the) errors

[21] a. He noticed every error
　　b. He didn't notice every error

In the presence of certain elements, of which the conditional modals *might* and *would* can be taken as representative, universal *any* (any_2) can be substituted for *all/every*:

[22] a. He might have noticed any_2 error (There is no error that he couldn't have noticed)
　　b. He would have noticed any_2 error (There's no error that he wouldn't have noticed)
　　c. He couldn't have noticed any_2 error (neg: [22.a])
　　d. He wouldn't have noticed any_2 error (neg: [22.b])

The syntactic order in [22.c] and [22.d] is modal-neg any_2, but the order of logical dominance is neg: any_2: modal.

The two sets of options represented by [18]–[19] and [20]–[22] are both excluded in certain syntactic contexts. Consider the following examples:

[23] There wasn't one error that he noticed

[24] There weren't many errors that he noticed

In these existential sentences, the negative must dominate the existential quantifier, so that [23] and [24] cannot be read in the sense of 'He overlooked one error' and 'He overlooked many errors' respectively. Indeed, one of the pragmatic functions of sentences like [23]–[24] is to disambiguate sentences like [18]–[19], or rather, perhaps, utterances like these. Now if we consider existential sentences in which universal quantifiers have been substituted for the existential ones, we find that they are quite different from normal existential sentences. Consider the following:

[25] !There was every error that he noticed

[26] !There would have been any error that he noticed

These sentences can be contextualized, but only in the same way as existential sentences with proper nouns and other definite NP's,[6] and they cannot be taken as existential analogues of [21.a] and [22.b] above. It we negate the matrix in [25] and [26], the result is totally ill-formed, as with proper nouns and definite NP's:

[27] *There wasn't every error that he noticed

[28] *There wouldn't have been any_2 error that he noticed

[29] *There isn't George

[30] *There isn't the theatre

If we substitute any_1 for any_2, however, turning [28] into [31],

[31] There wouldn't have been any_1 error that he noticed

we obtain a perfectly well-formed sentence. Now under the two-*any* analysis this is perfectly natural and precisely what one would expect; for here *any* is analyzed as existential in [31] but as universal in [28]. But under the unitary analysis we have an anomaly: any_1, interpreted as a universal quantifier, is the solitary exception to the constraint on quantifiers in existential sentences.[7]

The situation is similar in sentences with the main verb *have* (in one of its meanings). Consider the following:

[32] John has many friends

[33] John has some friends

[34] a. John hasn't many friends (neg dominating *many*)
　　 b. *ᵢJohn hasn'tᵢ many friends (*many* dominating neg)

[35] John hasn't any_1 friends

[36] a. John hasn't one friend (neg dominating *one*)
　　 b. *ᵢJohn hasn'tᵢ one friend (*one* dominating neg)

[37] *John has every friend

[38] *John would have any^2 friend(s)

[39] *John hasn't every friend

[40] *John wouldn't have any^2 friend(s)

In [40], as in [28] above, the substitution of *any*$_1$ for *any*$_2$ produces a well-formed sentence:

[41] John wouldn't have any$_1$ friends(s)

We see that with this use of *have* the constraints on the operators under consideration are the same as those for existential sentences. Again the rule is simple for the two-*any* analysis, while the unitary analysis creates an anomaly.

The affinity between existential sentences and *have*-sentences is so obvious that we are not surprised to find the same constraints operating, but there is also an entirely different sort of context for which the same rules that we have noted above seem to hold good. This is the comparative with a modifier of degree. For example:

[42] This book is much cheaper

[43] This book is a bit cheaper

[44] This book is £1 cheaper

[45] a. This book isn't much cheaper (neg dominating *much*)
     b. *^{much}-This book isn't much cheaper^{-much} (*much* dominating neg)

[46] a. This book isn't £1 cheaper (*neg* dominating *one*)
     b. *^{one}-This book isn't £1 cheaper^{-one} (*one* dominating neg)

[47] This book isn't any$_1$ cheaper

[48] *This book is all cheaper

[49] *This book would be any$_2$ cheaper

[50] *This book isn't all cheaper

[51] *This book wouldn't be any$_2$ cheaper

In [51], as in [28] and [40] above, the substitution of *any*$_1$ for *any*$_2$ produces a well-formed sentence:

[52] This book wouldn't be any$_1$ cheaper

We see that the same simple rule for constraints on quantifier options is statable for three different types of syntactic contexts if and only if our analysis provides for an existential *any* in addition to a universal *any*.

3.3 The two-*any* analysis is supported by a further set of data. There seems to be a rule in English that quantifiers in certain positions in embedded clauses cannot dominate certain logical operators in the matrix clauses.

The range of types of embedded clauses and the range of positions in them, as well as the range of operators that are subject to this constraint, remain to be delimited, though it seems that there is partial correspondence with the positions that are barred from unbounded fronting options, and it is clear that the operators include negation and some, at least, of the modals. (The constraint can in fact be made stronger, but there is no point in doing so for our purpose.) Consider the following examples:

[53] It is not true that two of their candidates were elected

[54] He did not say that two of their candidates were elected

In each of these sentences we have an existential quantifier (*two*) on the subject of a declarative clause embedded in a negative matrix clause. In each case the quantifier is within the scope of the negative and the reverse ordering is impossible. In other words, the sentences cannot be interpreted as [53'] and [54']:

[53'] Of two of their candidates, it is not true that they were elected

[54'] Of two of their candidates, he did not say that they were elected

Similarly with [55]:

[55] It may be that two of their candidates were elected

Here *two* must be within the scope of *may*, or in other words [55] can only be interpreted as:

[55′] There may have been two of their candidates that were elected

and not as:

[55″] There are two of their candidates that may have been elected

Here [55′] entails [55″], but not vice versa. So [55] would be contextually inappropriate if the two candidates were competing for a single seat. It is worth noting that the position of the embedded clause within the matrix makes no difference to the scope relationships. So [56]:

[56] That two of their candidates were elected is not true

is truth-conditionally equivalent to [53].

Let us now consider sentences with universal quantifiers. In [57] and [58] below we have configurations involving 'poss' and $\forall x$ in different orderings:

[57] All their candidates may have been elected

[58] Any of their candidates may have been elected

[57] has two readings, a weaker one corresponding to [58], with the order $\forall x$:poss, and a stronger one with the order poss:$\forall x$. If we compare [57] and [58] with [59] and [60], in which *may* has been transported into the matrix clause, we find that the weaker readings are eliminated: [59] is unambiguous, and [60] is ill-formed (on a non-generic reading):

[59] It may be that all their candidates were elected (*only* poss $\forall x$)

[60] (*)It may be that any of their candidates were elected

If [60] is understood in a generic sense, *ie* 'It may be that any of their candidates was always elected', it is well-formed (hence the parentheses round the star); on a generic interpretation of the predicate, *any* does not require any modal as a context; *cf*:

[61] Any of their candidates were always elected

[62] At that age they read (/they'll read) anything

The following pairs show the same contrast as between [58] and [60]:

[63] He may blame any of them

[64] (*)He may say that any of them are to blame

[65] He may suspect any of them

[66] (*)He may think that any of them did it

We have seen that embedding imposes constraints on the scope options of universal as well as of existential quantifiers. We can now return to non-assertive *any*. In the following examples non-assertive *any* stands in an embedded clause that lacks a negative, but there is a negative in the matrix clause:

[67] It isn't true that any_1 of their candidates were elected

[68] He didn't say that any_1 of their candidates were elected

As with [53] and [56] above, we find that the structural ordering of the clauses outweighs the linear ordering: [69] and [70] are truth-conditionally equivalent, respectively, to [67] and [68]:

[69] That any_1 of their candidates were elected isn't true

[70] That any_1 of their candidates were elected he didn't say

Now if we interpret any_1 as an existential quantifier, everything is straightforward: the quantifier in the embedded clause is dominated by the negative in the matrix clause. But if we follow Reichenbach, Quine, and their adherents, and take any_1 as a universal, the negative in the matrix clause will have to be dominated by the quantifier in the embedded clause, a state of affairs for which we have found no parallel.[8] Once again, therefore, the one-*any* analysis forces us to make an exception to a syntactic-semantic generalization.[9]

3.4 This has been only a brief excursion into what is still to some extent terra incognita, but it would seem to show two things: (i) that when a semantic problem has two solutions that are logically equivalent, there may be syntactic grounds for preferring one to the other, and (ii) that the analysis of non-assertive *any* as an existential-type quantifier deserves to be taken seriously.

However, the claim that any_1 and any_2 differ in quantification is not intended to imply that the two items have nothing semantic in common. The differences between any_1 and *some* (see above, p192), and between any_2 and *all/every* (see above, p192–3) may very well depend (in part?) on an element of meaning that is common to the two *any's*. This would help to account for the widespread intuition that the dominant element in the meaning of *any* is 'indifference as to the particular one or ones that may be selected' (OED, s.v. *any*)[10] There is also a more objective indication that the two *any's* have a feature in common that they do not share with *some* or with *all*. This is the fact (noted by Horn 1972:131) that both *any's*, but no other quantifier except *no* (which is equivalent to *not. . .any*), can be followed by *at all*. We may use the label 'arbitrary' for the shared feature, so that any_1 will be 'existential-arbitrary' and any_2 'universal-arbitrary'.

4. There remains the historical aspect of the problem. How did the present state of affairs come about? The answer to a question of this sort must be partly speculative, but we do have some facts to build on. We know that *any* was originally existential, since it is the later development of Old English *ænig*, a derivative of *ān* 'one' (OED, s.v. *any*). The Old English occurrences of *any* already show the association with negative, interrogative, and conditional contexts that is characteristic of present-day any_1, and there are also instances of Old English *ænig* after comparatives, *eg*:

[71] . . .he wæs mara þonne ænig mon oðer (. . .he was bigger than any other man) *Beowulf* 1353

However, there are apparently no clear instances of any_2. These facts would seem to indicate that in Old English, at any rate, *any* after comparatives represented any_1 exclusively.

How then did *any* acquire its universal sense? Here we must consider the history of certain other words which have something in common with *any*: *ever*, *either*, and *all*. To start with *ever*, from Old English *æfre*: this seems to have been originally universal, with the meaning 'always' which now survives only in a small set of special contexts (eg *for ever*, *ever since*, *evergreen*). But apart from this use, Old English already has the use in negative, interrogative, and conditional contexts that is characteristic of present-day *ever*. Here we seem to have a sense change that went in the opposite direction, from universal to existential.

It was probably the Old English expressions of absolute negation that made possible the switch from one sense to the other. Such expressions were formed in two ways: (i) by combinations of 'negative' and 'existential', as in *nān* 'none', from *ne + ān* 'not one', *ǣnig...ne, ne...ǣnig, nǣnig* 'not any' (*nb*: irrespective of the order of the constituent elements), *nāhwǣðer, nōhwǣðer* 'neither', from *ne...āhwǣðer* 'not...either'; and (ii) by combinations of 'negative' and 'universal', as in *nā* adv. 'never', 'not at all', from *ne* + *ā* 'not' + 'always', *ne...ǣfre, nǣfre* 'never', also from 'not' + 'always', *nealles* 'not at all', from *ne* + *ealles* (genitive of *eall* 'all') 'not + 'of all'.

With such combinations existing side by side, the way lay open for reanalysis (*cf* the morphological reanalysis that produced *an adder* from *a nadder* and, in the reverse direction, *a newt* from *an ewt*), and this could well have been the origin of existential *ǣfre* in Old English.

Either, from Old English *ǣgðer*, has undergone a similar process. Old English *ǣgðer* was always universal, meaning 'each of two', 'both', and the existential sense that is parallel to *any*₁ did not develop until later, when *neither* had come into use, displacing the older *nauther, nouther*, from Old English *nāhwǣðer, nōhwǣðer*.

Finally *all*, from Old English *eall*, was a universal in Old English and has remained a universal to the present day. Old English *nealles* 'not at all' did not lead to the development of an existential *ealles* 'at all', but we do have the exact analogue of this non-existent existential *ealles* in Modern English *at all*, apparently by reanalysis from *not at all*. The OED cites an early example from the Authorized Version:

[72] If thy father at all misse me (1 *Sam* xx. 6)

In the idiom *at all*, the later existential use has entirely displaced the earlier universal one, so that now we have a contrast between:

[73] They did not agree at all

with existential *at all*, and:

[74] They did not agree at all times

with universal *all*. Meanwhile, another idiomatic expression containing *all*, viz *at all events*, has developed a universal-arbitrary use: compare *at all events* and *in any event* (both universal-arbitrary) and contrast *in all cases* (unmarked universal): *in any case* (universal-arbitrary).

To return to *any*: it is reasonable to suppose that the development of the universal sense of *any*₂ is due chiefly to the analogy of the formerly very ambivalent items *ever* and *either*, which had come to share with *any* so many of their contexts of occurrence. And if it is right to suppose that *any* after comparatives has two alternative analyses (see above, *p*193), this potential ambivalence may have had its share in the process.

It seems that in quantification, as elsewhere in language, the course of history is full of twists and turns, eddies and cross-currents, and we can hardly expect that the result, at any given moment, should be 'un système où tout se tient'. The co-existence of any_1 and any_2 is just one manifestation of what a logician might regard as the general perversity of natural languages.

Notes

1. No English quantifier item is the exact equivalent of either of the two quantifiers of the predicate calculus; but the English items may be grouped into two sets, one akin to the existential quantifier and the other to the universal quantifier.

2. The distinction between [8.a] and [8.b] may appear to be vacuous; its significance comes out more clearly in a sentence like *Everyone might win a prize.* – Jackendoff (1971:497–8) claims that the difference between *You may take any of them* and *You may take all of them* (which is analogous to that between [6] and [8] above) cannot be accounted for if *any* is analyzed as a universal. But as Horn points out (1972:136), this criticism ignores the scope of the modal operator represented by *may*.

3. There is an error in Horn's paradigm (in 320.d), but it does not affect the point at issue.

4. The omission of interrogative and conditional contexts for existentials and of generic contexts for universals is presumably an oversight.

5. *Sic.* The awkwardness of the sentence serves to underline the need for a verb that will save us the cumbersome expressions 'includes in its scope', 'is included in the scope of', 'has wide/narrow scope with respect to'. The word 'dominate' seems suitable for the purpose: 'A dominates B' = 'B is included in the scope of A'. This also fits in with the use of 'domain' as a synonym for 'scope'. In what follows I shall make use of 'dominate' in the sense here suggested, as I have done in Chapter 5 (see § 5.2.3.1). The scope (or domain) of negation will again be indicated by angle brackets.

6. On definite NP's in existential sentences, see Quirk *et al* (1972:956*f*) and also, from a different point of view, stressing the non-syntactic factors, Bolinger (1977:133*ff*). Horn (1972:110*ff*) notes the relevance of existential sentences to the analysis of *any*, as well as the relevance of *have* (see below), but he gives only part of the evidence. 'Definite' represents a semantic category, of course, and does not simply refer to NP's with the determiner *the*.

7. The question arises, of course, why the two restrictions noted above should go together. Firstly, it may be suggested that universals are all definites (though not necessarily specific in reference). (For evidence from relative constructions to this effect, see Taglicht (1972). See also Milsark (1974) on definites and universals in existential sentences.) Secondly, while existential quantifiers are always indefinite, they must in addition be non-specific in reference when dominated by in-

terrogative, conditional, or negative. Perhaps we should posit some such category as 'indeterminate', the intersection of indefinite with non-specific, with a special affinity for certain syntactic contexts. On the relationship between existential, locative, and possessive constructions, see Lyons (1968:388*ff*). – There is one obvious exception to the restriction on definites that bars them from negative existential sentences, *viz* the NP's with minimizing superlatives, like *the least danger*, *the slightest reason*. These superlatives may be regarded as idiomatic substitutes for *any*$_1$. (See also Ladusaw 1980).

8. No parallel, that is, in the types of clauses and clause elements here examined. The constraint does not hold for the following, for example: *He didn't want to speak to some of them*. Here, under the most obvious interpretation, *some* dominates the matrix negative.

9. Some of the above arguments for the two-*any* analysis are used by Fauconnier (1975). More recently, the two-*any* analysis has received powerful support from Ladusaw (1980).

10. See also Jespersen (1933:181) and Vendler (1967).

References

Akmajian, A. (1979) *Aspects of the grammar of focus in English*, New York: Garland (MIT thesis, 1970)

Albrow, K. H. (1968) *The rhythm and intonation of spoken English*, London: Longman (Programme in Linguistics and English Teaching, Paper 9)

Allerton, D. J. (1978) 'The notion of givenness and its relation to presuppositions and to theme', *Lingua* **44**, 133–68

Allerton, D. J. and Cruttenden, A. (1979) 'Three reasons for accenting a definite subject', *Journal of Linguistics* **15**, 49–53

Baker, C. L. (1970) 'Double negatives', *Linguistic Inquiry* **1**, 169–86

Bar-Hillel, Y. (1970) *Aspects of Language*, Jerusalem: Magnes

Bolinger, D. L. (1958) 'Stress and information', *American Speech* **33**, 5–20

Bolinger, D. L. (1961a) 'Contrastive accent and contrastive stress', *Language* **37**, 83–96

Bolinger, D. L. (1961b) *Generality, gradience, and the all-or-none*, The Hague: Mouton

Bolinger, D. L. (1972) 'Accent is predictable (if you're a mind-reader)', *Language* **48**, 633–44

Bolinger, D. L. (1977) *Meaning and form*, London: Longman

Borkin, A. (1971) 'Polarity items in questions', *CLS* 7

Brazil, D. (1978) *Discourse intonation II*, Birmingham: University of Birmingham (Discourse Analysis Monographs, No. 2)

Burt, M. K. (1971) *From deep to surface structure*, New York: Harper and Row

Carden, G. (1970) 'A note on conflicting idiolects', *Linguistic Inquiry* **1**, 281–90

Chafe, W. L. (1970) *Meaning and the structure of language*, Chicago: U. of Chicago Press

Chafe, W. L. (1974) 'Language and consciousness', *Language* **50**, 111–33

Chafe, W. L. (1976) 'Givenness, contrastiveness, definiteness, subjects, topics, and point of view', in *Subject and topic*, ed. Charles Li, New York: Academic press

Chomsky, N. (1969) 'Deep structure, surface structure, and semantic interpretation', in *Semantics: An interdisciplinary reader in philosophy, linguistics, and psychology*, eds. Steinberg, D. D. and Jakobovits, L. A. (1971)

Coleman, H. O. (1912) 'Intonation and emphasis', *Miscellanea Phonetica* **1**, 6–26

Crystal, D. (1969) *Prosodic systems and intonation in English*, Cambridge: CUP (Cambridge Studies in Linguistics 1)

Crystal D. and Quirk, R. (1964) *Systems of prosodic and paralinguistic features in English*, The Hague: Mouton

Daneš, F. (1964) 'A three-level approach to syntax', *Travaux Linguistiques de Prague* 1, 225–40

Eckersley, C. E. and Eckersley, J. M. (1960) *A comprehensive English grammar for foreign students*, London: Longman

Fauconnier, G. (1975) 'Pragmatic scales and logical structure', *Linguistic Inquiry* 6, 353–375

Firbas, J. (1964) 'On defining the theme in functional sentence analysis', *Travaux Linguistiques de Prague* 1, 267–80

Fox, A. (1973) 'Tone-sequences in English', *Archivum Linguisticum* 4, 17–26

Givón, T. (1978) 'Negation in Language: Pragmatics, function, ontology', in *Syntax and semantics 9: Pragmatics*, ed. Cole, P.

Green, G. (1980) 'Some wherefores of English inversions', *Language* 56, 582–60

Greenbaum, S. (1973) 'Informant elicitation of data on syntactic variation', *Lingua* 31, 201–212

Greenbaum, S. and Quirk, R. (1970) *Elicitation experiments in English: Linguistic studies in use and attitude*, London: Longman

Grice, H. P. (1975) 'Logic and conversation', in *Syntax and semantics 3: Speech acts*, eds. Cole, P. and Morgan, J. L.

Halliday, M. A. K. (1967) *Intonation and grammar in British English*, The Hague: Mouton

Halliday, M. A. K. (1967–8) 'Notes on transitivity and theme in English', *Journal of Linguistics* 3, 37–81; 3, 199–244; 4, 179–215

Halliday, M. A. K. (1970a) *A course in spoken English: Intonation*, London: OUP

Halliday, M. A. K. (1970b) 'Language structure and language function', in *New horizons in linguistics*, ed. Lyons, J.

Halliday, M. A. K. and Hasan, R. (1976) *Cohesion in English*, London: Longman

Hare, R. M. (1970) 'Meaning and speech acts', *Philosophical Review* 79

Hodges, J. C. (1951) ed. *Harbrace College Handbook*, New York: Harcourt, Brace and Co.

Horn, L. R. (1969) 'A presuppositional analysis of *only* and *even*', *CLS* 5

Horn, L. R. (1972) *On the semantic properties of logical operators in English* (UCLA dissertation), publ. 1976, Bloomington, Ind.: Indiana U. Linguistics Club.

Horn, L. R. (1978) 'Remarks on neg-raising', in *Syntax and semantics 9: Pragmatics*, ed. Cole, P.

Huddleston, R. D. (1971) *The sentence in written English: A syntactic study based on the analysis of written texts*, Cambridge: CUP (Cambridge Studies in Linguistics 3)

Huddleston, R. D. (1980) 'Criteria for auxiliaries and modals', in *Studies in English Linguistics for Randolph Quirk*, eds. Greenbaum, S., Leech, G. and Svartvik, J., London: Longman

Hudson, R. A. (1973) 'The meaning of questions', publ. 1975, *Language* **51**

Hughes, A. and Trudgill, P. (1979) *English accents and dialects: An introduction to social and regional varieties of British English*, London: Edward Arnold

Jackendoff, R. S. (1971a) 'On some questionable arguments about quantifiers and negation, *Language* **47**, 282–97

Jackendoff, R. S. (1971b) 'Modal structure in semantic representation', *Linguistic Inquiry* **2**, 479–515

Jackendoff, R. S. (1972) *Semantic interpretation in generative grammar*, Cambridge, Mass.: MIT Press

Jacobson, S. (1964) *Adverbial positions in English*, Stockholm: AB Studentbok (Uppsala dissertation)

Jespersen, O. (1909–49) *A modern English grammar on historical principles*, London: George Allen and Unwin

Jespersen, O. (1917) *Negation in English and other languages*, Copenhagen: Videnskabernes selskab, Høst, reprinted in *Selected writings of Otto Jespersen* (1962) London: Allen and Unwin, pp. 3–151 (page refs to 1962 reprint)

Jespersen, O. (1933) *Essentials of English grammar*, London: Allen and Unwin

Jespersen, O. (1937) *Analytic syntax*, Copenhagen: Munksgaard (repr. 1969, New York: Holt, Rinehart and Winston)

Karttunen, L. (1974)'Until', in *Papers from the tenth regional meeting of the Chicago Linguistic Society*, 284–297

Karttunen, L. and Peters, S. (1978) 'Conventional implicature', in *Syntax and semantics 11: Presupposition*, eds. Dinneen, D. A. and Oh, C.-K.

Kelly, B. (1947) *An advanced English course for foreign students*, London: Longmans, Green and Co.

Kempson, R. (1975) *Presupposition and the delimitation of semantics*, Cambridge: CUP (Cambridge Studies in Linguistics 15)

Kempson, R. (1977) *Semantic theory*, Cambridge: CUP (Cambridge Textbooks in Linguistics)

Klima, E. S. (1964) 'Negation in English', in *The structure of language: Readings in the philosophy of language*, eds. Fodor, J. A. and Katz, J. J.

Kroch, A. S. (1975) *The semantics of scope in English*, Boomington, Ind.: Indiana U. Linguistics Club (repr. 1979, New York: Garland)

Kuno, S. (1972) 'Functional sentence perspective: A case study from Japanese and English', *Linguistic Inquiry* **3**, 269–320

Kuroda, S.-Y. (1969) 'Attachment transformations', in *Modern studies in English*, eds. Reibel, D. A. and Schane, S. A.

Labov, W. (1972) 'Negative attraction and negative concord in English grammar', *Language* **48**, 773–818

Ladusaw, W. A. (1980) *Polarity sensitivity as inherent scope relations*, Bloomington, Ind.: Indiana U. Linguistics Club

Lakoff, G. (1970a) 'Repartee, or a reply to "Negation, conjunction, and quantifiers"', *Foundations of Language* **6**, 389–422

Lakoff, G. (1970b) 'Linguistics and natural logic', in *Semantics of natural language*, eds. Davidson, D. and Harman, G.

Lakoff, G. (1971) 'On generative semantics', in *Semantics: An interdisciplinary reader in philosophy, linguistics and psychology*, eds. Steinberg, D. D. and Jakobovits, L. A.

Lakoff, R. (1969) 'Some reasons why there can't be any *some-any* rules in English', *Language* **45**, 608–615

Langendoen, D. T. (1970) *Essentials of English grammar*, New York: Holt, Rinehart and Winston

Langendoen, D. T. and Bever, T. G. (1973) 'Can a not unhappy person be called a not sad one?', in *A Festschrift for Morris Halle*, ed. Anderson, S. R. and Kiparsky, P.

Lasnik, H. (1972) *Analyses of negation in English* (MIT dissertation), publ. 1976, Bloomington, Ind.: Indiana U. Linguistics Club.

Lasnik, H. (1975) 'On the semantics of negation', in *Contemporary research in philosophical logic and linguistic semantics*, eds. Hockney, D., Harper, W., and Freed, B.

Leech, G. N. (1971) *Meaning and the English verb*, London: Longman

Leech, G. N. (1974) *Semantics*, Harmondsworth, Middlesex: Penguin (second edition 1981)

Lemmon, E. J. (1965) *Beginning logic*, London: Nelson

Lyons, J. (1968) *Introduction to theoretical linguistics*, Cambridge: CUP

Lyons, J. (1977) *Semantics*, Cambridge: CUP (2 vols.)

McCawley, J. (1972) 'A programme for logic', in *Semantics of natural language*, eds. Davidson, D. and Harman, G.

Milsark, G. L. (1974) *Existential sentences in English* (MIT dissertation), publ. 1976, Bloomington, Ind.: Indiana U. Linguistics Club.

Mittwoch, A. (1974) 'Is there an underlying negative in comparative clauses?', *Linguistics* **122**, 39ff

O'Connor, J. D. and Arnold, G. F. (1961) *Intonation of colloquial English*, London: Longman (second edition 1973)

Palmer, F. R. (1974) *The English verb*, London: Longman

Palmer, F. R. (1979) *Modality and the English modals*, London: Longman

Palmer, H. E. (1924) *A grammar of spoken English*, Leipzig: Teubner

Prince, E. P. (1978) 'A comparison of WH-clefts and *it*-clefts in discourse', *Language* **54**, 883–906

Prince, E. P. (1981) 'Toward a taxonomy of given – new information', in *Radical Pragmatics*, ed. P. Cole, New York: Academic Press

Pritchard, F. H. (1934) *Essentials of Modern English*, London: Harrap (repr. 1943)

Pullum, G. K. and Wilson, D. (1977) 'Autonomous syntax and the analysis of auxiliaries', *Language* **53**, 1–37

Quine, W. (1960) *Word and object*, Cambridge, Mass.: MIT Press

Quirk, R. (1965) 'Descriptive statement and serial relationship', *Language* **41**, 205–217

Quirk, R., Greenbaum, S., Leech, G. and Svartvik, J. (1972) *A grammar of contemporary English*, London: Longman

Reichenbach, H. (1947) *Elements of symbolic logic*, New York: Macmillan

Reinhart, T. (1976) *The syntactic domain of anaphora*, MIT dissertation

Reinhart, T. (1980) 'Pragmatics and Linguistics: an analysis of sentence topics', in *Philosophica* (special issue on pragmatic theory)

Reinhart, T. (1981) 'Definite NP anaphora and c-command domains', *Linguistic Inquiry* **12**, 605–635

Ross, J. R. (1973) 'Negginess', paper read at 1973 Winter Meeting of the Linguistic Association of America (quoted in Tottie 1977)

Scheurweghs, G. (1961) *Present-day English syntax: A survey of sentence patterns*, London: Longman

Sinclair, J. McH. (1972) *A course in spoken English: Grammar*, London: OUP

Sopher, H. (1976) 'Positional features of *too*', *Linguistics* **179**, 55–79

Stockwell, R. P., Schachter, P., and Partee, B. H. (1968) *Integration of transformational theories on English syntax*, U. of California, Los Angeles (repr. 1973 as *The major syntactic structures of English*, New York: Holt, Rinehart)

Strang, B. M. H. (1969) *Modern English Structure*, London: Edward Arnold

Sweet, H. (1898) A new English grammar, Oxford: Clarendon Press

Taglicht, J. (1972) 'A new look at English relative constructions', *Lingua* **29**, 1–22

Taglicht, J. (1977) 'Relative clauses as postmodifiers: Meaning, syntax, and intonation; *Forum Linguisticum* **6**, 73–107

Thomason, R. and Stalnaker, R. (1973) 'A semantic theory of adverbs', *Linguistic Inquiry* **4**, 195–220

Tottie, G. (1977) *Fuzzy negation in English and Swedish*, Stockholm: Almqvist and Wiksell International (Stockholm Studies in English 39)

Tottie, G. (1980) 'Negation and discourse strategy in spoken and written English', in *Papers from the 8th colloquium on new ways of analysing variation in English and other languages*, eds. Sankoff, D. and Cedergren, H.

Vachek, J. (1966) *The linguistic school of Prague*, Bloomington, Ind.: Indiana UP

Vendler, Z. (1967) '*Each* and *every*, *any* and *all*', in *Linguistics in philosophy*, Cornell U. P.

Index